理查德·琼斯

一位早期英国制度经济学家

赵迺抟◎著

宋丽智◎译

Richard Jones

中国金融出版社

责任编辑：戴　硕　董　飞
责任校对：李俊英
责任印制：丁淮宾

图书在版编目（CIP）数据

理查德·琼斯：一位早期英国制度经济学家（Lichade·qiongsi：Yiwei Zaoqi Yingguo Zhidu Jingji Xuejia）/赵迺抟著、宋丽智译．—北京：中国金融出版社，2013.6

ISBN 978 – 7 – 5049 – 6753 – 4

Ⅰ.①理…　Ⅱ.①赵…②宋…　Ⅲ.①琼斯，R. —制度经济学—思想评论　Ⅳ.①F091.349

中国版本图书馆 CIP 数据核字（2013）第 015075 号

出版
发行　中国金融出版社

社址　北京市丰台区益泽路 2 号
市场开发部　（010）63266347，63805472，63439533（传真）
网上书店　http://www.chinafph.com
　　　　　　（010）63286832，63365686（传真）
读者服务部　（010）66070833，62568380
邮编　100071
经销　新华书店
印刷　保利达印务有限公司
尺寸　169 毫米 ×239 毫米
印张　22.5
字数　280 千
版次　2013 年 6 月第 1 版
印次　2013 年 6 月第 1 次印刷
定价　48.00 元
ISBN 978 – 7 – 5049 – 6753 – 4/F.6313
如出现印装错误本社负责调换　联系电话（010）63263947

赵迺抟（1897 – 1986）
字廉澄，浙江杭州人，
我国著名的经济学家和教育家。

　　1922 年毕业于北京大学法科经济门，1929 年获美国哥伦比亚大学哲学博士学位。回国后被北京大学聘为研究教授，并任经济系主任长达 18 年（1931—1949），著有《理查德·琼斯：一位早期英国制度经济学家》（英文本）、《欧美经济学史》、《披沙录》等。他在北京大学经济系任教授 55 年间，学术上孜孜不倦，治学严谨，锲而不舍；教学上诲人不倦，桃李满天下。

译者序

中国近代经济学不是中国传统经济思想的延续，而是西学东渐的结果。它是一种典型的移植性变迁，是中外冲突融合的产物，是中国一步一步融入世界体系的结果。在这一转型的历史进程中，海外留学生群体发挥了独特的作用，他们的学术思想成为中国近代经济思想的重要组成部分。从海外留学生经济思想的角度演绎中国近代经济思想转型是中国经济思想史研究的崭新视角，可以大大丰富中国近代经济思想史的内容，同时也可以为构建具有中国特色的当代中国经济学提供历史借鉴。

但是，由于多种因素的影响，中国经济思想史学界缺乏对近代海外留学生群体经济思想的系统研究，近代海外留学生的经济学学术成就迄今没有得到足够重视。以赵迺抟先生为例，他是我国早期留美学生，是我国当代著名的经济学家，对欧美经济思想史和中国经济思想史的研究均有很深的学术造诣。其中，《欧美经济思想史》是他几十年研究和讲授西方经济思想史的结晶；长达数百万字的大型中国经济思想史资料专辑《披沙录》则凝聚了他毕生心血，实现了他"誓做淘沙者、拓荒者，为后人铺路架桥"的宏愿。非常遗憾的是，我们的历史参考文献中遗漏了赵迺抟先生非常重要的一部著作，即他在哥伦比亚大学完成的博士论文。

1923 年，赵迺抟先生进入哥伦比亚大学经济系，先后师从米歇尔教授和塞利格曼教授，分获硕士、博士学位。在攻读博士学位期间，赵迺抟先生转向制度学派的研究，在导师塞利格曼教授的指导下重点研究英国经济学家理查德·琼斯（1790—1855）的经济思想。琼斯的活动年代介于李嘉图和小穆勒之间，多为学者所忽视，材料并不丰富。赵迺抟先生为了研究琼斯的经济思想多方搜寻，搜集到琼斯的著作 16 种，研究琼斯的书籍 74 种及论文 52 篇，还有大量书信。其搜罗文献之勤、所得之富都是常人难以企及的。他不仅找到了人所共知的琼斯的一般经济学著作，还在文学类书架上找到了很少为人所知的琼斯的《文献存稿》。这部书稿是琼斯的密友惠威尔博士在琼斯逝世四年以后，于 1895 年编辑出版的，其中有不少琼斯生前未曾发表过的经济学著作。马克思在写作《剩余价值理论》一书时，曾设有专章分析琼斯的经济思想，可是他当时并没有看到这部《文献存稿》。

正是在大量占有文献资料的基础上，赵迺抟先生于 1929 年撰写成博士论文《理查德·琼斯：一位早期英国制度经济学家》（Richard Jones：An Early English Institutionalist）。该论文英文本 10 余万字，分为八章：第一章，制度学派的经济学；第二章，生平和一般背景；第三章，琼斯的政治经济学体系；第四章，地租理论；第五章，工资理论；第六章，利润理论；第七章，琼斯的其他理论贡献；第八章，琼斯的批判及其影响。论文对琼斯经济思想的渊源和体系做了深入的探讨和阐述。

该论文是琼斯经济思想研究的集大成之作，被国际上有名的《社会科学大百科全书》列为研究琼斯的第一部参考书。塞利格曼教授在讲授《经济思想史》课程中，讲到琼斯的经济思想时，往往要说到"一位中国留学生赵迺抟博士对琼斯研究的贡献"，并把他的研究成果纳入教学内容，还将他的这篇论文指定为参考书，要求同学们阅读。20 世纪 30 年代，制度经济学在美国盛极一时，当时学术界一般认为制度经济学是承袭于德国的历史学派，而该论文将一位英国经济学家确定为早期制度经济学家，自然引起西方学者特别是美国学者的极大关注，具有极高的学术价值。

中南财经政法大学邹进文教授敏锐地发现经济思想史研究中这一重要文献的缺失，于是他走访了赵迺抟先生之子赵凯华先生。赵凯华先生是北京大学物理系教授，为我国大学基础物理教育作出了重大的贡献并取得了突出的成就。他慷慨提供了父亲博士论文的打印稿，表示全力支持中南财经政法大学经济思想史研究团队的翻译工作。

我非常有幸，承担了这一重任。本着严谨的精神，希望向读者呈现出一个完美的译本。一方面，向赵迺抟先生严谨的治学和宽阔的胸怀致敬；另一方面，向关心翻译出版工作的赵凯华先生、我的恩师邹进文先生、很多经济思想史学界的同仁以及中国金融出版社的戴硕主任和董飞编辑致谢。

本译著为国家社科基金一般项目"海外留学生与中国经济学的发展研究"（12BJL016）和国家教育部人文社会科学研究青年基金项目"20世纪30年代中国经济思想的转变与发展研究——基于世界经济大萧条冲击的视角"（12YJC790161）的阶段性成果。

宋丽智
2013 年 6 月

宋丽智，1978 年 5 月出生于湖北十堰，经济学博士，中南财经政法大学副教授，曾任孝感市孝昌县发展和改革局副局长。

主要从事中国经济思想史、宏观经济政策等方面的科研和教学工作。主持 2012 年度教育部人文社会科学研究青年基金项目：《20 世纪 30 年代中国经济思想的转变与发展研究——基于世界经济大萧条冲击的视角》；出版学术著作《民国时期会计思想研究》（2009）；在《经济学动态》、《中国经济史研究》、《宏观经济研究》等刊物上发表学术论文十余篇。

目　　录

代传记

赵迺抟教授的学术道路

张友仁[*]

赵迺抟教授（1897—1986）是我国当代著名的经济学家和教育家。他在北京大学经济学系任教授长达 55 年，任系主任长达 18 年。他是《理查德·琼斯：一位早期英国制度经济学家》（英文版）、《欧美经济学史》专著的作者以及《披沙录》巨著的编撰者。他 1931 年到北京大学任教授。1986 年在《披沙录》最后一卷的修订和定稿工作中，不幸脑病发作逝世。55 年的时间里，他始终坚持在学术岗位上，孜孜不倦地从事经济科学的教学工作和学术研究工作。他是一位学贯中西、治学严谨、锲而不舍、诲人不倦、老当益壮的学者。他早已桃李满天下，学术著作也早已传播到海内外。

一、青少年时期

赵迺抟，号廉澄，或怜尘，浙江杭州人。1897 年 3 月 28 日生于钱塘江畔的杭州江干。父亲赵绳武，是一位知识分子，在浙江省 1897 年的乡试中考取为举人。他长期担任杭州江干小学校长，辛亥

---

* 张友仁，北京大学经济学院教授。

革命后在浙江省教育厅任秘书。母亲朱氏，也是一位读过一些经书和诗文的知识分子。赵迺抟自幼就在父母的督促下读书和练习书法，受到良好的家庭教育。

赵迺抟 6 岁时，就拜曾任翰林的吴震春先生（字雷川，后任燕京大学校长）为启蒙老师，入他所办的私塾，学了半年古文。那时，西学开始东渐，杭州已经办起一些新式学校。可是当时风气未开，社会上很多家长还不愿意将子弟送入新式学校求学。赵迺抟的父母思想比较开明，鼓励他投考新式学校。他于 1904 年考入杭州江干小学，在那里受到三年的初小教育。虽然，那时的初小学习的仍是以《四书》《五经》等古籍为主，但他在课外开始阅读一些书刊，受到民主主义思想的启蒙教育。

初小毕业后，他于 1908 年考入浙江省两浙师范学校附属模范小学高小读书。这所学校由沈钧儒先生任校长，校址设在杭州市内浙江省贡院旧址。他在小学读书时期，就打下了初步的语文基础，练就了一笔北魏体的书法。

1910 年赵迺抟高小毕业后，投考中学。他同时被浙江初级师范和杭州府中学两所学校录取。他起初是准备上浙江初级师范学习的，因为这样既能受到免费的师范教育，又能在毕业后从事教育工作，继承父业。后来，由于高小老师的苦劝，他才进入浙江省当时最著名的杭州府中学学习。这所学校的校长是著名教育家钱家治先生。他的儿子钱学森后来成为世界著名的科学家。赵迺抟一家后来同钱家治一家结下了深厚的师生情谊。

杭州府中学校址在现在的解放路中段路东，是当时浙江省的重点中学，有较好的教学质量，民国后改名为浙江省第一中学。他在那里学习了五年，打下了良好的中文和英文的基础，于 1914 年冬天毕业。在中学学习期间，他写了一些作品，在该校的《友声》刊物上发表过论说文一篇、英文作文一篇和词一首。

该中学有一位外籍英文教师马保罗，教他们班的英文。他推行奴化教育，激起了同学们的公愤，他们联合起来向校方请愿，要求解聘马保罗。他们还推举赵迺抟等几位同学作为代表，写了一封英文信给马保罗。信中历陈他的种种错误，要求他引咎离职。可是这位外籍教师不但不承认错误，反而将该班学生告到北洋政府大总统那里。那时的政府官僚都是唯洋人之命是从的，于是大总统命令浙江省第一中学开除学生。这时浙江省第一中学贴出了"奉大总统命令开除全班学生"的布告。学生们群情更为激愤，经过他们不断的团结和斗争，学校终于把他们改为留校察看的处分。

二、考入北京大学学习

中学毕业后，赵迺抟于 1915 年到上海投考大学。当时，北京大学是国内最著名的综合大学，虽然考试的难度较大，他却知难而进，投考北京大学。

由于他是旧制中学的毕业生，不能直接投考大学本科，而只能投考北大预科。他顺利地考入北大预科，在三年的预科学习期间，他每年的考试成绩都是第一名，因而年年获得奖学金。后来，他在《回忆录之一》（手稿）中曾经讲到当时北大预科的学习情况：

"北京大学预科，其前身乃译学馆，特别注重外文，所有课目，既不与大学本校的相应科门的功课相衔接，反而含有半独立的性质，大部分同学自以为能看外文原著、能听外文讲课、功课紧、纪律严，胜于本科生，颇有骄傲自满的情绪。"

在北京大学预科学习期间，他虽然主要是埋头读书，但是并不是不问政治。当 1918 年北洋军阀政府同日本帝国主义签订丧权辱国的《中日共同防敌军事协定》的时候，北京学生群起罢课，抗议这个卖国协定的签订。这是我国近代史上第一次学生反对日本帝国主义的爱国罢课斗争。他被同学们推举为北京大学的学生代表之一。同北京各高等学校的学生代表们一起前往中南海，向北洋政府的大总统冯国璋进行了面对面的斗争。在学生代表们义正词严的说理抗议面前，老奸巨猾的军阀冯国璋采取了花言巧语的手法，口头上答应了学生们的某些要求，把学生骗了回去；而在实际上却继续执行他的卖国求荣的政策。

1918 年赵迺抟以优秀的成绩毕业于北京大学预科，取得了免试升入北京大学本科的资格。当时，北京大学本科经济、商学门的主任是马寅初教授。赵迺抟受到他的创新思想的影响，选择了经济学作为自己的专业，准备进入北京大学法科经济门继续深造。可是那时他接到了父亲寄来的要他回浙江到衢州中学教英文并兼教务主任的来信和聘书，他考虑到家庭经济困难，准备前往工作。离开北京前，他到当时任教育部参事的前浙江第一中学校长钱家治先生处辞行，告以家庭经济困难，不能升学，将回浙江就业。钱老师听了为之十分惋惜，提出要留意帮他找个工作，使他能一面读书一面工作。在他刚回到浙江的第二天，就接到钱老师拍来的电报，说已经为他找到在晚间课余当家庭教师的职务，劝他返京升学。于是，他才得以在 1918 年秋天顺利地进入北京大学本科学习。

赵迺抟在北京大学本科读的是法科经济门。北京大学以前是一所官僚习气很深的大学，蔡元培先生于 1916 年底受黎元洪大总统的任命为北京大学校长后，大力进行整顿，改革北大的封建教育制度。蔡校长在就职演说中指出了大学的性质："大学者，研究高深学问者也。""大学生当以研究学术为天职，不当以大学为升官发财之阶梯。"于是他"广延积学与热心的教员，认真教授，以提起学生研究学问的兴趣。"蔡校长一方面广泛延请学有专长和热心教育的教授来校授课，另一方面辞退了学术水平低和教学态度差的中国教员和外国教员，从而充实了教授的阵容，提高了学生的学习兴趣。马寅初教授就是蔡元培校长在那时延聘的热心教授之一。

蔡元培校长还提倡"兼容并包"的办学方针。在这个方针的指引下，扶植了民主主义思想，也容许马克思主义思想的传播。他在为《北京大学月刊》撰写的发刊词中写道："大学者，'囊括大典，网罗众家'之学府也。"他主张，办大学应当仿照各国大学的通例："哲学之唯心论与唯物论，文学、美术之理想派与写实派，计学（经济学）之干涉论与放任论，伦理学之动机论与功利论，宇宙论之乐天观与厌世观，常樊然并峙于其中，此思想自由之通例，而大学之所以为大也。"

1918 年北京大学经济、商学门主任马寅初教授协助蔡校长，增聘学有专长的专任教员，解聘不学无术的旧官僚教师。他还在经济、商学门的办学中，贯彻了蔡校长"兼容并包"的办学方针。当时北京大学经济、商学门中，各种学派的经济学说都得到开课讲授的平等地位。赵迺抟在大学本科四年的学习期间，也兼容并包地加以学习，这给他以后研究经济思想史打下了牢固的理论基础。

马寅初教授等人还在北大开设许多实用性的经济学课程。马寅初教授本人开设的就有货币学、银行学、财政学、保险学、交易所论、汇兑论等。他还鼓励经济门学生于 1918 年创办学生银行，发行股票，经营存放款及汇兑业务，并且自己兼任顾问，还聘请会计学教师作指导。该学生银行设在北河沿北大第三院原译学馆大门的门楼上，赵迺抟也入了股（每股一元），并参加学生银行的工作，熟悉银行业务。在本科学习期间，他还参加了北京大学学生组织的雄辩会，并且曾任英文组组长，经常参加和举办英文辩论会。

1918 年，在赵迺抟进入北京大学本科的开学式上，蔡校长发表演说，指出：

"大学为纯粹研究学问之机关，不可视为养成资格之所，亦不可视为贩卖知识之所。学者当有研究学问之兴趣，尤当养成学问家之人格。"

不久，蔡校长又在 11 月 16 日庆祝第一次世界大战结束的大会上，发表题为《劳工神圣》的演说，其中讲到："我说的劳工，不但是金工、木工等，凡用自己的劳力，作成有益于他人的事业，不管他用的是体力，是脑力，都是劳工。所以农是种植的工，商是转运的工，学校职员、著述家、发明家是教育的工，我们都是劳工。我们要自己认识劳工的价值。劳工神圣！"

在蔡校长的教育思想的指引下，赵迺抟在北京大学本科学习中，专心研究学问，立志不做官，而做一名有知识的劳工，即脑力劳动者。

蔡元培校长为了改变旧中国的社会风气和旧北京大学学生追求升官发财的腐朽习气，于1918年在北京大学发起组织进德会。这个会的戒条按照会员种类有所不同。会员分为三种："甲种会员不嫖、不赌、不娶妾；乙种会员——于前三戒之外，加不做官吏、不做议员二戒；丙种会员——于前五戒外，加不吸烟、不饮酒、不食肉三戒。"进德会还"公定罚章"，违反戒条的要受到处罚，并且推举出纠察员来执行。赵迺抟在北京大学参加了进德会，做了乙种会员。他一生恪守进德会乙种会员的戒条。这对于他后来坚持不参加反动党派，不担任反动官僚，专心致志地从事教育工作和学术研究工作是有着一定的影响的。

赵迺抟的家庭经济收入是不能负担他攻读大学本科费用的，为了自己筹措学杂各项费用，他在大学本科学习期间，兼做了几项工作。从1918年开始，他在晚清名相翁同龢的后人翁振伯家里担任家庭教师，在晚间给翁同龢的几位孙子教课，历时四年，直到1922年。这就是前面所说的钱家治先生替他找的工作。同时，他经过同学俞九恒介绍，在北京安徽中学担任高年级英文教师。大学本科学习期间，赵迺抟还被由蔡元培先生兼任馆长的国史馆聘请为国史馆编辑，具体任务是翻译一部《希腊史》的部分书稿，以供编写中国历史的参考。他当时还为钱家治先生的正在读中学的公子钱学森辅导中文和英文，他的未婚妻、当时正在女子高师学习的骆雯（字涵素）则为钱学森辅导数学、物理和化学。大学本科时期的多种工作，虽然增加了赵迺抟的负担，但是这些工作对他本人也是很好的锻炼，同时还为国家培养了人才。在他当时教过和辅导过的学生当中，就出现了钱学森这样的世界第一流的科学家。

1922 年夏天，赵迺抟以优秀的成绩毕业于北京大学法科经济门，同时取得了北京大学文学学士的学位。毕业后，赵迺抟准备出国读研究院继续深造。根据他的经济情况，自费留学是不可能的，只好找官费留学的机会。于是，他在 1922 年回到浙江杭州，参加浙江省的留美官费生资格考试。那时，浙江省只有五个留学生名额，他以第一名的成绩被录取了。这年冬天，全国各省初试录取的官费生都集中到北京进行复试。赵迺抟参加了这次复试，又以第一名的成绩被录取为官费留美生。

由于出国留学还要等待一个时期，他在等待赴美留学期间，经蔡元培校长推荐和聘请，在民国大学经济系讲授了一年货币学课程。

1923 年他在北京与骆雯女士结了婚。骆雯是浙江诸暨人，专修化学，1923 年毕业于北京女子高等师范学校化学系，留在母校担任物理学助教。

三、留学美国，获哥伦比亚大学博士学位

赵迺抟于 1922 年取得浙江省留美官费生资格后，就申请美国的大学研究部的入学准许。当时既十分著名又在中国有重要影响的美国大学，是位于纽约市区北部的哥伦比亚大学。他获得哥伦比亚大学政治科学院作研究生的入学许可后，就于 1923 年 8 月乘轮船离开中国横渡太平洋前往美国，入哥伦比亚大学政治科学院，研究经济理论。

该政治科学院的著名经济学教授有塞利格曼和米歇尔等。初入学时，有的老同学告诉他说，米歇尔教授的课程要求十分严格，很难考及格的，最好不选他的课。赵迺抟却知难而进，选习了米歇尔

教授的"商业循环"等两门课程，还选习了米歇尔教授和塞利格曼教授合开的"经济思想史"课程。他选的这些课程，都取得了优秀的成绩。后来他在北京大学长期讲授"经济思想史"和"商业循环"等课程，就是在这时打下基础的。修满了课程的学分，再经过学科总的考试，取得优秀的成绩后，才开始选题写作硕士论文。在选题中，他也遇到了选择中国问题的题目还是外国问题的题目这样一个中国留学生往往都会遇到的问题。他自幼纵览经史百家，熟悉中国经济思想家的主要文献，如果选择中国经济思想史方面的题目来作硕士论文，对他来说显然是比较容易的。但是，他却选择了外国经济思想史的题目来作硕士论文。他在外国经济思想史的研究中学习到的研究方法，对于他后来研究中国经济思想史是大有裨益的。他的硕士论文题目是《重商主义与重农主义的比较研究》，选择了要求十分严格的米歇尔教授作为指导论文写作的导师。

他住在哥伦比亚大学附近暮吟赛特宿舍区，天天在哥伦比亚大学图书馆里为他设立的专桌上读书，直到闭馆。书籍仍放在专桌上过夜，第二天早晨再去继续阅读。晚上，他回到暮吟山麓的住处，仍抓紧时间学习和研究。那时，有的同学喜欢晚上前来闲谈，并且往往一谈就很久，影响了他的学习和研究。赵迺抟就在书桌上摆了一张字条，上面写着"会谈以十分钟为限"。他把时间抓得很紧，很少看电影和参加其他娱乐活动，因此，同学们给他起了个"暮山隐士"的外号。

他在哥伦比亚大学政治科学院做研究生期间，除了学习，还参加了一些体力劳动。他每天清晨五时到大学食堂去做些洗菜和切菜一类的工作，连续三年之久。暑假期间，他到纽约市郊区"春野"地方的农场，从事采摘苹果等劳动。这样，他既锻炼了自己，又获得了一定的收入，用以补贴自己的生活花费。此外，他还在纽约丹佛公司兼职。

赵迺抟刻苦钻研，很快就写出了硕士论文的初稿。米歇尔教授审阅后，认为内容不错，只是英文还欠流畅，要求在文字上加以提高。为了修改论文，他到纽约大学英文夜校进修，一面提高自己的英文水平，一面修改论文。经过两易其稿，向米歇尔教授送上论文的第三稿，被导师接受和通过，他终于取得了哥伦比亚大学1924年度的文学硕士学位。

在哥伦比亚大学，赵迺抟又继续攻读博士学位。要攻读博士学位，首先要通过两门外国文的考试。在美国，英文是不能算作外文的，因此，他参加了法文和中文的考试，获得通过。后来，他又参加了经济思想史、经济史、货币学和财政学等专业课程的考试，并一一获得通过，这样他才取得了写作博士论文的资格。于是，他又选择哥伦比亚大学经济系主任、《社会科学大百科全书》巨著的主编、著名经济学家塞利格曼教授为导师，在他的指导下从事博士论文的选题和写作。

从赵迺抟的博士论文选题上，我们可以看到他不畏艰难、努力攀登科学高峰的治学精神。他是从塞利格曼教授提出的，当时迫切需要深入研究的学术课题中，选择自己的博士论文题目的。塞利格曼教授说：自从英国古典派经济学大师大卫·李嘉图于1817年出版《政治经济学与赋税原理》以来，时间相隔三十余年，直到1848年才有约翰·斯图亚特·穆勒的《政治经济学原理》出版。在这两部名著出版相隔的三十多年里，难道就没有产生过有成就的经济学家吗？难道这个历史时期在政治经济学上是真空地带吗？不！绝对不是！他一口气就列举了约翰·洛克、罗勃脱·托伦斯、乔治·拉姆赛、理查德·琼斯等十几位有成就有贡献的经济学家的名字，并且指出：只是由于直到现在还没有人对这些经济学家作专门而深入的研究，所以在当时的经济思想史著作上，一般都没有讲到他们，在当时的经济思想史的课堂教学中也都缺乏他们的内容。塞利格曼教授提出，对于这些经济学家中的每一个人，都值得作专门的博士论文来加以研究，以补足经济思想史上的缺陷。

赵迺抟不怕困难，选择了在学术上开创了一个新的经济学派，可是在经济思想史上却缺乏专门研究的英国制度经济学派创始人之一的理查德·琼斯的经济思想，来写作自己的博士论文。

理查德·琼斯生于 1790 年，他生活在李嘉图的经济理论在英国占统治地位的年代里，他敢于大胆地向当时经济学界的权威挑战，认为抽象的土地报酬递减规律是根本不存在的，而李嘉图用它来解释一般地租的成因则更是错误的。琼斯主张用历史上形成的各种不同的经济制度来解释不同类型的地租。作为经济学流派中的少数派——制度学派的经济观点在当时是受到压抑的。琼斯的著作在当时只有《论财富的分配和租税的源泉》等少数几种得到流传。在学术界有权威性的帕尔格雷夫主编的《经济学辞典》中，虽然有理查德·琼斯这一个辞条，可是其中对他的生平和经济思想却写得非常简单。

科学研究要从收集大量的资料开始。赵迺抟写作关于理查德·琼斯经济思想的博士论文，首先要搜集和掌握全部有关琼斯的资料。他在藏书丰富的哥伦比亚大学图书馆中，不仅找到了人所共知的琼斯的一般经济学著作，而且在文学类书架上找到了很少为人所知的琼斯的《文献存稿》。这部书是琼斯的密友惠威尔博士在琼斯逝世四年以后，于 1859 年编辑出版的，其中有不少琼斯生

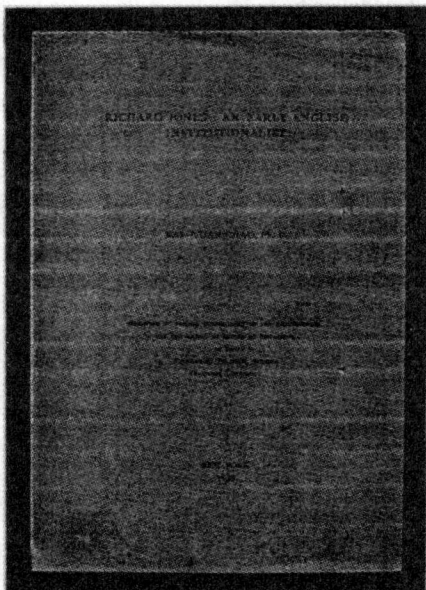

赵迺抟的博士论文
Richard Jones：An Early
English Institutionalist

前未曾发表过的经济学著作。马克思在写作《剩余价值理论》一书时，曾设有专章分析琼斯的经济思想，可是他当时并没有看到这部《文献存稿》。因此，此书的收集，对研究琼斯的经济思想提供了有利的条件。赵迺抟的收集资料工作，并没有到此为止，他刻苦努力，在尘封的书库的角落找到一包琼斯的亲笔书信，这是十分令人兴奋的收获。塞利格曼教授叫他将这一喜讯写信告诉英国当代经济学大师阿胥黎教授。阿胥黎教授见信后，非常高兴，曾于1926年春回信表示赞赏与鼓励，并表示自己年迈，对他的经济思想史研究寄予厚望。

赵迺抟收集到的琼斯的经济学著作有16种之多和大量的书信，又收集到有关琼斯的书籍74种和论文52篇。他对这些资料进行了认真的研究后，才开始写作博士论文。

这篇博士论文对琼斯的生平和经济学说的研究超过了以往的一切著作，是一部有创新性贡献的著作。因此，后来塞利格曼教授在讲授"经济思想史"课程中，讲到琼斯的经济思想时，往往要说到"一位中国留学生赵迺抟博士对琼斯研究的贡献"，并把他的研究成果纳入教学内容，还将他的这篇论文指定为参考书，要同学们阅读。

四、回国任教北京大学

赵迺抟于1930年圣诞节离开美国，动身回国。

早在他离开美国回国以前，就收到了南京中央政治学校的教授聘书。1931年1月他回到中国，就到南京建邺路就任该校经济系和财政系的合聘教授，开设"地方财政"和"土地经济学"两门课程。

1931年5月，赵迺抟接到北京大学聘请他为经济学系教授的聘书。1931年北京大学进行了大改组，由曾任教育部长的蒋梦麟先生任校长，他的北大校长任命书就是由他本人在离开教育部前签发的。蒋梦麟先生是浙江绍兴人，赵迺抟到北京大学就是出自蒋校长的提名，并得到周炳琳先生的同意后聘请的。改组后的北京大学，胡适任文学院长，周炳琳任法学院长。赵迺抟于 9 月到北京大学，被聘任为经济学系研究教授，后来又被任为经济学系主任。研究教授是当时北京大学特有的一种学衔，是教授中的一个等级，它的学术地位高于一般教授。1931 年，北京大学所聘请的研究教授只有 16 位，除赵迺抟外还有丁文江、王守竞、汪敬熙、李四光、许骧、葛拉普、冯祖荀、曾昭抡、刘树杞、徐志摩、周作人、陈受颐、汤用彤、刘复、刘志敳。赵迺抟教授是当时北京大学经济学系唯一的一位研究教授。1933 年北京大学成立校务委员会，他被任命为校务委员会的当然委员。接着，他又被任命为图书委员会委员、财务委员会委员和学生事业指导委员会委员等。

赵迺抟教授在主持北京大学经济学系工作时，继承了蔡元培校长"兼容并包"的办学方针，不仅以资产阶级经济学各流派的讲授为主体，而且允许开设马克思主义经济学说的课程。那时的北京大学经济学系就开设有"马克思经济学说""马克思学说研究"等课程。他在 1936 年同北大经济学系同学的讲话里就主张："经济学之研究，当注意于新陈代替之经济制度，从时间及空间阐明其相对性，切不可错认社会秩序及经济法则为固定不变的事理。"他还主张："民族经济的建设，必有赖于整个的计划。""经济政策，必以大多数人民之福利为前提。"对于研究经济科学的方法，他认为：当注意性质的研究与数量的研究两个方面，"静态经济学的训练及动态经济学的运用"两个方面。他的这些经济科学教育思想，当时被学生记录下来，以《赵主任的话》为题，发表在《北大经济学报》1936 年第 1 期上。后来，他在一篇文章中写道："不佞我治经济学有年，间尝以'死的思想，活的解释，静的理论，动的运用'与学子相勉励。"

对于治学的态度,他有下列的主张:

"一,对于经济社会发展之背景,当根据人类学之发现及历史学的启示,作一写实的叙述。二,当注意于新陈代谢之经济制度,不必空谈千古不灭之经济动机,尤不可错认经济法则及社会秩序有固定不变之性质。三,民族经济的建设,必有赖于整个的计划与编制。经济政策必以大多数人民之福利为前提,不应受党见之支配。四,必使道德的涵义浸濡于经济行为之中,对于社会全体之福利,因经济政策之实施而日益增进。五,对于经济学静态的研究与动态的研究,二者方法上的便利,必使其选用得宜,至于演绎与归纳,历史与统计,当兼收并蓄,不可偏废。"

从他担任系主任的时候起,北京大学经济学系在课程设置上,不仅有必修课,而且有选修课。随着年级的升高,选修课也逐渐增多。开设的课程,在学科性质上,既有理论性的课程,又有历史性和方法性的课程。在课程深浅上,既开设初级的基础课,供大学低年级学生修习,又开设高级的专业课和研究课,供大学高年级学生和研究生进一步修习。为了让教授们专心教课和提高教学质量,北京大学当时规定教授任课每年不得少于三门,并且规定教授原则上不得在校外兼课。赵迺抟教授虽然担任经济学系主任,在行政工作上要花费不少时间,但是在开课门数上并没有减少。每年他都要开设"经济学原理"和"经济思想史"两门必修课,此外每年还轮流开设"高级经济学""经济理论""商业循环""外国经济名著选读"等选修课程中的一门。他讲课,总要首先开出许多参考书让同学自学,然后抓住重点生动而清楚地加以讲授。同学们反映,他讲课内容丰富,条理清楚,记出来的听课笔记就像一篇文章。

除了课程教学之外,他还重视理论联系实际,将经济调查作为经济学系的必修课，并为学生安排毕业前的调查研究和毕业论文写作，以补充课堂教学的不足。在抗日战争以前的几年里，赵迺抟教授就曾亲自率领过三届毕业班的同学，分别前往青岛、塘沽和日本国各地作调查研究。他还指导同学收集资料、进行分析研究和写作毕业论文。

在课外，他还担任了学生组织起来的一些学会的导师。他既担任北大经济学会的导师，还担任其他学会的导师。如政治学系同学张镜航、哲学系同学范长江等在抗日战争以前组织的"国际问题研究会"，就曾聘请他担任导师。

早在抗日战争以前，北京大学就已经设立了研究院。赵迺抟教授兼作经济学研究生的导师，指导他们的学习和研究生论文的写作。同时，他还担任北京大学研究院社会科学研究部主任，主持北京大学整个社会科学类的科学研究工作和研究生培养工作。

赵迺抟教授在他所写的《回忆录之一》中，曾经客观地指出，北大经济学系从"九·一八"事变到"七·七"抗战这一时期在工作上有不少缺点，如资产阶级经济学的课程占主导地位，理论和实际的联系不够紧密，课程门类繁多和课程分量繁重等。这些缺点有的也是旧中国资产阶级大学教育难以避免的。但是，那时的北京大学经济学系在他的主持下，毕竟为培养有用的经济科学人才作出了重要的贡献。后来，这些学生中有些成为革命干部，在民主革命和社会主义现代化建设中作出了贡献。有的成为经济学家，在国内外从事教学研究工作和各项经济工作，并且取得了显著的成绩。还有的参加人民军队，成为将军。也正由于北大经济学系的认真办学，它的大学生和研究生的学历和学位，在国际上得到各著名大学的广泛承认。

赵迺抟教授在担任北大研究教授时，待遇较一般教授为优，月薪为大洋 500 元。他为了解决学生中的经济困难，提出每年拨出一

笔款项为他的母亲朱氏设立"赵母奖学金",奖励北大经济学系学业

优秀而又家境清寒的同学(见《北京大学周刊》1936年6月13日)。为此,成立了由胡适、周炳琳、陶希圣三位教授组成的董事会,并由董事会来决定获得资金的人选。为了这件事,胡适先生写了一封信给赵逎抟教授,信中说:

> 廉澄先生:手书敬悉。先生设立助学金,纪念令先母,这是最可敬佩的孝思。我很愿意追随诸公之后,做一个董事。我不久要出国,在出国期中,董事的事情请枚荪先生(按:即北大法学院院长周炳琳教授)代表我,敬覆。即祝
>
> 双安
>
> 胡适敬上
> 廿五、六、廿一

对于抗日战争以前北京大学学生掀起的正义的学生运动,他都深为同情,并且加以赞助。"一二·九"运动游行示威中,北京大学经济学系女同学黄淑生被反动军警用大刀砍伤,他得悉后极为悲愤,并立即赶往医院看望和慰问。

北京大学中文系马叙伦教授积极从事爱国民主运动,被南京政府勒令北京大学解聘后,1935年前后闲居上海,没有固定收入,以卖字为生,生活十分困难。他写信给赵逎抟教授,请他帮助申请庚子赔款科研基金。

马叙伦书赠的条幅

赵迺抟教授大力加以协助，使马叙伦教授取得一笔科研经费。马叙伦教授用秀丽的楷书录宋周邦彦词《氏州第一》一首写成一张条幅送给赵迺抟教授。内容如下：

波落寒汀，村渡向晚，遥输数点帆小。乱叶翻鸦，惊风破雁，天角孤云缥缈。官柳萧疏甚，尚挂微微残照。景物关情，川涂换目，顿来催老。渐解狂朋欢意少，奈犹被思牵情绕。座上琴心，机中锦字，觉最萦怀抱。也知人悬望久，蔷薇谢，归来一笑。欲梦高唐未成眠，霜空已晓。

怜尘尊兄先生雅属即希鉴正

廿四年夷初弟马叙伦

这首词的含义虽然比较隐晦，但是从词句中不难看出马叙伦教授在最困难的日子里，仍怀抱"壮心不已，志在千里"的雄心壮志。他长期从事抗日民主运动和中国人民的解放事业，新中国成立后荣任中央人民政府委员和教育部部长。赵迺抟教授和马叙伦教授的友谊是十分深厚的。

赵迺抟教授在担任繁重的教学工作和教学行政工作的同时，还坚持不懈地从事科学研究工作。这一时期，他在《北京大学社会科学季刊》《北大经济学报》《中国大学经济学报》《独立评论》等刊物上发表过：《〈国富论〉学说述原》《商业循环之理论》《价格经济学》《关于美国复兴计划》《中国银行之现状与展望》《白银问题之检讨》《消费者的信贷》等论文多篇。

五、抗战时期在西南联大任教

1937 年 7 月 7 日，卢沟桥上点燃起抗日战争的烽火，7 月中旬，赵迺抟曾和北大其他一些知名学者一起应邀到庐山参加南京政府召开的国是谈话会。会上，学者们纷纷敦促国民党政府奋起抗日。会后，北京大学派他到上海筹备北大、清华两校的联合招生工作。到上海后，由于"八·一三"淞沪抗战爆发，设在西藏中路青年会中的两校联合招生办事处不得已停止了工作。当时铁路交通中断，赵迺抟历经周折，辗转回到沦陷了的北平。

这时，平津相继沦陷，北大、清华、南开三校决定迁往长沙，联合成立临时大学。赵迺抟教授参加了迁校工作，担任北京大学旅行团团长，同汤用彤、罗常培、周作人等二十余位教授一起，经天津坐海轮到香港；原拟乘飞机去长沙的，因人数较多买不到飞机票，不得已坐江轮溯西江到广西梧州，得到在广西工作的北大校友的协助，乘汽车经桂林于 11 月到达长沙。在长沙临时大学，他仍担任经济学系教授。长沙临时大学借用长沙城内圣经书院校舍上课，文学院部分则设在南岳。1938 年 2 月武汉危急，长沙也遭到敌机狂轰滥炸，临时大学被迫停课。临时大学领导采纳了经济学系教授秦瓒的建议，决定迁往云南省的昆明市，成立西南联合大学。大学师生于 1938 年 3 月离开长沙，前往昆明。

从长沙到昆明，相隔三千余里之遥，加以崇山峻岭，交通极不方便，行旅十分困难。一部分年富力强的教授们，像闻一多、曾昭抡等教授率领大学同学徒步走湘西、经贵州高原，入云南，到达昆明。他们在崇山峻岭中迈步长征，在我国教育史上谱写了光辉的新篇章。

有一部分中老年教授，组成旅行团，坐汽车经桂林，出镇南关（现名友谊关）到越南同登，改乘滇越铁路火车，日行夜宿，历经三日三夜，才到达云南省昆明市。这个旅程要两度出入国境，事务繁多。大家推选赵迺抟教授为旅行团团长，周炳琳教授负责外交，魏建功教授负责文书，章廷谦副教授负责伙食，姚从吾、张佛泉两教授负责行李。他们终于在 1938 年春到达昆明。还有一部分教师和学生则经香港，乘海轮到越南海防，转乘滇越铁路火车到昆明。

1938 年春，国立西南联合大学在昆明成立，它是由北大、清华、南开三所著名大学联合组成，共分文、理、法商、工、师范五个学院。赵迺抟仍任经济学系教授。

在昆明，经过云南省工作的北大校友的多方协助，借到了几所中专学校和会馆，可是房屋仍不够整个大学使用，不得已只好尽先将理、工、师范学院设在昆明，而将文、法商学院暂时设在滇南的蒙自城外的海关旧址，成立西南联大蒙自分校。在蒙自分校成立校务委员会，三所大学各有两位代表作为校务委员，北大为赵迺抟和樊际昌教授，清华为陈岱孙和冯友兰教授，南开为陈序经等教授。分校校委会负责领导文学院和法商学院。

1938 年 9 月，昆明北郊的西南联大新建的简易的新校舍落成。新校舍中，只有图书馆和大饭厅是瓦屋，教室和办公室都是土墙和马口铁皮屋顶，学生宿舍是土墙和稻草屋顶。上课时如遇下雨，雨声叮当，干扰了教师的授课。后来，内地马口铁皮的价格飞涨，学校将马口铁皮屋顶拆下卖钱，教室和办公室也都改成和学生宿舍一样的稻草屋顶了。现在，云南师范大学校园内还保存有当年西南联大教室的复制品，供人参观。西南联大的新校舍虽然简陋，但总算有了比较集中的校舍，文学院和法商学院就迁到这所新校舍的北区里面。

在昆明，抗日战争最艰苦的年代里，敌机轰炸频繁，恶性通货膨胀严重，物质生活条件很差，可是西南联大在广大教师和同学的共同努力下，教学水平、科研水平有升无降，在国内外学术界产生了深远的影响。师生们的革命斗争又给西南联大赢得了"民主堡垒"的光荣称号。现在有一位美国学者易社强，他是哈佛大学博士、维吉尼亚大学教授，选择了西南联大校史作为他的研究课题。西南联大在我国教育史上留下了光辉的一页。

在西南联大，赵迺抟教授同在北京大学一样，仍同时讲授三门课程，不过课程名称和内容都有所变化。"经济思想史"是必修课，他每年都开设，给经济系三年级学生修习。他同时还开两门选修课，这是每年有变化的，其中有"商业循环""社会主义""经济理论"和"当代经济思潮"等。特别是他开设的"社会主义"这门选修课，吸引了许多同学前来听讲，西南联大新校舍北区仅有的大教室被挤得满满的。同时，他还指导大学生的毕业论文和担任经济学系研究生的导师。在抗日战争胜利的那一年冬天，原联大经济系主任陈岱孙教授飞回北平负责接收清华大学被日军占据的校园，赵迺抟教授就接替他担任西南联大经济学系主任。

在昆明，云南省主席龙云先生将他位于昆明市中心威远街公馆内北部住宅部分的东院借给北京大学使用，这就是才盛巷二号的北京大学办事处。才盛巷原名财盛巷，北京大学的教授们来了，才将它改名为才盛巷。龙云住宅同北大办事处之间虽有墙相隔，但是龙云同北大教授们的宿舍是同一排二层的砖木结构的楼房。龙云先生自己住在最西头的两间，这幢楼房，从东头起周炳琳、朱物华、赵迺抟教授各住一间，蒋梦麟校长住了三间。在那个院子里，还住有北大办事处秘书章廷谦副教授等人。

由于敌机的狂轰滥炸，教授们一度移居郊外。赵迺抟先生起初移居宜良县悬崖绝壁上的一处叫做岩泉寺的道观中，宜良离昆明百余里之遥，要坐火车前来上课。

后来，昆明北郊岗头村的北大教授临时宿舍修建好了以后，赵迺抟又迁到那个临时宿舍里。这是一个基本上由茅草屋顶和土墙构成的中式院落，窗子上没有玻璃，往往糊着学生试卷来阻挡风沙。在那里，赵迺抟同周炳琳、杨振声、吴大猷、饶毓泰、孙云铸、戴修瓒、张景钺和崔芝兰夫妇、雷海宗等教授、章廷谦副教授各住一间茅草房。蒋梦麟校长则住瓦房的三间。岗头村位于昆明北郊约十华里处。北大教授的临时宿舍北边是山坡和古寺，西边有小溪流过，教授们就在那里汲水和洗菜洗碗。他经常步行到昆明来上课。上课之余，他并不以"徜徉于山水之间，坐看云起日落"（赵迺抟教授诗句）而自娱，而是夜以继日地从事经济科学的学术研究。赵迺抟教授将他在那里写的文章的后面署有"写于昆明岗村茅斋"或"岗头村旷观自得庐"等字样。当时，北大物理研究所的一个实验室也设在岗头村，在吴大猷教授的指导下，杨振宁、李政道等未来的诺贝尔奖获得者也常来做物理实验。他们在实验工作之余，有时还到茅舍来替吴大猷教授生火做饭，和教授们一起过着清苦的生活。他们的生火技术并不高明，有时弄得满屋都是烟雾。直到抗日战争后期，我国和同盟国一起掌握了昆明的制空权以后，他才迁回昆明城内，先住在北门的螺翠山庄寄庐，后来搬回到才盛巷北大办事处。

在抗日战争后期，为了联合英美等同盟国家共同抗日的需要，军事委员会在昆明成立了译员训练班，抽调大学生去作短期的英语训练，主要是熟悉军事用语和提高会话能力，然后立即派赴前线担任英语翻译工作。赵迺抟教授应聘在该班教授英文作文，为抗日战争作出了一些直接的贡献。

1945 年暑假，西南联大经济学系的一些同学参加了云南澄江县政参观团，到当时的模范县澄江参观访问。他们邀请赵迺抟教授前往指导，他很高兴地去澄江抚仙湖边指导同学们进行调查研究。那时，澄江县北郊的一个山坡上就有由农民集体组织起来进行共同劳动统一按劳分配的农业生产合作社。中共中央在重庆办的《新华日报》上曾对领导这个农业社的李树华社长专文加以介绍。他和同学们爬到这个农业生产合作社所在的山头，进行参观和了解该合作社的生产和分配等情况。在昆明，他十分支持学生前往解放区。如经济学系学生陈忠经等人要去延安，缺乏现金，向他求助，他当即解囊相助，使他们得以顺利奔赴延安。解放后，陈忠经担任我国对外文委副主任、中共中央有关部门的副部长及国际关系学院院长等职。

在战时昆明艰苦的生活条件下，赵迺抟教授仍孜孜不倦地从事科学研究。他的学术专著《欧美经济学史》的初稿，就是在滇南的鹅塘写成的。他还从事其他经济理论、经济政策与经济问题的研究。他曾以"自笑漫谈经济策，不将心事付烟霞"的诗句，来抒发研究经济问题的情怀。这一时期，他在《北京大学四十周年纪念论文集》、《财政学报》、《现代周刊》等书刊上发表过《近四十年来经济科学之发展》、《经济理论与财政政策的联系》、《经济阶级和社会理想对于经济理论之影响》等学术论文多篇。这一时期，他还经常在《大公报》、《云南日报》等报纸上发表"星期论文"，其中有《静态经济与动态经济》、《科学发明与经济动态》、《经济循环中萎缩姿态的象征与因素》、《遗产税之性质及其社会意义》、《我国工业化的经济条件》、《对于我国地政问题的管见》、《现代企业的四大连锁及其四大过程》、《家庭经济之真铨》、《不经济的财政与不财政的经济》、《财政学之真铨与财政家之风度》、《经济建设的远景和近景》等五十余篇。这时，他还受聘为教育部经济学名词审查委员会委员，参加了经济学术语译名的审定工作。

在这个时期他发表的许多论文中，主张经济工作要"竭力为最大多数人民谋最大福利"，"务使人类之最大多数，得到精神上和物质上最大量的幸福"。他认为："斯后的经济政策应做到两个任务：其一，全社会所得或全国人民所得的分配问题，务使人民在生产过程中尽各种劳动后所得到的报酬，公允而均平。其二，一国生产资源的分配问题务必依据全社会的需要将一国的资源合理地分配于各种生产事业。进一步言，一国经济复员中应注意的经济建设，必须把握两大原则，即一方面提倡经济自由，一方面主张经济平等，使每一个人按照其能力和兴趣，可以尽量发展。如是则生活上的势力，相对自由，同时使每一个国民均可以维持相当生活水准，如是则生存的机会，绝对平等。"

21

他对当时国民党政府的经济政策有一些尖锐的批评。他认为，国民党政府的财政是"买办整治的财政"；国民党统治区的经济是"官僚资本的经济"；在它的统治下，"民族经济已被摧毁"，"中产阶级渐趋没落，劳动阶级所得之实际工资，亦有减无增"。他曾写文章谴责官僚资本："官僚资本实乃摧毁经济建设之利器，官僚资本更是摧毁民族资本的毒物。"他主张："既得权益的存在足以阻挠任何方案之执行，实有先行铲除之必要。""吾人欲维持社会之公平应首先严禁以政治的势力夺取商业上之不正当利益。""吾人以为必须铲除官僚资本然后建国事业方可推进。"因此，他在文章中公开主张："集中力量，铲除买办政治的财政与官僚资本的经济。"

六、抗战胜利后，从昆明回到北京大学

1945 年 9 月抗日战争胜利后，因交通运输条件十分困难，西南联大不能及时复员迁回华北，不得已仍在昆明继续上课。

赵迺抟教授和同学们比较接近，他经常指导同学们的课余学习和科学研究。对于革命的学生运动，他都出于正义而表示同情或给予支持。1945 年 12 月 1 日，昆明"一二·一"惨案发生后，他前往"一二·一"四烈士灵堂致祭，并且手书"魂兮归来"大字横幅一张，以及词为"徒手的学生中手弹而殉命，谁偿此赤血；无党之青年受党棍之欺压，惟诉诸青天！"的挽联一幅，以声讨国民党反动派杀害爱国学生的滔天罪行。他还被西南联大教授会选派为教授代表，前往会见新上任的云南省政府主席卢汉，要求严厉惩办凶手和保证大学师生今后的安全。

1945 年底，北京大学为了筹备复校工作，派赵迺抟教授提前回到北平，担任北京大学复校委员会委员。同时回到北平担任北大复员会委员的还有傅斯年、郑天挺两位教授。到北平后，他又兼任北

平临时大学补习班的总务长。这个补习班的任务主要是对抗战时期在北平各大学上学的学生进行补课和考试，考试合格后将他们分配到北大、清华、南开等大学继续学习，这个临时大学补习班的办公室就设在北大二院校长办公室原址。1946 年夏，这个大学补习班的工作宣告结束。

西南联大于 1946 年 5 月宣布解散，恢复北京大学、清华大学、南开大学三校的建制。教师们回到他们原来所属的大学，学生们按照自己填报的志愿，分别分配到北大、清华或南开继续学习。联大广大同学从 5 月起陆续离开昆明，他们坐救济总署的卡车出云南，横越贵州，入湖南，至长沙，换小轮船经洞庭湖到武汉，再换救济总署安排的军舰顺长江到上海；在上海换救济总署安排的海轮到秦皇岛，转乘火车回到平津。辗转跋涉，他们于 1946 年秋才陆续到达平津。

赵迺抟教授回到北京大学后，仍担任经济学系教授、系主任和经济研究所所长，继续从事教学、行政、科学研究和指导研究生的工作。同时，他还兼任大学一年级课业委员会委员、北京大学财务委员会主任委员等职。那时，北京大学一年级学生和先修班学生在第四院（现新华通讯社所在地）上课和住宿。1948 年间，北京大学又委派他兼任国会街北大第四院主任，负责指导和管理大学一年级学生和先修班学生的学习和生活。

1948 年国民党反动派在即将覆灭的前夕，在北平非法逮捕了北大经济学系同学孟宪功、李恭贻，他深为愤慨，并曾两次前往特种刑事法庭私设监狱进行探视和慰问。在探视中他对国民党特务的无理要求严厉地加以驳斥。

1947 年国民党政府抛出了一个所谓"经济改革方案"，妄图挽救国统区的经济危机。赵迺抟教授与北大、清华等校的陈岱孙、周炳琳、周作仁、陈振汉、樊弘、杨西孟、蒋硕杰、秦瓒、王毓瑚、刘大中、徐毓楠、吴景超、赵人儁、费孝通等教授共十五人，联名发表了《我们对于〈经济改革方案〉之意见》。在这份意见书中指出："此方案对于过去种种错误，未尝虚心检讨"，"此方案对于目前经济危机，并无救治之能力"，对国民党反动派的反人民的经济政策，加以揭露和抨击。

从抗日战争胜利到北京解放以前，赵迺抟教授在《北京大学成立五十周年纪念论文集》、《经济评论》、南开《经济周报》、《现代知识》等书刊上，发表过：《五十年来美国经济思潮的主流制度经济学派》、《欧美经济思潮之演变》、《古典经济学的盛衰》、《我国目前的经济是政治的牺牲品》、《论中国今日经济问题之症结》等学术论文。又在《大公报》、《中苏日报》、《益世报》、《平明日报》、《天津民国日报》、《华侨商报》、《民生导报》等报纸上发表过"星期论文"和"专论"数十篇。其中：《今后我国银行业的危机》、《铲除官僚资本三大理由》、《大学教育的歧途》、《物价与人心》、《我国经济建设的歧途》、《宪草修正案中经济条款评议》、《读经济紧急措施方案有感》、《经济紧急措施方案质疑》、《漫谈议价与限价》、《从速开征临时财产税》、《重论政府公布的经济方案》、《我国外汇政策的蜕变》、《评节约消费纲要》、《申论严惩贪污重于节约消费》、《大钞与物价》、《经济平衡与财政平衡》、《马克思〈共产党宣言〉百年纪念感言》、《经济科学非孤立科学，与政治有密切关系》、《我国土地改革的二大问题：制度与技术》、《我国币制改革的"三慧"》、《我国市场上的有效需求与游资》、《评"财政经济紧急处分"条文》、《如何推行"勤俭建国运动"——节约的美德必须由老百姓自己培养，浪费是万恶，必须由政府用权力向豪门巨富彻底根除》、《我国近二年来经济措施的失策》等。

这一时期，国民党反动派发动了反人民的内战，国民党统治区的经济日趋崩溃。赵迺抟教授所写的这些论文，有不少是批评国民党政府的经济政策以及抨击垂死挣扎的"经济改革方案"的。有不少论文的矛头是指向蒋、宋、孔、陈"四大家族"的。他在论文中主张:"铲除官僚资本","打倒官僚资本,实行经济革命"和"平均财富之分配"。他写道:"不扫除官僚资本,一切政治经济是无法改善的。"他严肃地指出:"社会若不铲除官僚资本,官僚资本必将覆灭社会。"

他在一些论文中,竭力反对国民党统治区的"恶性通货膨胀",反复陈述"物价高涨之弊害"。他指出:"物价问题,关系民生至巨。在物价之继续狂涨中,人民之生活标准,日趋降低,直使难以维持,大有民不聊生之势。"他在 1946 年写道:"八年以还,不佞曾于昆渝两地,数度讲演物价高涨之弊害,唤醒国人,不幸因情势之演变,竟酿成恶性通货膨胀,吾获知言之明,而举世受其殃,不亦悲乎。"他竭力主张:"管理通货","必以停止滥发纸币为第一要务"。

还有一些论文,竭力反对官僚买办政治的财政。论文中写道:"财政家不是买办,更不是账房",不能凭"一道手令,一句面谕,即可予取予夺"。把矛头直指反动统治的头子蒋介石。他在论文中尖锐地指出:"万不能用人民的血汗从金库消耗到火药库。"他坚决主张:"必须大刀阔斧向豪门资本算账";向"豪门巨富开征临时财产税"以及"严厉切实执行遗产税";同时,"严格限制"货币发行和"管制物价"。

在 1948 年夏国民党政府准备发行金圆券的时候,蒋介石飞到北平召集赵迺抟教授等经济学家征求他们对发行金圆券的意见,赵迺抟教授在会议上毫不客气地严厉指出:发行金圆券绝对不会成功!他还发表文章指出:这种"币制改革,决不能稳定物价"。后来,在 1948 年 8 月 20 日,即国民党政府发行金圆券的第二天,他就发表文章指出:金圆券的"命运必与法币相同",预见了金圆券必然彻底破产的命运。

这时，对于我国农村的土地改革，他发表论文主张："过去的租佃关系，必须废除。"他还在论文中指出："土地改革必须对于地权的制度和利用的技术双管齐下，才能成功。"

七、《欧美经济学史》的写作和出版

《欧美经济学史》是赵迺抟教授撰写的一部经济思想史的学术著作。

《欧美经济学史》是他多年来在北京大学和西南联合大学主讲经济思想史课程的基础上写成的。初稿写于滇南的鹅塘极其艰苦的生活条件下。初稿写出后，他仍在西南联大继续讲授此课，每讲一遍，就修改一次。复员回到北京大学后仍继续讲授此课程和修改此书稿。直到1948年夏才在北平完成了《欧美经济学史》的定稿工作。此书是赵迺抟教授二十余年来研究和讲授经济思想史的结晶。

全书除绪论外，共分重商主义与重农主义、英国经济思想、美国经济思想、德国经济思想、奥国经济思想、法国经济思想等六篇；重商主义、重商主义经济学家、重农主义、重农主义经济学家、重商主义与重农主义之比较、18世纪英国之经济状况、英国经典学派之创立——亚当·斯密，马尔萨斯之经济学说、李嘉图之经济学说、继承派与祖述派之经济思想、独立派与批评派之经济思想、约翰·穆勒之经济学说、钱文思之经济学说、马歇尔之经济学说、美国经济思想绪言、殖民地时期及国家成立时期之经济思想、国内经济发达时期之经济思想、美国现代经济学派、府库主义之经济思想、德国古典学派之经济学说、德国社会主义学派之经济学说、国家主义派之经济学说、历史学派之经济学说、边际主义之理论、孟格之经济学说、费沙之经济学说、庞巴维克之经济学说、奥国学派之优点

与缺点、法国经济思想引言、法国正统学派之思想、法国社会主义
之思想、法国和谐经济之思想——巴士夏、连带责任主义之思想等
三十三章。书后附有详尽的文献目录，包括欧美经济学史之文献、
中文欧美经济学史参考书、研究中国经济思想史之文献等附录。

本书对欧美近代各流派经济
思想家的学说包罗较为完整，其
中着重对七十多位欧美经济学家
的生平和经济学说做了专门的考
证和论述，共约 45 万字。不仅论
述了重商主义、重农主义、古典
学派资产阶级经济学说和庸俗派
资产阶级经济学说，而且也论述
了空想的和科学的社会主义经济
学说。对于社会主义的经济学说，
既有介绍和论述法国的空想社会
主义的专章，又有介绍和论述马
克思和恩格斯的科学社会主义的

赵迺抟所著的
《欧美经济学史》初版

专章。本书在资料考证上，详实可靠，有些资料不仅注明了出处，
而且还引用了原文，初学的读者可以节省许多查找原书的时间。因
此，这是一本很好的经济思想史的大学教程。1948 年，此书在北京
校阅了多次，完成了清样。本书原拟在商务印书馆出版的，不意被
北大校友吴俊升闻讯后，以正中书局出版较快等理由坚决索去，作
为正中书局的"大学用书"出版。1949 年初，本书即将在上海发行
时，正值上海解放前夕，正中书局迁往台北，并将纸型和书稿运往
台湾，在台北发行。因此，本书没有在祖国大陆发行，在大陆极为
罕见。可是，本书在台北却一而再、再而三地出版和发行了九版之
多，在台湾和海外得到较为广泛的流传。赵迺抟教授并没有得到本

书的任何稿费。该出版社对此曾表示：赵迺抟现在并不在"自由世界"，不能发给他任何稿费；只有在他到达"自由世界"以后，才能付给稿费。赵迺抟教授闻讯对之一笑了之。台湾学术界的有识之士，对此曾提出意见，认为这种说法和做法毫无道理，并为之打抱不平，但亦均无济于事。

八、解放后延聘新人开设新课程

北平解放前夕，南京政府企图将北京大学迁往南方，受到广大师生们的抵制，赵迺抟教授和北大许多教授们一起反对将北京大学迁往南方。北平城解放前不久，南京政府派来专用的飞机，要接北大教授们飞往南京，也受到教授们的抵制。赵迺抟教授同许多教授一起拒绝搭乘飞往南京的专机。北京大学只有极个别的几位教授才搭此专机飞往南京，如化学系的钱思亮教授，他后来在台湾担任台湾大学校长，他的儿子北大经济系一年级学生钱纯，后来曾任台湾的财政部长和行政院秘书长。专机是傍晚在北京南苑机场起飞的，胡适校长和南京政府官员们夜间在南京机场迎接到的绝大多数并不是教授，而是乘此机会挤上飞机的一般党政工作人员，因而使他们非常失望。赵迺抟教授同广大师生一起，留在北平迎接了北平城的解放。

1949 年初，北平解放了。北京大学经济学系停止开设介绍资产阶级经济学基本原理的"经济学概论"课程，新开设了讲授马克思主义经济学的"政治经济学"课程。这时，赵迺抟教授主动开设了"价格概论"新课程，讲授马克思主义政治经济学中所不着重讲解的关于价格的形成、需求与供给、竞争和市场等理论。价格理论是市场经济学的核心问题，他的"价格概论"的课程内容涵括了市场经济学的极重要部分。可是，那时人们热衷于计划经济，在计划经济的思想支配中，市场经济不但不被重视，而且被当做资本主义经济来看待，因此，他的"价格概论"课程在当时也得不到同学们的重视。

解放之初，赵迺抟教授还诚恳地接受经济学系同学们的建议，积极延聘经济学家中的共产党员和民主人士到北京大学来担任经济学系的兼任教授等职务，开设新中国经济建设迫切需要的各门新课程。他们是王学文、薛暮桥、郭大力、狄超白、千家驹等著名经济学家。他还曾主动提出聘请王亚南教授来经济学系任教，但因其他原因而被清华大学先一步聘去。他还接受同学们的建议，邀请各有关的经济部门的负责同志，如南汉宸、何长工等来经济学系作专题报告。这些新的课程和专题报告对培养学生们参加新中国经济建设的能力，以及对于北大经济学系的教学改革，都起到了很好的作用。

从 1949 年夏起，他不再担任北京大学经济学系主任职务，只任教授，主要从事学术研究。

1951 年党号召知识分子参加伟大的土地改革运动。他响应号召，自愿报名和北京大学经济学系的师生们一起到广西省柳城县参加土地改革工作队的工作。在参加土地改革工作中，他具体了解到旧中国封建剥削的残酷和惨重，提高了阶级觉悟和思想认识。

在 1952 年的知识分子思想改革运动中，他认真学习，作了比较深刻的思想检查，并且表示要彻底批判自己的资产阶级经济学学术思想，争取对社会主义革命和社会主义建设事业作更多的贡献。

1952 年夏，我国高等院校进行院系调整。新的北京大学经济学系由原北京大学、清华大学、燕京大学、辅仁大学四所大学的经济学系的政治经济学专业调整而成。赵迺抟教授被教育部分配在北京大学经济学系继续任教授。

新的北京大学从城内迁往北京西郊燕园，经济学系的教师队伍得到扩充和增强。这时，"经济思想史"课程的教学工作已经后继有人。赵迺抟教授考虑到自己年事已高，就大力扶植后学，将自己数十年来积累的教学参考资料毫无保留地提供给当时担任"经济思想史"课程教学工作的中年教授徐毓楠长期使用。这些教学材料直到1958年徐毓楠教授病故以后，才由资料员杨瑛同志从徐毓楠教授的研究室中整理出来，送还给赵迺抟教授。

九、潜心研究中国经济思想史

赵迺抟教授专长西方经济思想史，可是他却从不低估中国经济思想史的重要性，他积极主张用科学的方法来研究中国经济思想史。凭借他渊博的经济学学识、深厚的国学基础、科学的研究方法和严谨的治学作风，他在研究中国经济思想史上有着很多有利的条件。

解放以后，赵迺抟教授在党的知识分子政策的感召下，反复考虑自己如何贯彻党的政策，为我国学术文化事业更好地贡献力量。他想到，中国经济思想史在当时是尚未开辟的一个新的学术领域，全世界对中国经济思想史都还缺乏研究。在这个领域中，虽然原始的文献资料浩如烟海，汗牛充栋，可是它们大都未经整理，因此，研究中国经济思想史的工作必须从收集和整理原始的文献资料入手。早在1952年，赵迺抟教授就开始收集和整理中国经济思想史的原始资料。1953年的一天，毛泽东、周恩来邀请北京各大学的教授们到中南海怀仁堂观看京剧，赵迺抟教授也应邀参加了，京剧演的是《萧何月下追韩信》。观剧回来后，赵迺抟教授非常高兴地同北大经济学系的同志说："我看出了这台戏的深刻含义，毛主席、周总理是多么希望知识分子在社会主义建设事业中发挥更大的作用啊！"从此，他更坚定了研究中国经济思想史的志向，决心在这个领域中做一名淘沙者，踏踏实实地从收集和整理资料工作做起。

1955年11月27日，中央文委和国务院二办副主任范长江同志到北京大学作关于知识分子政策的报告，赵逎抟教授坐在会场前排听得十分认真。会后，范长江同志到燕东园 29 号教授宿舍去看望他昔日的老师赵逎抟教授，向他表达党对他的关怀。赵逎抟教授感动得流下了热泪，更加下定决心，要"肩负起整理祖国文化遗产的工作，来报答党的关怀和信任"。于是，他早起晚睡，夜以继日，孜孜不倦地批阅数以万卷计的古典书籍。到 1958 年底，他已编成《近代重要经世学者之生平简介》、《历代经世学者之姓名及其重要著作》等书稿，取得了初步的成果。

赵逎抟教授对中国经济思想史的研究并不以此为满足，他修订了自己的研究计划，要进一步进行中国经济思想史资料的汇编工作，打算将分散在经部、史部、子部、集部中各种大量著作内的所有经济思想资料，统统整理出来，编成一部大型的中国经济史文献方面的学术专著。

他将这部大型学术专著定名为《披沙录》，取其"批阅万卷，沙里淘金"的意思。起初，全书计划分为七卷，后经修改，改为五卷。《披沙录之一》分上下两集：上集为《中国历代经世学者人名录》，辑录各种史书——《食货志》、《十通》、《明经世文编》七种、《清经世文编》十四种——当中经世学者的籍贯、生平及著作。下集为《中国经济思想文献要籍简介》，扼要介绍了经书、子书、专集、史志、政书、类书、经世文编、诏令、奏议、会典、言行录、实录、笔记、经济专题著述、经济思想史以及近代人有关经济思想史的论著。本卷为研究中国经济思想史的基础知识资料专著，供学者查找我国古今有关经济思想的论著及片段或零星的各种思想观点。《披沙录之二》为《春秋战国至汉初诸子经世思想》，包括了儒家、墨家、法家、兵家、杂家、道家以及汉代诸子的著作中有关经世思想的论述。《披沙录之三》为《唐宋元明清五代经世资料》，选录了这五个朝代全部文集、奏议、论说、传记等文献中有关经济思想的资料。

《披沙录之四》为《通鉴中的经世资料》，包括了资治通鉴、续资治通鉴、明鉴、清鉴各大部头书籍中有关经世的资料。《披沙录之五》为《历代本纪及列传中的经世资料》，选录了历代重要史籍中有关生产、流通、财政、金融、农田水利以及教育等方面的资料。

在"文革"中赵迺抟教授也受到迫害，手稿全部抄家时被抄走，有一部分文献资料被毁，住房大部分被占，编书工作一度完全无法进行。可是，只要环境一有可能，他就偷偷地进行辑录和抄写。粉碎"四人帮"以后，他朝气焕发，干劲倍增，重整旗鼓，加速进行《披沙录》的编写工作。这时，杨瑛同志在整理经济学系仓库时发现了赵迺抟教授被查抄的全部手稿，予以发还，这使他喜出望外，从而减少了他重新编写的许多劳动。他在1978年初步完成了《披沙录》的初稿，全书长达600万字，均用工整的蝇头小楷写成。这是他历时二十余年孜孜不倦、呕心沥血地钻研的结果。他后来又将《披沙录》书搞加以修改和精简，起初将全书压缩为300万字，后又压缩到200万字左右。

赵迺抟教授编写《披沙录》，自称"本无问世之意"，只是要"做淘金者、拓荒者，为后人铺路架桥"，希望身后存放在北京大学图书馆中，有朝一日能为后人所用，他也就"死而无憾"了！可是，出乎他意料的是，随着党的拨乱反正和科学的春天的到来，《披沙录》受到各有关方面的重视。《人物》杂志1981年第2期上有一篇文章认为："这是一笔宝贵的财富。"《光明日报》于1980年1月14日，以《锲而不舍，为而不有》为题，撰文加以报道，并用这八个字来概括赵迺抟教授二十多年来坚韧不拔的努力。《光明日报》又在1980年7月19日以《研究中国经济思想史的一块基石》为题，对《披沙录》加以介绍和评价。该报导的"编者按"中写道：

"北京大学经济系赵迺抟教授经历二十二个年头，编纂数百万字的《披沙录》……现在即将出版。这对热心中国经济思想史的研究工作者来说，是一大喜讯。中国经济思想史的科学著作很少，要在这方面有所成就，只能从系统地收集有关的资料开始；否则，研究工作只能建立在沙滩上。作为这一项事业的拓荒者赵迺抟教授，用他的心血铸造了一块基石，我们怎能不为这位年过八旬的老人这种呕心沥血的精神所感动呢？"

《北京日报》于 1981 年 1 月 13 日，以《愿将垂暮日，努力追长征》为题，对赵迺抟教授的学术研究工作作了专门的报道。

赵迺抟教授抗战前北大经济学系的老学生邓立群同志这时担任中共中央书记处书记，他曾多次来北大看望赵迺抟教授，并且说：你是我真正的老师。那时，邓立群同志还兼任中国社会科学院副院长。赵迺抟教授孜孜不倦地编写《披沙录》的消息被广泛报道后，中国社会科学出版社专程来将书稿约去，准备不惜工本在该出版社迅速出版。可是，北京大学领导闻讯后，认为北大教授的著作，应在北京大学出版社出版。他本人则服从校方意见，同意在北京大学出版社出版。

1981 年 10 月《披沙录（一）》，在北京大学出版社正式出版，并由全国各地新华书店发行。本卷约 40 万字，第一版印行了一万册。该书的出版，不仅受到中国经济思想界的重视，而且也得到我国图书馆学界的好评。

华东师范大学图书馆学系的卢中岳先生，在《广东图书馆学刊》1982 年第 1 期上发表了《谈〈披沙录〉目录学方法的特色》一文。文章写道："《披沙录》是一本颇具特色的经济学科论著书目索引。"文章认为：《披沙

披沙录之一

录》的第一个特色，是在揭示资料上已深入到第三级，将一本书的片断论述揭示出来，"以往出版的较好的学科论著书目索引，一般是将一个学科的图书目录、报刊论文索引与论文集中的篇目索引结合在一起。……这种结合在反映书刊资料上只反映到二级，即以一本本图书为单位揭示资料，和以图书报刊中的一篇篇文章为单位揭示资料，对于一篇文章中某一片断或某一部分资料的揭示，绝大部分的学科论著书目索引未能深入到此。《披沙录》在揭示资料篇目上深入到这第三级，即一篇文章中有某一部分或某一片断有相关的论述，同样把这篇资料揭示出来，并在全书内同时运用这一级、二级、三级的方式揭示资料篇目。"《披沙录》的第二个特色，是全书同时运用多种目录学方法。"它同时采用了书目、篇目索引、主题索引、提要、人物小传等，将古今的目录学方法比较有机地结合起来。"《披沙录》的第三个特色，是对若干目录学方法有所发展，"最明显的是，将提要与索引相结合。""此外……人物为标题的带有主题性的篇目索引，在目录学方法上也是颇具匠心的。"

图书馆学专家卢中岳先生还认为："《披沙录》的特色还不止于此"，它还有揭示资料的一些特色。"一是通史式的揭示资料……将古代、近代、现代的资料融为一体……使人有此一编，就能检索从古至今的经济文献。""另一是全面系统地揭示资料。尽管科学研究要求全面系统揭示资料，在目录学理论上主张书目索引要全面系统揭示资料，但真正做到此的是微乎其微。这主要表现于学科论著书目索引在揭示本专业的书刊资料上是做到了较为全面系统，然而对非专业书刊中有关本专业的资料则大都未能做到全面系统地揭示。《披沙录》对专业和非专业书刊中的资料都能做到较为全面系统揭示。"最后，这位图书馆学专家令人信服地指出：

"要把古今非专门书刊文献中，将有关经济的文献揭示出来，这是巨大的工程。《披沙录》能将其揭示出来，是此书最有价值之处和最可贵之处，也即编者披沙拣金的结果。"

《披沙录（二）》于 1986 年在北京大学出版社出版。上卷为《春秋战国时期诸子的经世思想》，包括儒家、墨家、法家、兵家、杂家、道家等的经世思想；下卷为《汉代诸子的经世思想》，包括陆贾《新语》、《淮南子》、桓宽《盐铁论》、杨雄《法言》、王充《论衡》、荀悦《申鉴》、王符《潜夫论》等的经世思想，以及汉代各个时期的经世思想与政策等。

到 1985 年，88 岁高龄的赵迺抟教授还不辞辛苦地继续修改《披沙录》以后各卷。他将《披沙录（三）——唐宋元明清五代经世资料》修改为 60 余万字，《披沙录（四）——通鉴中的经世资料》修改为 40 余万字，并已陆续交给北京大学出版社准备付印。《披沙录（五）——历代本纪及列传中的经世资料》的定稿工作则仍在继续进行中。

十、庆祝从事学术活动 56 周年

1981 年时，赵迺抟教授在北京大学经济学系已经连续任教达 50 周年，加上他在其他学校的任教和从事学术活动，则已达 56 周年。1979 年，他的学生和同事，钱学森、邓力群、千家驹、何锡麟、陶继侃、姚曾荫、陈振汉、赵崇龄、胡代光、易梦虹、徐旋、赵靖、闵庆全、罗真崑、杨道南、范家骧、赵辉杰、马雍、张盛健、洪君彦、傅骊元、厉以宁、巫宁耕等倡议出版一部学术论文集，以资纪念。他们在倡议书中写道：

赵迺抟教授治学谨严，一丝不苟，埋头著述，锲而不舍。对于中西学术思想之源流，具有精湛的论述。诲人不倦，数十年如一日，桃李满天下，在祖国经济科学的教育事业中作出了巨大的成绩。为此，创议出版《经济理论和经济史研究》学术论文集，以纪念赵迺抟教授任教 56 周年和在北京大学连续任教 50 周年。

由于他的许多学生和同事的积极响应和踊跃撰稿，《经济理论与经济史论文集》一书于 1982 年由邓立群、钱学森等领衔，在北京大学出版社出版。书中收集了知名学者、教授邓立群、钱学森、滕茂桐、刘方棫、智效和、叶方恬、巫宝三、赵靖和常卓超、马雍、李德彬、蒋建平、朱懋庸、张友仁、范家骧、蒋光远、姚曾荫、陶继侃、傅骊元、张秋舫、陈振汉、厉以宁、巫宁耕、沈振宏、赵辉杰、张盛健、易梦虹、闵庆全、杨道南、田万苍和王茂根、宁嘉风等 32 人撰写的经济理论和经济史方面的学术论文，共 28 篇，40 余万言。本书内容新颖、充实，论述清晰，对于经济科学，特别是对于经济理论、经济史和国际经济的学习和研究，有一定的参考价值。

赵迺抟教授长期以来坚守在经济科学的教育岗位上，这位园丁的辛勤劳动早已结出了累累硕果，国内外许多教授、经济学家和经济工作者都曾荣列他的门墙，他对我国的高等教育事业和科学研究事业都作出了很大的贡献。北京大学经济学系有鉴于此，于 1981 年 5 月 27 日在北大办公楼礼堂举行了"赵迺抟教授从事学术活动五十六周年（在北大任教五十周年）庆祝大会"，庆祝他在长期的学术活动中作出的显著成绩。会上，北京大学校领导、历届校友、经济学系师生以及在北京的经济学界知名人士，都到会向他表示热烈的祝贺。中共北京大学党委副书记王路宾同志代表北京大学校领导、经济学系的师生代表和校友代表，还有钱学森等曾经接受过他教导的同志们纷纷发言，对赵迺抟教授热爱祖国、献身学术、辛勤耕耘的高尚精神，给予高度的评价。

赵迺抟教授虽然年事已高，但是雄心壮志，不减当年。1979 年秋，他曾写诗勉励自己："夕阳无限好，人间爱晚晴；愿将垂暮日，努力追长征。"同年又自称："行言八三不言老，奋笔著述赴长征。"他借此抒发自己愿意在实现社会主义现代化事业的新的长征中，为繁荣我国经济科学事业贡献自己全部力量的心情。

十一、鞠躬尽瘁　死而后已

正当赵迺抟教授以九十岁的高龄，夜以继日地从事《披沙录》最后一卷的进一步修改定稿工作的时候，不幸脑病发作，住入北医三院专为一级教授增盖的病房，经过多方抢救无效，于1986年12月17日晨在北京逝世。他已真正做到了为发展我国学术文化事业，鞠躬尽瘁，死而后已。

赵迺抟教授毕生从事经济科学的教学和研究工作，是无党派民主人士、中国经济思想史学会名誉理事。他一生从事教育工作，坚持学术研究直到生命的最后一息，在祖国的经济科学教育事业上，作出了很大的贡献，为国家培养了大批人才。

按照赵迺抟教授生前的遗愿：一，把毕生收藏的大量古今中文经济科学书刊，全部献给北京大学，供后人使用；二，将《披沙录》各卷的全部稿酬，献给北京大学设立经济学奖学金，奖励后学。

我们深切怀念赵迺抟教授，我们要学习他热爱祖国、治学谨严、刻苦钻研、一丝不苟地献身教育和学术事业的高尚精神。

2000 年 6 月写于北京大学朗润园

理查德·琼斯：
一位早期英国制度经济学家

前　言

本书试图展现理查德·琼斯的经济理论，他是一位 19 世纪早期的英国经济学家。琼斯对于经济问题的制度分析方法深深吸引了我的注意，其原因在于两点。首先，1920 年到 1922 年间我在北京国史馆做编辑时，那里关于中国经济史研究的丰富历史文献给我留下深刻印象。但同时，我失望地发现英国古典经济学与中国经济制度没有什么共同之处。因此，我急切地想要寻找任何同时强调历史和制度的英国经济学家。

其次，在哥伦比亚大学师从塞利格曼教授、西格尔教授、米歇尔教授和斯姆克维奇教授后，我意识到现代经济理论的发展趋势是要重点关注比较研究、历史对策和制度分析等方法。在这些教授的引导下，我试图探究这些现代思潮能否追溯到古典学派统治经济思想的时期。

我要特别感谢 E. R. A. 塞利格曼教授，他将本论文的选题推荐给我。没有他的引导，我的研究工作几乎无法进行。我还要感谢 E. M. 伯恩斯博士对于本项研究所给予的宝贵建议和建设性指导。没有她的批评和不懈的指导，工作不可能顺利完成。我还要对向我提出建议的 R. W. 苏特先生和帮我校稿的厄玛小姐表达感谢。还要特别感谢我的朋友 S. S. 史劳特夫妇，他们在研究的准备过程中帮助了我。还要特别感谢我的妻子对我的理解关怀和不断鼓励。

赵迺抟
1930 年 4 月 30 日于纽约

目　录

第一章　制度学派的经济学

第一节　制度经济学的主要特征

经济理论遵循批评、重建和认可制度安排的循环。自由放任理论最早明确提出把对重商主义的批评和重建作为一种方法。自由主义的胜利为古典学派的发展打下了基础，他们强调人类的理性、推测人类自然状态并着手解释经济均衡。古典政治经济学讨论竞争的影响，作为人们在追逐利润过程中自利行为的检验。它的基本假设是经济力量的不可变性和普遍性。

但是当今的经济学家对于抽象的经济理论并不是很感兴趣。近年来，他们已经忽视了原有的演绎法而转向越来越多地以事实发现作为研究方法。他们强烈倾向于直接基于人类经济福利的研究领域。很多研习经济学的学生深信经济学的学习应该是通过分析现存状况而寻求经济学原理。大多数年轻的经济学家 [1] 认为区别对待经济理论和经济制度的研究是不对的。他们主张价值和分配理论在经济学中保持重要地位的同时，相关经济制度的补充发展是应该值得期

---

① 近期对制度经济学研究的重要贡献如下：Mitchell："The Prospects of Economics" in The Trend of Economics，1924，edited by Tugwell；Hamilton："The Institutional Approach to Economic Theory" in American Economic Review，1918；Edie："Some Positive Contributions of the Institutional Concept" in the Quarterly Journal of Economics，1927；Thorpe：Economic Institutions，1928。

待的。

制度经济学宣称要满足广义上表述作为一个整体的经济安排的需求。他们把重点放在习惯的形成过程。他们断言习惯主要由现实生活中的纪律形成，而那些被大多数人共享的习惯就被称为制度。制度因为其被普遍接受而变得必不可少。制度经济学试图结合经济现象解释社会秩序的特征。它的调查必须要超越经济体系特征下的买卖行为，并且允许买卖行为在特定的条件下发生。制度经济学绝不能止步于简单的对于惯例、风俗、习惯、思想和行为模式这些我们称之为经济秩序安排的研究，它必须阐述共同组成现代工业社会组织的各种制度之间的相互关系。

制度经济学有四个主要特点。首先，这一经济方法的基础是被广泛接受的人类行为理论。制度方法只是研究群体行为的常规方法，经济学家可以充分利用制度研究是因为制度是大部分人共享的，是大众现象。如果我们想要理解大多数人的行为，制度研究就是重要的任务。

在社会科学中，我们关注过去人类行为的变化，同时我们对未来人类行为的进一步改善也是饶有兴趣。社会生活的变化主要基于人类行为的改变。如果现在一个国家大部分人的生活和他们祖先有很大的不同，这并不是因为现在出生的人们有着更发达的头脑。我们的反射、本能和能力与我们的穴居祖先是非常类似的。而我们现在获得了更高级别的经济福利应该归因于我们思考和行为的习惯与我们的穴居祖先截然不同。通过长时期的变化积累，自身能力得到更有效的运用，我们进化了。正是这些广泛流行的被一代又一代人修正并重新认识的社会习惯，使得我们的行为与我们祖先的行为大不相同。同样，我们后辈的行为与我们的也将大不相同。

只要我们对社会变革感兴趣，我们就必须关注制度下人类行为的累积性变化。习惯在我们的经济活动和其他社会生活中占有重要地位。现在，个人支出很大程度上取决于适当的习惯，而不是个人行为原因。"习惯、惯例、声望——所有这些名词都揭示出社会认可、公众观点或者非胁迫性的尊重优势竞争力对于群体选择行为的影响。"①

个体是社会的产物。他不是自我满足的，并不拥有自然和稳定的需要，而是会根据他所在群体的社会意识不断改变自己的喜好。具体来说，我们行为的大部分是模仿，这得益于别人的发明。现代文明的重大特征就是保存新发现，结果促成了其他人类行为经历的累积性储备。货币经济制度给人类本性打上了烙印，使得我们对于一般刺激有了标准反应，以至于我们对于什么是好的、什么是美的、什么是真的产生了绝对化的观点。在高度标准化的社会习惯中，"制度"一词是最为合宜的术语。因此，行为主义观点使得经济理论逐渐成为研究经济制度的理论。

其次，经济理论应该与现代管制问题相关。问题的转变和一般需求管制使得制度经济学成为一个适当的方法。问题转变的一部分原因是由于人们发现制度是能够导致改变的社会安排，还有一部分原因是由于经济活动一度被自发地认为是由微妙的惯例和思维习惯所控制。在经济领域以及其他科学领域，我们渴望知识成为管制的工具。管制意味着规划经济生活的演进以来适应我们民族的发展目标。经济生活太错综复杂了，不同行业组织状况也是千差万别。用竞争来保证买方能够得到诚信商品和合理价格、卖方能够得到其劳动力和资本的公平回报，这并不能总是令人满意。

我们目前的经济组织有一些弊端。②工业社会的一个突出特点是不确定性，正如消费者欲望的反复无常导致的需求和经济周期的不

---

① Z. C. Dickinson：Economic Motives, 1924, p. 216.

② S. H. Slichter："The Organization and Control of Economic Activity"，p. 328, in The Trend of Economics, edited by Tugwell.

确定性。我们现存的经济组织使得需求成为异常变量，安排预期生产变得特别危险。现代工业的另一个重要特点是存在浪费。浪费存在的根本原因是在现实自由企业的条件下，管理者主要关注一般经济政策和策略，而不是企业内在的管理。但是现代工业最引人注目的一点是在增加产出过程中企业与员工合作的失败。显然，现在比一百年前更急切需要更好的管制经济活动的方法。

制度经济学是从历史发展的角度处理管制问题。[①]原始人类氏族是扩大的家庭，由血缘关系维系，其管制体系相应紧密和完全，产生了原始制度中的共产主义。罗马帝国以其管制体系而闻名，延伸至军事管制，直至其囊括了整个西方世界。中世纪城镇的主要管制机构是商人行会和手工业者行会，同时，教会坚持"公平价格"。随后，商业主义被称为"制约体系"。这一学派关于管制的假设是所有特别重要的生产分支都应得到人为的支持，而最为重要的生产分支是国际贸易、航运和制造业。个人主义的兴起反对重商主义不正当的制约，他们认为个人可以选择自己在什么地方和什么行业里工作，经济应该自己决定哪个生产分支需要改进，而对于质量和手艺的管制应该留给消费者，因为他们拥有选择大权。但是，即使如同亚当·斯密这种真正的个人主义者，他也没有宣称自由企业体系是完美的。他证明一些管制是正确的，因为国家防御比国家财富更为重要。

当今工业实质上是一个受到公众关注的实体，公众在它发展过程中所拥有的投资并没有得到个人主义的充分保护。社会有充分的理由设计有效率的方法来保护或者增进它的利益；管制必须被实验、修正，从而使我们的经济生活计划更好地满足我们的要求。而经济生活特殊领域的管制需要特殊的制度。如果我们想要合理地解决通货膨胀问题，我们必须理解社会的财政金融组织。为了达到这个目

---

① J. M. Clark：Social Control of Business, Chap. Ⅱ.

的，经济学家应该去分析现存制度的运行情况。只有这些理论家首要关注了制度的累积性变化，我们才能接受他们的理论，认为其是科学的。

再次，经济理论应该统一全部的经济秩序，只有制度经济学可以达到这种要求。在用一般的术语描述经济组织时，很显然制度世界里存在各种特殊因子，如银行、货币市场、公司。它们各自运作，但在经济整体中展现了各自特色。长期以来，经济学家处理经济理论是一回事，而处理经济问题，如保险、税收、公共财政、信托基金、劳动力等又是另一回事，二者之间存在着显著的差别。专著很少用到论文里的观点，而论文只把专著作为示例。如果我们能够把经济学看成是累积性的变化，所有对于特殊制度的研究就会成为一个整体的有机组成部分。

最后，制度经济学关注的是问题产生发展的过程。这是一个动态观点，认为经济现象是变化的过程。它处理演进过程就如同处理波浪式的波动一样。演进过程的处理适用于那些没有很多扰动因素、不重复的按照确定的方向发展的变量，如人口的增长。而波浪式波动的处理则针对那些可重复的、根据时间改变运动方向的变量，如价格的波动。

在研究变化的过程中，制度经济学同时考虑了定性和定量的变化。在一定情形下，如经济组织、生产技术和时尚对于需求变化的影响，定性分析与定量分析相比并不是次要的，因为经过几代人后社会结构的永恒特征似乎已经不见了。例如，现在土地对所有人都是自由的，个人领土根据几乎绝对的权利重新分割。另一种情形，如价格、利率和收入分配，定量分析就更为重要了，统计汇编的扩展和进步将会对研究起到促进作用。

人们不可以忘记，在经济学的研究过程中渗透着生命精神，前进和后退、进步和衰败，这些都将影响对于社会制度兴衰的控制。

价格结构、工资体系正如制度一样拒绝保持明确的内容，不仅对于所发生的内容，还包括伴随其发展的内容。演进中的经济学必须包括文化发展进程理论，因为这一理论由经济利益所决定，由经济制度变革所累积而成。科学是与生命过程相关的，而不是机械的、没有思想的。总的来说，我们正处于制度经济学重建的初期，应该响应基于人类行为的现代心理学的科学方法，通过额外的经济实践经验来使得经济生活的管制原理达成一致。

第二节　理查德·琼斯的制度方法

非常有趣的是，我们注意到近期有所发展的经济学说中很少有找不到早期先行者的。

塞利格曼教授说："19世纪20年代和30年代的英国经济学家远不止简单赞同古典学派观点的水平。他们中的很多人能力很强，并无所顾忌地抨击很多占统治地位的假设和结论，从而另辟蹊径。他们的成果已经被现代思想家们重新发现。"①

这一表述是正确的。正如理查德·琼斯，他是抨击李嘉图学说的最重要的经济学家之一，也是现代制度经济学的创始人。他的财富分配理论完全基于他对现存习惯的分析。他认为竞争完全主宰分配的假设是大错特错了。当分配理论固定不变时，分配也就没有明确的规律可考察了。我们不得不考虑各个国家不同的制度。例如，要讨论地租理论，琼斯介绍了各个国家很多不同的经济组织。他是将经济社会的发展回归到经济习惯和习俗。

他说："我们要时刻准备着才不会很惊讶地看到地租的不同体系产生于不同人群、不同环境，将整个社会维系在一起，决定着社会的性质和如何统治，反映出全

---

① Seligman："On Some Neglected British Economists"，Economic Journal，1903.

球绝大部分人群的突出特征，包括社会属性、政治属性和道德属性。"①

他几乎讨论所有经济问题时都会频繁使用"经济习惯"（habits）、"经济习俗"（custom）和"经济传统"（tradition）等术语。他关于贸易平衡体系的论文被认为是早期英国经济制度研究的原创性贡献。而劳动力的非流动性和资本积累问题也是从经济制度的角度进行研究。

琼斯的归纳哲学是"去看看吧"。他坚信决定人们地位和成功并支配人们行为的经济原理只能在实践中被认知。同时，他也指出了经济力量的相互关系，给出了经济现象的切实研究。他建议给予经济动机物理上的、社会上的和政治上的解释。琼斯声称那些单凭自己的意识、观点、感受和动机进行研究的学者一定是浅薄的推理者。他们个人的观察是狭隘的，推理是短暂的，他们甚至认为从此他们就可以预测绝大部分人的行为、进步和财富，从道德和物理特性区分不同人群，理解各种复合因素如天气、土地、宗教、教育、政府等的影响。②

琼斯的归纳法引导他去比较发达国家和不发达国家的不同状况。从劳动力状况、地租支付、资本积累到国民财富，他在他所有的工作中始终强调比较法的运用。在讨论生产力和分配不公问题上，他总是会考虑到不同国家的社会和国民属性。他坚持说："如果我们试图理解诸如工资、地租等问题，不畏艰难去观察各个国家如何雇佣劳动力和支付工资，或者土地主如何使用分配土地的做法将给我们的成功提供很多信息。"这种将不同国家的经济因素进行比较的做法很可能归纳为原理，从而为后进国家在现代经济进步中同步跟进提供可能。

---

① Richard Jones：Distribution of Wealth，1831，p. 4.

② Distribution of Wealth，Preface；Literary Remains，edited by Whewell，1859，p. 188.

琼斯对于经济原理和经济问题没有任何区分。他说理论和实践经常被认为是相悖的。但是，严格来说，理论是检验现实的结果，理论永远都不会和现实相悖。因为他极力强调实践和观察，所以他自然而然倾向于将演绎法的重要性最小化。

演绎法和归纳法孰轻孰重的不同观点取决于不同的情况。有些情况下人们倾向于演绎推理、系统展示、概括和教条化；有些情况下人们倾向于历史偏好、归纳和统计观察。[1]后者偏重特殊研究，甚至微观研究；前者偏重系统规划。每个方法都有利有弊。采用哪种方法取决于特殊问题的性质和个体研究者受到的训练和教育。通过科学方法，工业生产的就业率原理可能与合意就业原理相同。因为财富生产者将使其投资结果达到一个特定点，即所谓的边际利润点。所以，在制造业中，每个人将指出他仅有的能源基金，一部分运用演绎推理法投入到固定资本中去，一部分运用历史经验法投入到原材料中去。学者们所谓的边际利润正如外在世界一样会因为个体不同而不同。[2]

归纳法的使用将扩展我们对于社会相互关系的眼界。它谨慎地观察有限的时间和地点，避免断言理论是普遍的和永恒的。它强调历史的重要性，目的在于发现人们和国家犯了怎样的错误，如何在未来避免类似的错误。归纳法也是可以比较的，即它可以比较经济制度怎样在不同国家起到相同的作用。最后，归纳法可以进行统计，它以统计数据为基础，测量经济力量、估测经济活动的结果。[3]

琼斯关于这一问题的态度可以从他对历史和统计的观点上得到

---

① Wagner："On the Present State of Political Economy", Quarterly Journal of Economics, Vol. I , 1886.

② Edgeworth："The Scope and Method of Political Economy", Inaugural Lecture delivered in 1891 at the University of Oxford.

③ R. M. Smith："Methods of Investigation", Science Economic Discussion, 1886, The Science Company, New York.

例证，而历史和统计都是可以通过经济调查得到的。在对历史事件长期考察过程中，我们分析了经济制度的即时效应和长远效应。无论是本国还是外国历史文献都蕴涵了大量不为人知的经济启示。

琼斯说："我们必须承认，政治经济学需要通过综合而艰难的实践找到所有貌似普遍的定律。我们要牢牢记住，通过不断重复的观察国家历史上正在发生和已经发生的事情，可以将导致大量现象的混合原因分割、检验并得到彻底认知。"[1]

"历史提供了广泛的事实，如果谨慎处理，这些事实将引导和修正我们的诉求。基于人类实践的大量事实会为我们构建经济系统真理提供丰富的材料。如果我们能够彻底考察这些材料并谦虚谨慎地从中得出推理，那么我们对于从政治经济各部门获得合理认知的绝望将只不过是知识分子的胆怯而已。过去是我们自己被现实所磨炼，经济研究就是在讲述过去的故事，并使得我们国家和其他国家的实际情况显而易见，从而得到大多数我们经济使用并敬仰的指令。"[2]

埃奇渥斯坚称琼斯是哲学历史学家，而不仅仅是编年史记录者。[3]

追溯历史并不是简单的堆砌事实，而是要遵循活生生的事实和制度的逐步发展。历史观点包括正确讨论每个时期所拥有的是什么，而不包括对过去的崇拜和对现在的贬损。相反，历史方法可以很好地协调经济进步愿望。种族、时间和地点在历史方法中发挥了重要的作用。

琼斯确实是第一个使用"经济解剖学"这个术语的人。随后，这一术语被德国历史学派的领军人罗雪尔所采用。

"通过对经济进行解剖，我们可以挖掘经济力量深层次的根源、制度的组成和习惯的成因。而我们对一个国家经济结构的这一准确认识将是我们认识世界上不同人过去财富的关键。"[4]

---

[1]　Richard Jones：Distribution of Wealth, 2nd edition, Preface, p. 19.

[2]　Literary Remains, p. 559.

[3]　Dictionary of Political Economy, edited by Palgrave and Higgs, Vol. Ⅱ, p. 491.

[4]　Literary Remains, p. 560.

琼斯在 1833 年做出这样的陈述，而 20 年后罗雪尔几乎用原话采纳了这一观点。罗雪尔说：

"我们的目标简单说来是描述人们的经济本质和经济愿望，探讨被采纳满足这些愿望的法律和制度特性以及采纳后所取得的或多或少的成就。因此，我们的任务是进行社会或者国民经济的解剖学或者生理学研究。"①

琼斯的《国民政治经济学》和德国经济学家 F. 李斯特的《政治经济学国民体系》两书观点非常相似。在一次演讲中，琼斯的开场白是这样的：

"我在努力追溯历史和观测不同人群在现在和过去如何创造和处置他们各自的国民财富。我坚信我们能够运用最可靠的方法，调查得到是什么原因决定了过去不同国家的相关财富，或者说是什么原因决定了我们国家的财富。"②

琼斯还强调处理国民财富的人为因素有赖于人类的技巧而不是物质财富。几年后，大胆攻击古典经济学派的李斯特也有同样的表述。

"我已经认真并努力地研究了那本关于现实生活的书，并与我之前的研究结论、经历和反应相比较。问题是体系的创建并不是基于多元化的世界，而是在于事物的属性、经验教训和国家的要求。"③

从以上两个例子，我们有理由认为德国历史学派采纳了和琼斯一致的科学研究方法。

任一给定时期内正确的经济学原理与那一时期特殊环境是相关的，而不能被认为对于所有时期都是永恒正确的。这一认识在教授历史学派和现代制度经济学时是非常关键的。关注现实世界的经济学说是经验认知的一个分支，它并没有普遍性。④我们对于经济状况

---

① Roscher：Principles of Political Economy, Vol. Ⅰ, p. 111.

② Literary Remains, p. 340.

③ List：The National System of Political Economy, Preface.

④ Cunningham："The Relativity of Economic Doctrine", Economic Journal, March, 1892.

及其变化的认识只不过是经验化的，如果我们总是认为它是一般性的而加以运用，我们可能会犯错。

琼斯非常强调时间和地点因素，同时也强调调查分析和实际应用。

"政治经济学老师首先要检验发生在不同国家的现象，那样他的理论才有安全的基础。这是他的分析和调查部分。接着，他必须要说明这些原理如何在任一给定国家的特殊阶级中得到应用。这是他的实践运用部分。如果他忽视了两部分中的任意一个，他的表现都是不完美的。"①

基于此，琼斯认为李嘉图地租理论的可操作性是有限的，是受限制于时间和地点的。他指出，基于个人所有权和自由竞争假设下的理论是不能在所有权共有和习惯规制地租的东方国家中运用的，也不能运用于如分成制佃农体系下那种土地具有习惯使用权的地方。同样，考虑到时间的限制，琼斯指出李嘉图的地租理论也不能很好地运用于中世纪，那时土地很大范围上是公共持有，土地主和耕种者的关系也不是自由竞争的。

琼斯说："我们应该综合考虑事实情况，那样才可能得到真正全面的理论。如果我们采用不同的方法，如果我们追求一些普遍原理，如果我们因狭隘的观测而沾沾自喜，那么将会发生两件事情：第一，我们所谓的一般原理将会经常被发现没有一般性，我们声称全球通用的主张在发展过程中经常出错；第二，我们将错过大量有益的知识。"②

经济学研究领域已经发生了变化，而且这一变化是历史发展造成的。因为作用于人类本质的动机力量不只是机械力量，它们在不同时期有不同的修正。毫无疑问的是，早期经济学家对于经济状况的历史变化认识不足。他们也没有充分认识到，特别是在相比工业

① Literary Remains, p. 575.
② Literary Remains, p. 569.

化国家落后的社会中，竞争是有限的而且是受到法律和习惯制约的。我们应该充分认识到历史学派鼓励和采取的缜密研究所有部门经济事实的做法是发展一般性经济理论所必不可少的。[1]但是历史方法的追随者不会很快地承担起研究经济制度的重任，因为他们认为只有极少的制度会对全人类或者整个文明时期起到有益或者有害的作用。

尽管基于历史研究的推理优于对于现存事件的观测，但是也存在弊端，因为关于事件本身经常有或多或少的不确定性。对此，琼斯坦诚地指出历史是滞后于现实的，或者说从来就没有记录到现实，而现实的很多信息对我们是最为宝贵的。[2]对于为理论研究提供基础来说，一个不完全不完美的记录可能比没有任何信息更加糟糕。我们是透过迷雾看过去，无法像我们经常交叉检验现实那样清晰。[3]这是狭义上历史方法的缺陷。

统计方法是琼斯提到的第二种方法。琼斯不仅仅是提出使用统计方法，而且他在 1833 年建议组织一个统计学会。

"统计不同于历史。历史陈述了所有对我们推理有用的事实的细节，但是却让我们自己去推测其原因、猜测其影响。它不愿意反省其在英国对于统计调查系统化、保存和传播统计信息方面做得远远不够的事实。从这方面看，同时也从其他诸多方面看，自然科学研究者已经树立了辉煌而有益的榜样。在哲学观点指导下，几乎没有一个部门没有从收集、记录现实的人类社会中受益。我们期望人类和他们的关注点将会很快有足够的兴趣达成一致；统计学会将被增加成为促进英国科学进步的群体之一。"[4]

---

[1] Sidgwick：An Address delivered in 1885. 在 1886 年的科学经济讨论中，塞利格曼教授提交了一篇题为《经济思想的连续性》（*The Continuity of Economic Thought*）的论文。论文讨论了两个问题，第一个是关于经济学说的相对性，第二个是关于政治经济学的连续性，并得到了两个结论。对于第一个问题，他抨击了古典学派的绝对性；对于第二个问题，他阐述了经济科学研究的历史方法和演进方法。

[2] Literary Remains，p. 570.

[3] J. N. Keynes：Scope and Method of Political Economy，p. 326.

[4] Literary Remains，p. 571.

我们发现在英国统计学会 1885 年周年纪念册中，以下有趣的陈述揭示出琼斯是英国科学联合会统计分部的常任委员：

"1832 年，英国科学联合会成立统计分部。随后，也就是协会成立第三年，协会在剑桥开会任命一个永久的委员会来管理协会事务。统计分部委员会主席是巴贝奇先生，秘书长是 D. W. 白求恩先生，其他组成成员有历史学家哈兰、马尔萨斯教授、辛普森和牧师理查德·琼斯，他们都是杰出的经济学家，后辈有约翰·卢布克和 M. 因克泰利克。"（伦敦统计学会 1885 年周年纪念册，第 15 页）

他进一步观察到如果统计调查的精髓能够在世界广泛传播，如果同样现象被所有文明国家同时注意到，而且对于政治问题有同样的认识，那么我们得到可靠而有用结论的时间将会缩短。[1]借助统计方法，经济制度的历史研究和对不同国家不同经济结构的比较分析将变得简单而更加有用。经济科学和统计的正式合并有着极大的优势。如果统计学家倾向于只考虑事实，而经济学家却忽视现实；如果统计学家经常乐于收集现象而不留意规律，而经济学家经常忽视现象直接跳到规律；如果统计学家主要关注干巴巴的数据和图表，而经济学家主要关注于假设、猜想和偏狭的概括，那么，这一合并将纠正经济学家和统计学家容易犯的错误。[2]

有趣的是，当今的经济学家们和一个世纪前的琼斯表述了相同的观点，他们都认为统计是非常重要的。到了杰文斯时代，演绎经济学必须要进行纯粹的经验统计验证的观点更为明确。[3]政治经济学数量化并区分总体与个体的表现是杰出的，在归纳方面趋于统计化，在演绎方面趋于数学化。[4] 用统计描述经济调查是至关重要的。举例来说，对于产量、工资和价格的统计是完整描述社会情况的基本要

---

① Literary Remains, p. 181.
② Leslie: "Economic Science and Statistics", The Athenaeum, 1873.
③ Jevons: Theory of Political Economy, Introduction, p. 22.
④ J. N. Keynes: Scope and Method of Political Economy, p. 341.

素。统计在经济理论的作用首先是提出无法被演绎解释的经验规律，其次是通过检验结果补充演绎推理并提交测试经验。

此外，统计在解释特定、具体现象的经济学运用中发挥了更为重要的作用。当琼斯预测近期数量统计经济学的发展时，他已经洞悉了统计的重大作用。例如，他提出运用统计调查方法研究人口问题。

在统计中，分类方法非常重要。分类是最好的可能排序，可以使得我们的观点同时或先后出现，既能够最好地掌握现有知识，又可以最为直接地获得其他知识。①我们只能根据所发现的事物之间的真实关系对事物进行正确分类，而寻找事物之间真实关系的重要性完全不亚于发现事物的真实本质。分类的价值与一般的科学推理的价值同样广泛。科学的扩展仅能达到准确分类所能扩展的程度。②

琼斯的经济学说是基于他的三重分类。他总是在他的地租理论、工资理论、资本运用理论以及现实问题如什一税折合偿付的讨论中运用这一方法。③

毫无疑问，琼斯是研究经济制度的最为重要的经济学家之一。他关于人类本质的观点根源于习惯和文化。他将人类行为作为大众现象进行研究，关注于制度因素对于人类行为的作用。他了解经济历史和同时代英国以外的情况，总是把时间、地点作为讨论经济问题的要素。他并不寻找均衡水平，但是对于经济制度的累积性变化非常感兴趣。他鼓励在知识和信息进步中使用统计方法。总的来说，相比于他同时代的经济学家，琼斯对于经济学研究拥有更为广阔的视野，他更加关注经济与其他科学之间的关系。

---

① J. S. Mill：Logic，Vol. Ⅱ，p. 258.
② Jevons：Principles of Science，Vol. Ⅱ，p. 345.
③ 详见附录 A。

第二章　生平和一般背景

第一节　社会背景——同时代思想

如果我们要去评价一个经济学家的学说，那么我们决不能忽视他所处时代的社会情况。琼斯的经济理论可能在今天看来很一般，但是当时能够有他所表述的那些思想是不同寻常的。李嘉图去世后的两代人兴起的学派接受李嘉图的政治经济学作为既定真理和公共政策的安全指南。事实上，古典政治经济学从来没有享受这样的青睐和声望，也没有在李嘉图后二十年间得到实践。[1]马丁纽小姐的著作《政治经济学》以新的形式普及了李嘉图学说。几年时间这本著作发行了1万册。内阁部长、报纸编辑和政治家似乎都在相互较量，使得自己的主张得到书中观点的支持。政治经济学俱乐部成立时假定政治经济学原理已经被发现，俱乐部成员组织起来是为了传播原理，他们的职责是严密监控与李嘉图观点相悖的学说并不允许其发展传播。[2]1821年至1845年可以被认为是原理和教条的时期。举例来说，琼斯刚刚出版他关于地租的著作，李嘉图的忠诚信徒麦克库洛奇就在《爱丁堡评论》上发表了严厉的批评，谴责琼斯是异教

---

① Mitchell：The Prospect of Economics, in The Trend of Economics, edited by Tugwell, p. 11.
② Ashley：Address to the British Association, Economic Section, Leicester, 1907.

徒。①政治经济学俱乐部成员的使命是努力限制有害出版物的影响，②而李嘉图学派的影响一直占据主导地位。从以下1831年托伦斯的表述显然可以看出政治经济学当时被认为是已经建立起来的科学：

> "在人类心智进步过程中，任何科学分支创始人的争议时期必须先于一致时期。而对于政治经济学，争议时期已经过去，一致时期迅速到来。因此，二十年来对基本原理几乎不存在怀疑。"③

德昆西称赞李嘉图是伟大的真理发现者。詹姆斯·穆勒认为李嘉图体系极端严密。麦克库洛奇也是基于李嘉图学说，在《爱丁堡评论》上批评当时的经济法规。

经济学领域一度存在着李嘉图神话。毫无疑问，这种对于李嘉图价值夸张的估计在一定程度上源自制造商和其他资本家与旧土地贵族对抗过程中李嘉图体系给予前者的莫大支持。④这是工业革命的一个阶段，人口增加，制造业发展，农业因谷物法的实施而保持繁荣。这就是1817年李嘉图出版他的著作《政治经济学原理和税收》时英国的现实情况。他似乎运用自由竞争行动下精确的理论为看上去无政府的状态安排了明了的秩序，所以这部著作立刻取得了全面的认可。

李嘉图认为人口数量恒定，并假设世界由仅受环境影响的人组成。李嘉图体系认为所有城市居民都希望获得便宜的食物和高利润，而英国的商人早已倾向认为商业中习惯和情绪是有害的，因此已经准备好接受自由企业的理论。

19世纪初哲学激进主义也影响了英国经济学派的兴起。哲学激

---

① 详见第八章。

② 虽然政治经济学俱乐部的每次会议讨论主题都涵盖了俱乐部揭示的一些政治经济方面的问题或疑惑，但是李嘉图的价值与劳动力理论、地租理论和马尔萨斯的人口理论这三大理论对于几乎所有的问题都产生了巨大的影响。

③ Torrens：Essays on the Production of Wealth, p. 13.

④ Ingram：A History of Political Economy, p. 133.

进主义认为所有的政治理论都可以从几个简单的人类本质的公理中推理得出。这一理论的领导者边沁认为给出应该怎样的建议是很容易的，但是阐明是怎样的情况却非常困难。因此，很多追随边沁的经济学家都在讨论"应该怎样"而不是"是怎样"。考虑"是怎样"就是观察，"应该怎样"就是推理，而推理导致了抽象研究。

功利主义再次加强了古典政治经济学派的统治地位。二者结合强调了最终以人类本质为手段的精密计算，反对以习惯或者直觉指导行动，个人主义得到了新的发展，个人判断基于经济主体的最优选择。它有三个前提观点：物质世界是恒定的（正如报酬递减规律）；社会组织稳定，未来没有很大的变化；人类本质是计算机器。这三个观点彻底地渗透到了当时的思想。1848 年正统的政治经济学大体上保持了 1817 年李嘉图的观点。

在这种哲学环境下，理查德·琼斯出现了。他提出了一种非正统的经济学理论，应对一些自由竞争哲学下无法企及的问题。他更感兴趣于制度的累积性变化，而不是抽象理论。在李嘉图学派的发展壮大过程中，他反对李嘉图的一些结论，特别是只在最近的一个非常时期或者小范围运用的有关地租的理论。[①]他强烈要求进行历史调查。但是人们对于他的呼吁置若罔闻，因为大家不准备接受他的学说。为了全面理解他，我们必须追溯他的学术背景和他的经济理论的发展。

第二节　个人背景和友谊

理查德·琼斯出生于 1790 年，是坦布里奇韦尔斯市一位律师的

---

① Dictionary of Political Economy, Vol. 11, p. 310.

儿子。他的早期生活没有在任何传记中详细记载，[①]所以我们无法知道他的早期受教育情况。1812 年 10 月，他在剑桥大学凯斯学院就读。因为他思维敏锐、极其健谈，所以他最早选择法律作为专业。[②]但是他的身体状况与这种职业不相匹配，于是最终他就读了剑桥大学文学与哲学专业，并结识了很多他受益终生的朋友。

追溯琼斯利用归纳法解决经济问题的学术背景，我们发现这一思想是他在剑桥读本科时发展起来的，而且是他大学同伴共同支持发展起来的。琼斯自己也总是说他的思维习惯中最好的部分是在大学培养的。[③]他幽默风趣且品德高尚，自然成为很多圈子的红人，特别是在知识分子中。[④]当他就读凯斯学院时，在三一学院有一个由 J. 赫希尔、G. 皮科尔和 C. 巴贝奇组织的分析学会。1812 年，他们开始组织"周日哲学早餐会"，琼斯也参加了他们的活动。这种大学同伴关系影响了琼斯的思维发展。

琼斯最为亲密的朋友是后来编辑他的《文献存稿》的惠威尔博士。他们都对归纳法感兴趣。琼斯在 1816 年获得硕士学位后离开大

① 以下是一些传记记录：
Men of the Reigh, by T. H. Ward.
Gentlemen's Magasine, March, 1855, p. 360.
Annual Register, vol. 97, 1855, p. 247.
Encyclopedia Britannica, vol. 15, p. 500, 13th edition.
Dictionary of National Biography, vol. 30, p. 157.
W. Whewell, edited by Todhunter.
Dictionary of Political Economy, edited by Palgrave and Higgs.
Peasant Tent, Preface, edited by Ashley.
Literary Remains, Preface, edited by Whewell.
Memorials of old Haileybury College.
Political Economy Club, 1821 – 1920, edited by Higgs, London.
② 埃奇渥斯小姐回忆录里关于琼斯个性的亲切描述（第 3 卷，第 55 页）证实了琼斯著作中表达的"完人"的印象："他提出了成堆的想法，并能快速地完全地表达它们，充分扩展，不错过任何好想法。"
③ Literary Remains, Preface, p. 20.
④ 比如说由赫希尔、E. 雅各布、亚历山大·达尔布莱、皮科尔博士、巴贝奇先生、爱德华·瑞恩、约翰·马斯格雷夫和 T. 格林伍德组成的学术探讨圈子。

学，他担任圣职并在苏塞克斯的很多神职部门实践，深受爱戴。

正如他的学术背景，特别是归纳法思想，滋生于他的大学生活，他的经济理论基础形成于他在苏塞克斯乡下生活的那段时间。如同社会交往和学术朋友帮助他建立了思维方式，苏塞克斯的自然风光和森林美景使得他乐于去观察现实社会。琼斯总是说他对于自然风光的热爱永远都不会削减，而且比其他任何事情都更富有乐趣。因此，他决定定居在以多样化闻名的苏塞克斯。①南部微风轻拂的开阔的丘陵地、险峻的常克顿伯瑞山、宽广绵延的旷野、荒弃的城堡和修道院、逝去的雄辩时代、海水永恒冲洗着的海岸，所有的这些合并起来使得苏塞克斯成为充满魅力的临海地域，因其美丽的山林而深受人们喜爱，因其错综复杂的力量较量而引人深思。琼斯担任苏塞克斯很多乡下教区的传教士职责。1822 年开始，他在布拉斯帝德做了一段时间的助理牧师，深受郊区居民的热爱。1823 年，他在布赖顿与夏绿蒂·艾特瑞结为夫妇。

琼斯在邻居中非常有名，他对于农业问题也很感兴趣，被称为最睿智的农业家。苏塞克斯南部丘陵地带以产羊而闻名。琼斯的农业知识都是他对于政治经济学深思熟虑的结果。他有计划多年的目标，并储备了大量新颖的观点，留待后半生去完善。公众生活中那些令人兴奋的事情并没有分散他的学术精力，从 1822 年开始，在布拉斯帝德，他开始规划他的经济学说。写作《地租》一书时，他的亲密朋友华惠尔一直在鼓励他并提供很多建议供他参考。同时，华惠尔还帮助他解决从大学出版社到发行费用的问题。

①　Bygone Sussex, p. 9.

第三节　他的理论和实践活动

琼斯的著作《地租》在 1831 年一出版就获得成功，这使得他在 1833 年被任命为当时新成立的伦敦国王学院的政治经济学教授。1833 年 2 月 27 日，琼斯发表其就职演说。马勒为我们描绘出琼斯开始教授生涯的生动场景：

"牧师琼斯，国王学院政治经济学教授，6 周前发表就职演说。大约 300 人出席并给予最高评价。大家请求出版他的演说内容，而琼斯的应允是很不明智的，因为演说内容读起来并不像发表演讲时那么好。下一个琼斯的讲座只有大约 60 人出席，其中只有三四个人为此课程付费。所以，如果没有捐助，没有人认同这门课程。结果在上周三，琼斯先生独自和另外一个教授待在教室里，讲座没有进行。"①

如此不受欢迎的原因在于当时国王学院的政治经济学专业绝不是一个热门专业。西尼尔·纳索是琼斯的前任，由于出版了推荐爱尔兰教堂改革和一种新的爱尔兰什一税拨款款项的小册子，他被迫辞去政治经济学主席的职位。当琼斯被任命接替西尼尔职位时，国王学院当局想用"政治哲学"取代"政治经济学"一词。但是琼斯坚持如果"政治哲学"一词被采纳，他将在政治制度方面采取自由态度。保守党历经西尼尔事件，对此极为恐慌，所以他们让步了。

1835 年，琼斯继任马尔萨斯的职位，成为哈利伯瑞东印度学院政治经济学和历史学教授。他是得到玛丽亚·埃奇渥斯小姐的推荐，

---

① Political Economy Club, edited by Higgs, p. 249.

由兰斯多恩勋爵任命该职位的。①在东印度学院与在国王学院的气氛完全不同。琼斯的所有学生都崇拜和尊敬他，他们普遍认为琼斯是所有教授中最聪明的，也许也是最受欢迎的。②

从他在教室开讲的那一刻起，所有学生都知道他需要绝对的安静和集中注意力，不能忍受最轻微的打断。公正地说，人们不得不承认，他是讲演非常精彩的人之一，所以不去认真聆听他讲的每一个字也是很困难的。以下是他的学生 J. W. 雪拉对他的生动描述：

"谁能忘记那些讲演过程中绝妙的伴奏，诸如反复脱掉和穿上长袍和外套的斗争、隆隆的吼声、咳嗽与窒息，尽管难以忍受，但是都不能掩盖清晰的思路、明晰而不受妨碍的课程安排、纯正的感觉和男人的判断力，这些使得讲座极为有价值和指导意义。那些关于政治经济学的内容要优于关于历史的内容。事实上，后者并不缺乏栩栩如生的人物刻画和有价值的总体评论，但是它们太过于要求细节和完备化。所以，可以说，如果一个学生从琼斯讲座中得到他唯一关于印度的历史知识，那么他已经成功通过考试，尽管他可能对这一课程所知甚少。"③

琼斯不仅仅是高效率的、引人入胜的演讲者，他还是日常生活中知名的评论家，特别是晚餐后的发言者。在整个晚餐过程中，他通常是非常安静地坐着，显然处于抑郁状态。但是，学院地窖出产的一杯以上的好酒就会激发他的想象力。虽然他的谈话机敏而有趣，充满故事和逸闻，但是他无意识地一遍一遍重复使得他的教授兄弟们并不开心。他的故事总是一系列连在一起的，他的教授兄弟们太熟悉这些故事的顺序了，所以当一个故事结束后他们都知道下一个

---

① 1835 年，埃奇渥斯小姐在给 P. 埃奇渥斯的信中提到这样的事实："你已经看到我们敬仰的朋友马尔萨斯先生去世的公告。他是多么地爱你！他的政治经济学教授职位由我的一个非常有能力胜任此职的朋友琼斯先生接替。你已经在读琼斯的著作《地租》。我非常高兴最早将这本著作和琼斯本人推荐给兰斯多恩勋爵。正是在兰斯多恩勋爵所在机构，琼斯得到任命。"（The Life and Letters of Maria Edgeworth, edited by A. J. C. Hare, vol. II, p. 616.）

② 他从不提问，也不期望学生提前准备。他考察学生是否取得进步的唯一方法是每个月检查一次他们的笔记。

③ Memorials of Old Haileybury College, p. 173.

会是什么，于是不得不相互对视一笑。而毫无疑问的是，琼斯误认为这是大家感兴趣的表示。琼斯的衣服和背心总在晚餐中溅上油点，人们说他"背心上带着他最后一星期的伙食账单"。

不了解琼斯作为传教士的行为就无法对其个性作出全面描绘。在这一领域，他当然是不同寻常而又独一无二的。他的布道从不超过十五分钟。以下是雪拉提供的生动描绘：

"哈利伯瑞教堂的讲道坛位于圣餐桌之前，面对人群，背对栏杆。它可以灵活地升起，如同那种一打开盖子就立刻弹出人物的玩具盒子。所以，站在上面的牧师就是这样出现了。哦！谁能描述琼斯出现的场景呢？首先，他总是碰倒凳子发出惊人的轰鸣声，接着是气喘吁吁的声音、叹气声和喃喃自语，最后呈现在人们面前的是一个巨大的躯干，满脸通红，棕色假发，时不时会被讲道坛上升遇到的问题所扰乱。他有时也会被讲道坛的不便激怒，前仰后合之后掉了下来，他的语气如同积极的船长在暴风雨中对待疏忽的水手。接下来的布道的主要特点在于一旦他感觉到热或者不舒服就突然结束，从来不考虑演讲的完整性或其他方面问题。"①

除了加入葡萄酒的因素以外，对琼斯的描述都是无趣和乏味的。但是不能因为嗜酒的习惯而认为琼斯没有有规律的行为。在任哈利伯瑞大学教授期间，他于 1836 年被任命为什一税（tithes）委员。除了有讲座的日子，每天清晨他都会坐四轮马车去布罗克斯伯恩的大东方火车站。他魁伟的身躯总是定时出现在肖尔迪奇总站，在特定时间走下火车，然后坐上出租马车去他的办公室。在他的职员和其他官员中，琼斯非常受欢迎。

琼斯在什一税折合偿付（commutation of tithes）中充分体现了他的管理才能。在计划实施过程中，琼斯为和解牧师群体的纷争作出巨大的贡献。这并非简单的工作，因为什一税折合偿付法案改变了现有什一税的一些评估准则，剥夺了神职人员未来因为土地生产增

①　Memorials of Old Haileybury College, p. 180.

加而增加的什一税。琼斯在这一事件上能够颇具影响力得益于他在国王学院任教授时广泛接触了坎特伯雷大主教威廉豪利、伦敦主教布姆费尔德和其他教会高官，因此他知道这些人对于这一问题的看法。1836 年的法案委托什一税委员会负责什一税的折合偿付，前两年采取自愿原则，随后强制执行。他们立刻开始工作，实践的成功证明这一想法是明智的，执行是公正有效的。折合偿付行动大部分在很短时间里取得效果。这归因于杰出人物的领导，很大程度上是指琼斯花费的大量精力、敏锐的头脑和清晰的思路。委员会每年向内政大臣汇报他们取得的进展。最先由琼斯撰写这些报告，以一页为限阐述观点。助理委员和其他下属官员提交的报告格式和说明都主要由他起草。他主要致力于获取每个教区的什一税地图，将土地分成小份分配什一税。这些地图盖有委员会印章，成为教区内外评估什一税的法律依据。

1851 年，什一税委员会取消了分立存在的情况，合并成为一个享有不动产权的委员会，琼斯不再是其成员。离开办公室时，他写下了关于什一税委员会工作的备忘录，指出还有什么工作没有完成，这是给他的继任者的一份说明书。①随后琼斯成为资产委员会秘书，后来又成为英格兰和威尔士的一个慈善委员会委员。他的公共服务能力毫无疑问是杰出的和值得尊重的。

因为是从理论经济学研究转向应用经济学研究，所以，琼斯出版的讲稿没有一定的格式。他从事大量公共服务和对社会现实问题的迷恋耗费了大量时间，因此，他没有达到他朋友们的期望，也没

---

① 在 1851 年年度报告中，琼斯指出在当前什一税委员会截止之后什一税和地租税相结合的情形一定会持续一段时间。这一情形中有些是永久的，有些是暂时的。折合偿付行动的最终成功一定会是在经历了一个合理时期后以法案形式公布什一税，禁止法庭接受索赔。

有展现出他可能拥有的巨大能力。1855 年，琼斯在哈利伯瑞大学去世。①四年后，他的朋友惠威尔搜集了他已经出版和还未出版的讲稿和论文并结集出版，题名为《文献存稿》。②

① "1855 年 1 月 26 日，琼斯教授逝世。他不是病得很厉害，还没有 65 岁，他只是厌倦了自己的自然活力……圣约翰·赫歇尔和惠威尔博士参加了他的葬礼。水晶棺葬于安维尔村庄，离大学大约两英里远。"（Memorials of Old Haileybury College, P. 125.）

② 琼斯出版的著作如下：

An Essay on the Distribution of Wealth, and on the Sources of Taxation, 1831;

An Introductory Lecture on Political Economy, delivered at King's College, with a Syllabus of a Course of Lectures on the Wages of Labor, 1883;

A few Remarks on the Proposed Commutation of Tithes, with Suggestions of some Additional Facilities, 1833;

Remarks on the Manner in Which Tithes Should be Assessed to the Poor's Rate under the Existing Law, 1838;

A Letter to Sir Robert Peel, 1840;

Text – Books of Lectures on the Political Economy of Nations, delivered at the East India College, Hailerbury, 1852.

第三章　琼斯的政治经济学体系

第一节　理论方法的一般特点

琼斯在政治经济学理论方法上与众不同的特点在于他对经济生活发展上的认识，以及他强调研究经济组织应该注重动态分析而非纯粹静态分析。政治经济学是有关社会系统现象的科学。人性和社会制度不是一成不变的，它们随着社会环境和人们日常活动模式的变化而不断变化。不同国家的不同社区或者不同时期下的同一社区都会表现出多种经济发展进程。任一给定社区的经济结构、发展方向、阶级、性别、选民、动产和不动产的分割、生产力的进步、停止或者退步、生活必需品和奢侈品的数量和质量等都取决于政治、道德、智慧以及工业化水平的不同。而若采用历史研究的方法，就必然使经济学与其他学科的研究紧密地联系起来。琼斯的工作正是遵从了这种理念。

琼斯不但是制度经济学家，还对经济福利问题有着极大的兴趣。相比财富问题，他更关注福利问题。福利不仅意味着提供充足的可用的产品，还意味着令人满意的工作生活充满着各种有趣的活动。

"在这些规定生产和财富分配的法案中，我们可以看到其关注于人类利益并表达出对这些利益在哲学意义上的尊重。我们不再将财富视为一堆静态的东西；也不会再将地租、工资或者利润原理仅仅视为代数运算；但是只要这些社会因素因为生产习惯或者分配模式的改变而改变，我们就会对其进行追踪调查。在调查国家财富时我们总会紧紧地将其与人类社会的进步与财富相联系，我们也将紧密地关注国家政治因素的改变，以及人类谋取独立进步和幸福的能力与机遇的改变。"①

他也认同亚当·斯密的有关贫穷的观点：国家财富和政治实力不断增长的过程中，底层阶级的退步和赤贫总是很难被发现的。在对农民地租问题的总结中他表示，客观存在的贫困和悲惨的生活不仅会导致耕种者更加无助，还将对国家的发展造成巨大的障碍——使国家的财富总量、人口数量的增加和文明的发展停滞不前。

琼斯提出了和谐经济的学说，后来这个学说得到了法国的巴师夏和美国的凯里的认同。他的学说是基于他对相关经济问题的乐观估计：

"对于地租、工资、利润这样的年度生产分配现象，当我们进行深入研究的时候，我们至少会慢慢感觉到这样一种忧虑：错误的观念正在慢慢地逼近；当国家的各种资源处于增长的时候，没有哪个造成必然衰退的原因会时常影响任何一个阶级的财富；利润分配的问题是不会有永久的对立面的；在一个人所生存的组织环境中，不需要有什么力量来削弱上层阶级的希望和影响，如果对其有了正确认识，诚信的政府和明智的法律就会拿出一些令人振奋和具有启发性的方案，使得社会上所有阶层都能持久和谐、共同繁荣。"②

在整个分析的过程中，他强调了三个重要论点：第一，农业的进步使生产力可以紧跟上文明进步的步伐；第二，和李嘉图学派的观点不同，他认为地主和资本家之间是没有经济利益冲突的；第三，他倡导比马尔萨斯的人口论更为科学客观的人口理论，他的第二需求学说旨在消除马尔萨斯政治经济学中悲观的论点。

---

① Literary Remains, p. 561.
② Distribution of Wealth, Preface, p. 35.

第二节　琼斯的分配理论

在琼斯生活的年代，对于谷物法的争斗是当时英国经济政策中收入分配问题的焦点。实际问题在于政府是否需要维持农场主和地主的高收入，或者是否降低进口税以增加制造商和商人们的收入。同样，当时的分配问题也是经济学家关注的焦点。理论问题在于是什么决定了社会利益在地主、资本家和劳动者之间的分配?①

琼斯的分配理论与当时的经济学家的学说大相径庭。他从一个完全崭新的角度看待这个问题。他引入分配问题的目的不仅仅在于弄清楚什么因素决定了社会利益在各个不同阶层中的分配份额，而主要在于发现当时不同分配制度下不同国家生产力的差异。

"实践上，生产当然先于分配。但是，虽然一些财富的分配总是在生产之后进行，但是追溯历史，土地和劳动力的分配曾在人类早期对社会的性质和人们的习惯产生了巨大的影响。在很多情况下，生产是不会受到影响的，而在我们可以充分解释现存生产力的不同和不同国家的具体操作之前，我们必须考虑这一影响并将其理解透彻。"②

卡尔·马克思把生产过程看做是塑造社会的重要因素，相反，琼斯将分配过程视做组成社会的基本因素。"我们可以预测：在不同的收入分配方式取代先前的方式之前，所有迅速改变人类特性或者社会生产能力和资源问题的期望都是不切实际的。"③

琼斯还认为，那些研究财富分配原理的人们，不能像那些研究

---

① Mitchell W. C："the Prospects of Economics" in The Trend of Economics，edited by Tugwell，1924.

② Literary Remains，p. 554.

③ Literary Remains，p. 555.

影响生产数量的因素的人那样取得成功。①他认为，在解释分配定律方面，迄今很少会有对立的观点。政治经济学已经不再受信任了。这些结论所依赖的事实论据被认为过于善变和反复无常以至于几乎不可能对它们进行准确的分析，更近一步说，无法得出更加可靠、持久的普遍原理。真理被错失了，因为那些杰出的人士在讨论财富分配问题的时候把注意力集中在了一个狭小的范围之内，以至于构筑了一个有问题的上层建筑学说，这个学说不是完全错误就是被限定在极小的应用范围之内。②在这种窘境之下，琼斯重拾分配理论这个研究选题，但他依靠经验指导和广泛的观察，采用了截然不同的研究计划。

琼斯的《论财富分配》由两部分组成。第一部分关注农民的地租，第二部分则是农场主的地租。这两个部分共同构成了他著作的第一本。他本来想写四本关于财富分配的著作，但是后面三本没有以著作形式出版，而是在他死后以大量讲义的形式出现。从严格意义上讲，他的政治经济学体系是不完整的。为了论述这个问题，他首先使用"地租"这个术语，因为这个问题方面任何一点微小的进展就足以显示世界上较大一部分国家仍然处于那种应该称为农业的状态。在这样的社会形态下，土地的所有者和占用者之间的关系决定了大多数人民生活情况的细节，以及他们的政治制度的精神和形式。③接下来就是工资问题。这个问题被放在第二部分而不是第一部分，因为在他看来，只有调查清楚不同地租的形式和现状，才能对世界上大部分人如何得到他们的报酬有清楚地认识。④至于收益理论，琼斯集中于研究资本在生产过程中是如何积累的，而不是在分配过

---

① Distribution of Wealth, Preface, p. 5.
② Distribution of Wealth, Perface, p. 23.
③ Distribution of Wealth, Perface, p. 23.
④ Distribution of Wealth, Perface, p. 24.

程中的积累。他说："在进行这项工作的时候，我并没有把自己限定在一个单独研究影响利润率最为重要的因素的范围内。"①最后，在税收方面，他论述了税收归宿和公平原则，而最重要的是他强调：在不会抑制或降低生产的条件下，整个国家应该共同享有公共的财富。

在整个财富分配理论分析中，琼斯将注意力主要集中在其他国家的经济制度而不局限于英格兰。除了偶尔尝试对李嘉图的劳动价值理论进行驳斥以外，他不会试图去讨论价值理论。②他专注于可用物品的生产，而事实上，他对分配的研究是研究生产的一个重要步骤。③

第三节　琼斯的生产理论

尽管琼斯选择用《论财富分配》作为书名，但是他对生产理论更感兴趣。因此，在讨论不同类型的土地保有期和不同的劳动力群体时，他总是比较不同制度下不同国家的相对生产力状况。同样地，对于资本，虽然一开始是从分配的角度考虑的，但在事实上比较了辅助资本与流动性资本在生产过程中的重要性。所以，他的分配理论里面总是蕴含着生产理论。

琼斯认为一国生产力决定于以下两个条件：④第一，原始资源是否肥沃；第二，使用资源的劳动效率或者是使用生产出来的商品的效率。在早期社会，土地质量影响财富的创造，但在后期这个影响

---

① Distribution of Wealth, Perface, p. 26.

② "这个理论的检验对我们目前的研究目标来说不重要。然而我认为，由于许多人认为这个理论并不完善，与不同商品的可交换价值比起来其他因素必须考虑在内，包括直接或间接赋予的劳动力数量。"（Distribution of Wealth, p. 206.）

③ 和其他历史学派的作者一样，琼斯并没有将一般的分配原理用公式表达出来。

④ 但是这两个条件都没有论及平均资本生产力理论。

已经很小以至于不用将其考虑在内。"在大部分情况下，相对财富量取决于劳动效率而非土壤或者水资源的差异。"① 他认为，当政治经济学家们把研究限定在与财富的创造、影响劳动效率的因素相关的范围内，并且在对不同国家富饶程度的差异进行详细论述时没有犯严重的错误，则他们的理论是有道理的，这也为亚当·斯密的政治经济学体系进行了辩护。②

追随亚当·斯密的思路，琼斯进一步讨论了决定国家财富增长的一个重要的因素——劳动效率。他提出了三个影响效率的因素，即生产力提供的持续性、管理技能以及扶助能力。③他还讨论了制约人均生产量的环境因素。他指出，全民的财富显然不仅仅取决于工业的繁盛或者在生产中的投入份额，还取决于从事非财富生产的劳动力的比例。"如果一个国家四分之三的人都是军人或者仆人，纵使另外四分之一可能是多产的劳动者，这个国家也终将贫穷。"④琼斯还对生产力和非生产力进行了区分，但他聪明地运用了这两个术语。他指出，我们不能犯下这个普遍的错误，即认为社会中没有参加生产的人是没有生产能力的，而"没有生产能力"这个说法是对人格的侮辱。

在比较各国的劳动生产率时，他对激励动因和机械优势进行了区别。他说：

"在我们比较不同国家的劳动效率时，对比运用含有更大机械优势的同一激励动因的创造手段的差别就显得至关重要。通过比较法国和英国的马匹的相对数量，

---

① Literary Remains, p. 334.

② 下面的引言表明了琼斯对亚当·斯密在生产问题上的认同程度："斯密是这条新路（生产理论）的领路人；在他之后，这一方向的研究和他的观点大同小异。"（Distribution of Wealth, Perface, p. 4.）"在生产问题论述的最后一个分支中，集中展现了大量的相关知识，构建了很多服务于理论或者实践的原理，虽然它们在特定条件下的应用可能会遇到困难。这些知识理论共同构建了一个政治学思想体系，它的完整性和持续性对于人们具有启发意义，这个想法可以被大多数人所接受。"（Distribution of Wealth, Perface, p. 5.）

③ 所有这些因素都取决于资本的运用，这个问题将在下一章中讨论。

④ Distribution of Wealth, p. 346.

我们无法比较两国的生产力，直至马匹可以促进生产，即除非我们能够获悉这些马匹的应用价值确实在两国农业和其他行业体现出来了。"①

在当时，没有哪位作者能像琼斯那样把这么多的注意力集中在技术问题之上。他坚信在那个充满活力的时代，可获得的技术决定了人们征服利用自然的能力，也正是这些成就促成了物质文明的发展。由于我们的经济生活水平是技术应用和自然开发的产物，因而经济科学和经济制度的发展与技术的进步息息相关。所以，在讨论生产的时候，不能忽视技术这一问题。

琼斯赋予"生产"更广泛的含义。一篇文章只有放在读者手中才能算做全部完成。茶叶在从中国贩运到英国之后，才被英国人消费；它通过个人和各种形式附属资本的中介运作从而进入消费者手中。②这种包括在生产过程中的交易现象在他那个年代并不常见。③在琼斯看来，生产不一定仅指物质资料的生产，新的效用的创造也可以囊括在其中。我们也可以将能增加现存效用总量的活动视为生产。

琼斯一直强调国家经济社会组织和生产力之间的重要联系。他首先概述了劳动、技术知识和机械设备的持久性标准，用来判断一国生产力是否完善。接着他讨论了伴随社会经济结构变化的政治、社会、道德、智慧等因素的变化。他指出，对于政治经济学家来说，解释这些影响因素是一项特殊的任务。如果这些选题被研究者完全回避，经济科学就无法成功发展。他认为国家的经济习惯是国民财富研究中的一个重要因素。"我们思考用什么模式能对国民财富进行抽象概括时，这种对各个民族经济习惯的分析显然有着巨大的作用。"④他进一步指出，随着国家生产力的改变，人们也必然改变他们

---

①　这段话是琼斯用来揭示 M. 杜班的谬论的，M. 杜班认为英国和法国的生产力差别仅仅在于激励动因不同。

②　Literary Remains, p. 192.

③　继詹姆斯·穆勒之后的英国作者都倾向于遵循他在研究生产交易过程中的思考方式。

④　Literary Remains, p. 340.

的习惯。在这个变革或者说进步的阶段，社会上不同阶级的人认识到阶级之间有了新的关系，他们被指定了新的身份，他们被新的道德和社会问题所困扰，也同时置身于一个新的社会政治环境中。琼斯始终坚信，制度的积累性变化是解释生产力问题的关键。

第四节　琼斯政治经济学的其他特点

尽管琼斯批评那些试图给出准确定义的做法，但他总是乐此不疲地创造新的术语。①除"契约平衡体系"（Balance of Bargain）和"国家解剖学"（National Anatomy）外，琼斯首次使用了'阴暗体系'（dismal system）这一术语，这个说法后来也被卡莱尔采用，只不过稍微改动为"阴暗学科"而已。琼斯说："对这个事实的看法是源于对这些'阴暗体系'极度的不信任。而这个理论告诫人们说，人们总是在一种无法抗拒的冲动主宰下，将自己能够创造的物质总量推到极限。"②

琼斯还设计了一个经济理论用来解释历史。

"对于真正重视政治经济学的人而言，他们能运用这个学科洞察物质环境，而这些物质环境又能影响人们的道德情操。他们乐于站在更高的角度，追寻政治经济学在实际中的影响，从而催生人类的共同需求。在国家的长期发展中，这个共同需求将大多数人们牢牢地束缚在他们耕种的土地之上，也长期影响着广大人类的政治、智慧和道德品质。"③

---

①　"如果有读者在研究中真的对我们所观测的事物感到迷惑，那么我将非常遗憾。但是我可以确定，如果一开始就给他一个定义作为推理的根据，那么将没有给他任何真正的帮助。"（Distribution of Wealth, Preface, p. 47.）琼斯认为给出定义就像往学生眼里撒入灰尘一样，使得他们转移注意力，远离了更为重要的地方。

②　Distribution of Wealth, Preface, p. 17.

③　Distribution of Wealth, p. 66.

在一次演讲中，他提及了关于政治的经济学解释：

"在国家政治进程中，逐渐增加的自由与责任间有密切的联系；简而言之，自由就是说在一个由人和社团构成的组织中，没有人会长时间地占有本不属于他的东西。这些可以被普通人模糊地认识到，而政治经济学家则能看清楚其中的细节。他们通过追踪生产和财富分配模式的演变，循序渐进地观察自由和责任之间的联系、相互间的独立性、对人类物质的共同作用，所有这些都是国家的重要部分。"①

他还认为评价一个政府的形式或法律的优劣不属于我们的职权范围；但是，他认为我们有职权去探究什么情况下政府和法律的建立方式可行或者不可行，或者为什么在一个经济形态下持久繁盛的制度和法律移植到另一个没有一定物质支持的社会就会衰退甚至消亡。"我们这门学科在很大程度上是宪法立法和法学的哲学基础。立法者如果缺乏我们提到的这些知识，很可能只能成为一个雄辩的幻想家而非务实的政治家。"②

总之，琼斯的政治经济学理论体系与其同时期的理论截然不同。他的分配理论并非只是主要用于解决当时英国的分配问题，他更多地从生产角度而不是分配角度进行研究。他将大量的精力花费在研究落后国家的经济制度上，以用于反驳当时李嘉图学派的学说。在他的生产理论中，他强调了科技对于生产力的重要性。他还讨论了经济习惯和其他社会状况对生产的影响。他对和谐理论和历史的经济学阐释都表达了积极乐观的态度，这可以说是琼斯理论方法的特点之一。

---

① Literary Remains, p. 593.
② Literary Remains, p. 576.

第四章　地租理论

众所周知，琼斯的政治经济学体系是建立在对制度经济学的研究基础之上。然而，我们有必要深入探究：为什么琼斯更关心英格兰之外的其他国家的经济制度？他是如何发展地租理论的？为了回答这两个问题，首先让我们回顾一下当时的财富分配理论。

根据李嘉图财富分配原则，假设工资是恒定的且由生活水平决定；由于需要越来越多的劳动力为大量的工作人口提供生活必需品，所以利润逐步递减；未来属于地主阶层，工人和资本家越来越贫穷的同时地主越来越富有。地租理论被视为古典分配理论的基石，工资理论和利润理论都与之密切相关。它建立在自由竞争的假设基础之上，认为地主和承租人都分别由竞争关系驱动。地主争取获得他所能够得到的最大化的地租，而承租人则希望地租越少越好。他们都是精明独立的个体，有能力且愿意在最好的市场上供给他们的货物和服务。熟知不同土地、市场和贸易的所有优势的承租人，愿意并且能够转移到能给他带来更多利益的土地、市场或交易之中。[①]这种地主与承租人的关系体系也被定义为普遍形式的土地保有权。

由于古典分配理论的核心是地租理论，琼斯自然也将其作为研究对象。因为，如果他能够证明李嘉图地租理论是不正确的，那么整个古典分配理论将会因为失去根基而完全瓦解。另外，李嘉图地租理论假设英国的土地制度是土地保有权的普遍形式，琼斯的下一

---

① Price：A Short History Of Political Economy in England ，p. 80.

步便是希望通过研究调查英国之外的其他国家的不同经济制度来推翻李嘉图的假设。他将研究经济制度作为攻击的武器，将地租理论视做战场。因此，琼斯农民地租理论的主要研究对象不仅是农民地租本身，还包括收集经济材料支持他的论点，反对李嘉图学派的普遍性原则和自由竞争学说。

琼斯阐明了李嘉图地租学说中主要的谬论，如下：（1）地租的增加经常不是来源于土地创造的新增财富，而是来源于财富转移，且是在到达地主手中之前就已经存在了的财富发生的转移。（2）地租总是作为额外增加的资本运用到报酬递减的农业；（3）只要不改变耕种土地的相对生产能力，任何东西都无法增加地租；（4）农业的改善不能增加地租；（5）农业的改善可以减少地租，至少在某一段时间里，减少地主收取的租金；（6）增加地租不能增加一个国家的资源；（7）每一次地租的增长仅仅只是一次价值转移，只对地主有利，而对消费者有害；（8）地主利益总是与社会的其他阶级对立。后文将详细论述以上观点。

第一节　农民地租

琼斯将他的地租理论分成两部分：农民地租和农场主地租。他谢绝给"地租"下一个定义，说道："曾有人向我提意见，说我对'地租'一词没有给出正规的定义。这个疏漏是有意而为之的。在这个问题上，试图从定义中得出结论必将导致错误。"①

在他的农民地租研究中，有四点值得我们注意：第一，自由竞争的经济法则已经完全失效，习惯和制度研究占据主要地位；第二，

---

① Distribution of Wealth, Preface。琼斯不想将其地租思想抽象为定义。事实上，他的地租理论是指土地的收入。

历史研究方法已经得到更多的重视，取代了演绎推理法；第三，明确指出工资和地租的紧密联系；第四，资本、生产、分配的重要性得到充分考虑。

从历史上看，农民地租伴随着国家进步而产生，因此也被称为初级地租。从经济意义上看，农民地租是指土地占有者利用土地获得自己的工资。最初的地租来自于土地——土地占有，而并不是土壤的优势。土地占有是一种政治制度，然而土壤的优势属于自然现象。

> "当人们开始以农业团体的形式联合起来的时候，他们似乎总是首先采用的政治概念是一种对他们居住地区土地拥有绝对权利的概念。他们的环境、他们的成见、他们对公道或者权宜之计的想法，引导他们（差不多普遍地）把这项权利授予他们的共同政府，以及从政府中取得他们的权利的那些人。"①

无论是古老的民族还是新的国家，这些都是事实。整个亚洲，所有的君主都对其统治的领土拥有专属权。中国的皇帝被奉为"天子"，是唯一的土地所有者。在美国，土地是联邦政府的财产。只有通过联邦政府的允许才能占用土地，地点应由政府人员指定，同时还需提前缴纳费用。然而，美国政府不把陆续来的大批申请人改为佃户，也不会让类似所有者的人产生。

在经验和历史的帮助下，琼斯得出了一个结论，人类社会进步的真实历程中，地租总是来源于土地占有，因为那个时候大量人口必须以耕种土地的形式获取收入。他坚持认为，正是这种必然性逼迫人们缴纳地租，而且地租的多少与他们占用的土地优劣毫不相干，且每寸土地平等，不允许搬迁。在这里，琼斯假设地租的形式与数量由直接契约决定。他并没有进一步讨论级差地租和边际地租。

琼斯将农民地租划分成四类，分别是：劳役地租、分成制佃农地租、印度农民地租和爱尔兰小农地租。这种分法看起来微不足道，

---

① Distribution of Wealth, p. 5.

然而约翰·斯图亚特·穆勒随后采纳了该观点。穆勒在论述产品分配理论中习惯的重要性之后，紧接着用了四个章节详细研究农民的雇主。

劳役地租也被称为服务地租，由于没有资金或产品作为支付款，雇农必须出卖一定量的体力劳动。琼斯的调查研究覆盖了从俄罗斯到德国的东欧地区。①他以动态变化的眼光探讨不同国家的劳役地租。观察了各国的情况之后，琼斯简短地总结了各个体系下地租最显著的特征。他利用归纳法的优点，开始研究特定的现实情况，最后得出一般性的结论。从经济学观点分析，琼斯对劳役地租主要有四点质疑。首先，工资依赖于地租，两者密切相关。其假设是农奴的时间需求翻倍，他自己的土地没有充分耕种，因此配给的生产不得不减少。其次，这种租赁形式明显地破坏了众劳役勤劳工作的习惯。另外，地主们宽松的监督、条件的简陋，都使农业劳动力效率越来越低下。最后，低效的农业劳动力只能产出少量的非农阶级赖以生存的原料。

除了以上经济方面的因素之外，琼斯进一步从三个方面评述了国家政治和社会情况对劳役地租的影响。劳役们遭受了持续的压迫和专横的统制、贵族阶层巨大的权力和社会影响力和那些国家政治体制的第三社会等级的欲望综合起来使得劳役地租前景黯淡无光。他也提出了改善劳役地租的尝试性建议，包括用产品或者现金替代

---

① 在描述俄国农奴的卑贱情形之后，琼斯坚称这一状况变化很快。劳动力必须每周工作3天作为地租。总体上说，皇家主管的农奴的生存条件比私人拥有的农奴好很多。1782年，皇家农奴估计有1500万人。1977年，匈牙利的农民占有大约一半这个国家的耕地面积，都缴纳劳役地租。直到玛丽亚·特里萨女王当政为止，他们的情况差不多和俄国农奴的情况相似。她命令每块土地（35～40英亩）的业主应该得到的劳动力数量固定为每年104天。此外，农民必须供给4只家禽、12个蛋和1.5磅奶油。在德国，这些劳动者的情形更加充满希望。一些农奴在"管家"的管理下非常兴旺。还有一些农奴被称为"男农奴"和"贫下中农"。男农奴缴纳劳役地租，每年有若干天耕种地主的土地。贫下中农佃户的劳役地租已经折合为货币地租或者谷物地租。地主不能增加地租，也不能拒绝续租土地，除非佃户的继承人是一个白痴，或者拖欠地租。

劳役地租。

第二类农民地租是分成制佃农地租。它现存于一些国家，比劳役地租先进。分成制佃农用劳动力从土地上赚取自己的工资，勉强维持生活。他们缴纳一种产品地租给土地所有人。地主除了供给佃农土地之外，还供给农具和牲畜等帮助他的劳动。因此，人们可以认为缴纳给地主的报酬由两个部分构成：一部分是农具和牲畜等资本的利润，另一部分是地租。琼斯研究了欧洲大陆西部和古罗马的分成制佃农地租情况。①

为了全面评价分成制佃农地租，琼斯从多个角度衡量了它的优缺点。就优点而言，人们把照管耕种的全部责任托付给分成制佃农，这一情况不仅表明社会对他的优越评价，而且给他的境况带来很大的改善。此外，由于地主的地租收入依赖于生产总量，他显然乐于减轻佃农所受的压迫来保存佃农自身的能力。②至于缺点部分，显然

---

① 追溯希腊的分成制佃农地租，琼斯咨询了很多权威人士，包括色诺芬和亚里士多德。他试图发现摧毁奴隶耕种体系、形成分成制佃农地租的原因。随着希腊的统一（先是由于马其顿的影响，后来是罗马的影响），个别地主拥有的土地自然而然地扩充到较大的地区范围，由奴隶主代理人管理而能获利的情况一定越来越不切实际。最后引进一个佃农，他从土地所有人那里领取土地和农具等资料，负责向土地所有人缴纳一定比例（通常是一半）的产品。导致罗马佃农制产生的那些原因同样在希腊发生作用。对此，琼斯仔细地研究了卡托和维吉尔关于农业的文献。引入分成制佃农制度以前，维吉尔推荐主人和奴隶分担耕种。随着帝国逐渐强大和私有财产数量的增加，对于奴隶耕种的监督越来越没有效率，下等奴隶深思熟虑后放弃了土地。克鲁梅拉是唯一一个主张让所有这些私人财产放任自流的人。

法国分成制佃农占用土地所依据的条件随时代不同而不同，但是通常可以取得产品的一半，他原来的名称"Medeetarius"就是从这里衍生出来的。意大利分成制佃农的数量比法国少很多。分成制佃农可以耕种的土地英亩数由谷物和耕地情况决定。

② 查尔斯·纪德高度评价分成制佃农地租的益处。他的表述主要如下：首先，分成制佃农地租统一了土地主和佃农之间的利益。他们无论好坏收成都要分享，这就是他们之间真正的关系，这是利益分享模式中最为古老但也最值得敬仰的模式。其次，佃农再也不会因为支付地租的方式而贫困，因为他们用实物支付。他只是将土地自身的给予提供给土地主：如果什么都没有产出就什么都不提供；如果产出很多就多提供。再次，分成制佃农制度通常固定的将产出分为两半，而不管价格竞争的影响和地租数量的争执。它还保证长期的租约。最后，交往更加亲密，土地所有者和佃农彼此更加熟识。基于以上原因，我们可以认为分成制佃农制度是社会和平的一项因素，且能够解决一定的土地问题。（Dictionary of Political Economy, Vol. Ⅱ, p. 738. ）

在耕种的产品中存在着利益分歧，几乎弄糟每次人们想要改进的尝试。①佃农不愿意听从地主的建议，地主也不愿意把更多的生产资料托付给一个有成见的并且通常是很无知的佃农。佃农害怕新事物是当然的，他只是依赖一种他所熟悉的耕作制度生存，一次实验失败就可能使他挨饿。然而，这种畏惧思想，使得有关方面几乎不可能把改良措施引进分成制佃农的业务实践。一方面佃农害怕制度改变，另一方面地主犹豫不前，抱着同样有害的消极态度，不肯采取为了有效地推进任何制度而必需的步骤。当工具等生产资料由一方提供，而由另一方用来谋取他们的共同利益时，很自然的，使用一方会有些浪费和疏忽，那提供一方则会嫉妒不平。②

衡量了分成制佃农地租的优缺点之后，琼斯指出了它所蕴含的特点，作为抨击以土壤肥沃差异为基础的李嘉图地租理论的利器。然而，分成制佃农体制下的地租与土壤肥沃程度、资本回报和雇佣的劳役没有任何关系。任何一国，若所有的土地完全一样，即使地主们已经拥有了少量的资本和大量的土地，能够绰绰有余地养活一批佃农，他们仍然会孜孜不倦地通过工业生产方式榨取更多的收入。为此，琼斯也探讨了工资问题。在实行分成制佃农制度的国家，主体人群的工资收入和他们所付的地租相关。同地主签订的合同约定了产品分配，也决定了佃农的工资。同样地，这些国家的地租也由工资数量决定。

印度农民地租是一种产品地租，由靠土地赚取自己工资的劳动

---

① 亚当·斯密在《国民财富》（The Wealth of Nations）第3本第2章指出："随着土地的进一步改进，土地主从他们共同分享的产品中省下工具投入的部分，这将不是这种耕种方式的益处，因为土地主什么都没有投资却要分得产出的一半。"

② 亚瑟·勇已经指出了分成制佃农制度的缺点："没有什么语言来表达对于分成制佃农制度的喜爱，成百上千的评论可以用来反对这一制度。在这个最为悲惨的土地出租模式中，受骗的地主收取卑劣的地租，农民处于最贫穷的状态，土地被悲惨地耕种着，国家和团体一样遭遇剧烈的动荡。哪里流行这样的制度，哪里理所当然就会造就无用的和悲惨的人民。"（Travel，Vol. Ⅱ，p. 153.）

力上交给土地所有人——君主。这种地租起源于统治者作为他的领地内唯一的土地所有者。

琼斯的印度农民地租调研仅局限于亚洲国家。[①]他发现印度农民地租没有任何恶性的直接影响。这种地租通常是适度的，如果和平地、公正合理地征收，这种地租将成为一种土地税，留给佃户一项有益的可以世袭的财产。但是，该地租形式拥有极其恶劣的间接影响。一方面滋养了亚洲地区的专制统治，另一面将百姓推向了无助、衰败的深渊。同其他种类的地租一样，在实行印度农民地租的国家，大部分人们的收入由其缴纳的地租决定。同样地，地租也由工资收入水平决定。在印度农民制度下，地租的存在和发展，完全不是依靠土地的不同质量，或者每块土地上使用的农具和劳动力所取得的不同收益。

第四种地租是爱尔兰小农地租。在爱尔兰小农地租的标题下，我们可以包括所有的约定由农民佃户用货币缴付的地租，他们从土地取得自己的生活所需。爱尔兰小农地租受制于合约，不管产品的数量或者价值是多少，他必须缴付一笔规定数目的钱给地主。爱尔兰流行这种地租制度的原因很简单，是因为其临近英格兰以及这两个国家之间的关系，使得爱尔兰农民可以用自己的产品换取现金。

---

① 琼斯发现印度政府统治下，耕种由印度地主管理并收取地租。由于官员们的腐败，这是一种灾难性的制度。在波斯，农民缴纳给伊朗王的地租是产品的五分之一。在土耳其，地租随宗教信仰的不同而不同，土耳其人缴纳产品的十分之一，基督教徒缴纳五分之一。对于中国农民地租，琼斯坦承了解得还不够充分，不能正确地评判这种皇家所有制在中国受到的那种特殊的修改。我们知道，孔孟之道下，真正的地主只能是皇帝。诗经有云："普天之下，莫非王土。"当政府就是地主时，土地税和地租是没有区别的。在清朝，毗邻的土地持有者共同耕种，并向政府交税。土地被分配给八旗子弟，用劳役缴纳地租，而不是如琼斯认为的用产品缴纳地租。在中国，土地属于君王，在不同朝代分割成一块一块授予经营农业者的子孙后代。经营土地者有一种土地保有权，从他大概 30 岁开始耕种，直到他 60 岁，政府回收土地。大约 2500 年后，普遍的土地私人所有制出现了。基于历史事实，最早的支付地租形式是分成制农民地租。耕种者保留二分之一的收成，并将剩余的二分之一作为地租缴纳给地主。这一制度从秦代持续到现在，从商鞅"废井田"变法成功开始。既然这样，琼斯所指的产品地租是正确的。

这种地租制度大致有三个不利之处。首先就是人口问题。推行劳役地租和分成制佃农地租的地方，地主为了自身利益对佃农的干预是导致阻遏的外部原因。推行印度农民地租的地方，罪恶的、错误的管理是导致阻遏的外部原因。而推行爱尔兰小农地租的地方，没有外部原因可以有助于抑制农民人口增加，最终结局悲惨。第二个缺点是，用来维持地主与佃农之间合同条款的惯例、传统等方面的诉求是稳定不变的。第三个缺点是，地主和佃农之间没有明显的或直接的共同利益可以使得农民在遭逢不幸时得到地主的援助。爱尔兰小农地租最重要的优点是，一旦佃农经济状况转好，他的社会地位同时得到提升。

完成了以上各种地租制度调研之后，琼斯明确指出任何一种制度都无法成为地租理论的基石。在历史和经济数据的帮助下，他大胆地表述了自己的观点，靠土地赚取收入的做法并不是导致土地优劣分级的起因，也不是催化剂。伴随着农业进步，形成年度地租的农业产出稳步增长。地主也意识到，如果承租人生产越多，他们越富裕，反之亦然。增长的产出转化成了更多的地租，也构成了一种全新的物质财富。[①]在所有形式的农民承租中，地主阶层的利益永远与土地承租人和整个社会息息相关。以上所有观点源自对不同国家不同经济制度的调查研究，也被琼斯用来对李嘉图地租理论进行批驳。

在这里，我们必须注意，后文中也将指出，琼斯关于地租的概念与李嘉图不同。前者指更大众化的地租概念，而后者仅限于狭义的经济地租概念。

---

① "地租的增加使得土地资本开始积累，产出的增加不仅仅是表面上一国资源的增加，还自然而然地是生产阶层资源的增加，实质上也等同领土的扩张。"（Distribution of Wealth, p. 203.）

第二节　农场主地租

在研究地租过程中，琼斯成功指出李嘉图地租理论缺乏一般适用性的局限性。紧接着，他论述了农场主地租的状况。他认为，资产阶级的产生导致了农场主地租的出现。那些人用自有资金垫付劳动力工资，并负责管理一群人口的各种工作。在这种情况之下，地租仅由剩余利润组成。也就是说，人们不再从事其他的职业，而是通过向土地投入一定量资本和劳动力来赚取利润。①

在讨论农场主地租之前，我们必须简单说明农场主地租和农民地租的不同之处。第一，琼斯认为地租来源不同。农民地租源于土地占有，而农场主地租源于资产阶级的出现。第二，习惯和合同对于农民地租尤为重要，而农场主地租的关键因素是竞争。第三，从经济阶段的发展来看，前者属于物物交换时期，而后者属于货币经济时期。第四，考虑到分配过程，前者是一种两部门的生产分配，而后者涉及三部门。第五，工资对农民地租的影响很大，但是对农场主地租却没有影响。第六，农民地租制度的核心人物是地主，而农场主地租制度的核心人物是资本家。最后，琼斯认为，如果从国民经济的角度出发，多种形式的农民地租适用更为广泛、更为重要。它不仅建立了地主与承租人之间的经济关系，还影响了政治和社会状况。

---

① Distribution of Wealth，p. 177。琼斯从亚当·斯密学习到了剩余价值思想："地租是超过农场主必要的正常利润之上的生产。"（Wealth of Nations，Book Ⅰ，p. 145.）

"地租"和"剩余"两个术语可以交换使用。如果收入以剩余形式出现，它马上就会被认为是一种地租。如果地租被认为是有差别的，那么所有有差别的收入都被称为剩余。如果剩余收入被定义为残差，那么所有残差收入都可称为地租。（Johnson's Rent in Modern Economic Theory，p. 19.）

　　琼斯从开始就提出了一些关于农场主地租的问题。如同地主在农民地租中的地位，资产阶级在农场主地租制度中也相当重要。因此，对于资产作用的研究占据了琼斯为探究地租增长而写的第二本著作的三分之二。李嘉图认为差别报酬是产生地租的唯一原因，然而，琼斯持反对观点。琼斯还指出地租增长的真实原因，针对李嘉图理论的阶级斗争论提出了自己的社会和谐论。

　　琼斯认为，地租仅由剩余利润组成，并提出了三种增长地租的来源。首先，耕作中更多资本的积累促进了生产。其次，资本运用更加有效率。最后，生产阶级拥有的份额越少，相应地，地主所得份额越多。①事实上，琼斯坚持认为，地租增长的真实原因显然不是因为耗费了昂贵的成本以获取贵重的农产品，而只是取得了更多的生产总量。

　　在耕作中投入更多的资本是增加农场主地租的第一种来源。琼斯质疑了李嘉图关于土壤优劣和报酬递减理论。李嘉图认为地租就是"因占用地主原始且不会被破坏的土地进行生产而向地主缴纳的一部分产出。""投入相同数量资本和劳动力，产出总是有所不同的。"还有，"人口的增加迫使一国开发劣等土地，为了提高食物供给量，优质土地的地租也会进一步提高。"②李嘉图地租原理包含两个互补的阶段，其一是对于劣质土壤的诉求和外延利润，其二是报酬递减原理导致的集约利润。琼斯首先对报酬递减原理提出质疑。他认为，向发展中国家增加资本投入无法避免地提高了优质土地的地租。这种现象既与土地相对肥沃程度无关，也与向劣质土地投入资本数量而获得的产品总量无关：

---

　　①　亚当·斯密已经论述了农场主地租增加的三种来源。

　　②　J. R. MaCulloch: The Works of David Ricardo. London, John Murray, 1888, pp. 34, 36, 37. 阿尔弗雷德·马歇尔指出那些经李嘉图分类的土地固有的、不可被破坏的属性已经被一代一代的劳动人民大幅度修正，要么磨灭了，要么更加丰富了。(Principles of Economics, 8th edition, p. 147.)

"假设 A 前期一共投入了 100 英镑进行耕作，一年后产出 114 英镑，资本的正常利润是 10 英镑；B 投资 100 英镑，产出 115 英镑；C 投资 100 英镑，产出 120 英镑，依此类推到 Z。综上，每个人收入超过 110 英镑的部分即是剩余利润，或者说是地租。那么，B 的地租是 5 英镑，C 的是 10 英镑等。假设在不定期间内，将这些耕地投入的资本增加为 200 英镑，土壤的相对优劣等级不变，产量成比例增长。最后，A 获得了 220 英镑，B 为 230 英镑，C 为 240 英镑。所有超出 220 英镑的部分即是剩余利润或地租，则 B 的地租变为 10 英镑，C 为 20 英镑，每个人的地租都增加一倍。"①

尽管耕作中投入资本总量的不断积累能使各种等级的土壤按原来的生产比例扩大生产量，但它在提高地租的同时，并不能证明投入劳动力和资本的回报逐渐递减。琼斯总结道，为了更好地耕种土地而投入更多的资本和劳动力，随之而来的是土地产量普遍增加，这是导致地租增加的自然而然的原因。

琼斯还指出，假设我们承认土壤肥沃程度的差异是产生地租的唯一原因，那么除了改变土地自身相对生产能力之外没有任何办法能提高地租。因为其他增加地租的方法都只能增加土地的总产量，并不能改变土地相对生产能力。

"我们一直试图证明，一国所有土地产量的增加均来源于更多资本和劳动力的投入。在由资本家控制农场的众多国家里，用这种方法提高土地租金的现象比比皆是。因此，耕地自身相对生产能力的变化、任何劣质土地或者古老土地上农业劳动力获得的产量递减等因素都不必考虑。虽然这种观点没有任何依据，但在实践的每一个阶段，同一耕地上不断增加的额外的产量必然伴随着不太有利的劳动力和资本消耗。"②

---

① The Distribution of Wealth, p. 182.

② Distribution of Wealth, p. 196 – 197. 罗杰斯认为肥料的使用是检验报酬递减效应的一个因素。"18 世纪产量的大幅增长完全归功于天然肥料的使用。"（Six Centuries of Work and Wages, p. 476.）F. L. 巴顿也提到，种植作物的轮换可以推迟报酬递减规律出现的时间（Diminishing Returns in Agriculture）。

琼斯不仅拒绝承认土地相对生产能力的差异是产生地租的唯一原因，他甚至否认相对土地的肥力是固定的。"我们还必须考虑打理不同庄稼的技术进步所带来的影响力，并且思考如何将这种影响应用于改变农场肥力。"①一块土地不一定适合每一种农作物，对于肥力而言，不同的土地有不同的优势。土壤的生产能力随着耕种作物种类的改变会出现不同程度、相反方向的波动。另外，土壤的好坏必须视具体情况而定，把产品运输到市场的成本受到农作物体积、是否容易变质等因素的影响。例如，有些产品体积大、易腐烂，而有些产品会因为野蛮装卸受损。最后，运输成本鉴于市场不同也有所不同。一块土地不一定适合每种市场。②农作物杂交的技术日益完善，影响了农场的生产力。这也是琼斯批判李嘉图地租理论的有力论据。

琼斯直接关注了消费模式对于农场生产能力的反应，这是消费理论研究上的重大贡献。如果人们经常改变饮食习惯，那么衡量土地肥沃或贫瘠的标准就不复存在。因为适合作物 A 生长的土地不一定适合作物 B。优质土地的缺乏仅仅是相对于需求而言的。消费习惯的根本性变化通过影响消费者需求，从而改变优质土壤的相对稀缺性。我们无法判断一块土地贫瘠与否，除非掌握了耕种者的技术和计划、资本和劳动力数量的配置、产品的需求是否可以带来耕作利润等情况。不同土地的优劣很可能受到种植方法和不同农作物相对价值的影响。拙劣的种植方法会迅速破坏所有土壤，适宜的种植方法也能使贫瘠的土地变得肥沃。③"肥沃"一词只有限定在特定的时间、地点下才有意义。

接着，琼斯强调了报酬递减规律操作上的"极点"问题。在到

---

① Distribution of Wealth，p. 188.

② L. L. Price："Some Aspects of the Theory of Rent，" Economic Journal，Vol. Ⅰ.

③ 阿尔弗雷德·马歇尔指出即使产量没有发生改变，对于产品需求的微量增加就可能会使得毗邻的两块土地的肥沃等级截然相反。（Marshall：Principles of Economic，8ᵗʰ edition，Macmillan & Co. p. 157）

达某一个特定的点之后这个规律是适用的，给土地追加资本和劳动力的产出逐渐递减。然而，我们不能认为，任意时点上追加的劳动力产出比例都比之前的低下。

"人的身高是有限的：身高超过了某一点后，一个自然人在不消耗体能的前提下再长高是一种妄想。假如要讨论一位年轻人每长高一英尺，便会带来身体机能的衰退，我们的论据是不足的。但是，我们至少比一些人的论证更加充分些，那些人已经注意到劳动力投入一旦超过了某一点，向土地中增加新的劳动力，其生产能力递减，并认为这就是自然法则。同样地，资本投入量的增加也会导致生产率的递减。"①

他进一步说明，如果劳动力投入数量增加而产出报酬相应减少的命题是正确的，那么我们可以得到两个结果：要么是大部分人口从事农业，要么作为地租缴纳给地主的总产品比例必然增加。如果没有观察到以上两种情形，那么地租增长必有其他原因，或者不是从农业劳动力投入增加而报酬递减这一点寻求起因。随后，琼斯查询英格兰统计史，找到了三个重要事实。第一，耕地的分配伴随着区域土地的租赁。第二，农业雇佣的人口比例减小。第三，缴纳给地主的产品比例缩小。综上，琼斯得到了一个结论：英格兰地租一直在增长，耕种雇佣的劳动力大量减少，作为地租缴纳给地主的产品占总产出的比例递减。地租的普遍增加与增加劳动力投入、产出递减没有关系，真正的原因与之截然不同。英格兰地租的增长是由于种植的改进和产量的增加。②

报酬递减规律的重要性质之一是资本和劳动力效率保持不变。

---

① Distribution of Wealth, p. 190.
② 这个观点甚至被约翰·斯图亚特·穆勒所接受。尽管穆勒早期的观点来自那些坚信报酬递减是普遍规律的经济学家们，但是在观察现实后他让步了。他说劳动力投入的增加使得土地产出以递减比例增加这一农业普遍规律已经被否定了，事实有力地证明，与文明的早期阶段相比，目前属于先进阶段，更多资本被用于农业，土地报酬不是递减而是递增。毫无疑问，与我们早期历史相比，为全体人类生产食物的人口比重小了很多。（Principles of Political Economy, Book Ⅰ, Chapter 12.）

在这一点上，琼斯回复说种植技术的进步提高了产品获利的数量，可能会使得持续投入的资本和劳动力比以前更加经济有效。[1]因此，要理解报酬递减倾向必须参照农业技术发展的特定阶段。农业的发展可能会抵消递减倾向，将"极点"向远处推移。

报酬递减总是伴随着总报酬递增。生产报酬并没有绝对的递减，仅仅是指增长率递减。地租增加，即使同时土壤相对生产率的差异在减少，每个阶级的总产量也是递增的。[2]事实上，李嘉图与琼斯的观点分歧就在于，前者计算的是速率，而后者评估的是总量。[3]一个考虑平均报酬，另一个只考虑总报酬。平均报酬达到某一定点之后将会递减，而总报酬总是随着支出的增加而增加。

不管如何，在报酬递减规律问题上，现代经济学家如塞利格曼教授、费特教授都试图使李嘉图和琼斯达成一致。与琼斯相反，他们坚信存在报酬递减规律，并修正了李嘉图的观点，认为这个规律并不像李嘉图所言仅限于农业。塞利格曼教授说道，报酬递减规律是普遍存在的，一切有价值的东西都符合该规律。它不但可以解释地租，也同样可以解释资本利息和劳动力工资。[4]除此之外，塞利格曼教授谨慎地评论道："定点就是充分效用的点。充分效用很少出

---

[1]　根据罗杰斯的估计，英格兰土地的产出大概是 500 年前的 7 倍，而产出的增加得益于生产方法的进步。事实上，正如约翰·斯图亚特·穆勒经常指出的，很少有普遍文明的进步不能抵消报酬递减规律的。（Nicholson's Tenants Gain Not Landlord's Loss，p. 39.）

[2]　如果 100 英镑使用在 A、B、C 三种土地上，取得产出 110 英镑、115 英镑和 120 英镑，接着使用 200 英镑，取得产出 220 英镑、228 英镑和 235 英镑，产品的相对差别将减少，土地在肥力方面将比较接近，然而产品数目的差别将从 5 英镑和 10 英镑增加到 8 英镑和 15 英镑，并且地租会相应增长。（Distribution of Wealth，p. 196.）

[3]　阿尔弗雷德·马歇尔说："李嘉图关于报酬递减规律的措辞是不准确的，这种不准确很可能不是思考上的疏忽，而是写作上的疏忽。在他写作期间，他认为其他情形无论如何都没有英格兰特定情形重要，他的目标在于解决特定的实践问题。当然，他无法估计到一系列伟大的发明开发了新的供给资源，而且，在自由贸易的辅助下英国农业大举改革。但是，英格兰和其他国家的农业历史可能引导他更加关注变化的可能性。"（Principles of Economics，p. 163.）

[4]　Seligman：Principles of Economics，p. 375.

现，该点也往往难以达到。"①费特教授深入探究了技术报酬递减和历史报酬递减的区别。李嘉图拒绝讨论该问题，而琼斯则没有考虑到这个问题。费特教授说：

"在任意给定的时刻，技术报酬递减规律的用途不可能轻易地无限增加。历史报酬递减是指，现期的人类劳动与前一段时期相比没有得到充足的回报。如果现在做一天农活的产出少于 50 年前，那么就发生了历史报酬递减。实际上，今天的劳动力产出远超过 50 年前的水平。如果按照现行的资本和劳动力价格集约使用更少的土地和设备，新增加投入的资本就不会报酬递减。所以，从历史角度出发，报酬递增是普遍存在的，但是我们无时无刻都有必要依照报酬递减规律来使用资源。"②

因此，李嘉图和琼斯关于报酬递减规律的争论得到了和平解决。李嘉图的观点就技术报酬递减而言是正确的，但是就历史报酬递减而言是错误的。琼斯在历史层面的思考是正确的，但却忽视了技术报酬递减。报酬递减法则并不唯一，要充分讨论至少需要考虑如下几个方面：技术的、创业者的和非宗教的报酬。③

琼斯关于报酬递减规律的批判极大地推动了人们对该命题的进一步审视和修正。在他的那个时代，这个规律仅仅是粗略的可能性论述，在一个给定的时期是正确的，而与产业历史性进步没有关系。递减规律被认为是发展趋势的陈述，而不是必要的描述或者是不可避免的事实。

琼斯从三条不同线索出发，更进一步抨击了所谓的农业劳动力

① Seligman：Principles of Economics，p. 252.

② Fetter：Economic Principles，p. 69.

③ 这一观点是 F. L. 巴顿在他的著作《农业报酬递减》（*Diminishing Returns in Agriculture*，1926）中提出的。他说："第一个方面包括所有关于自然的、实验的或者技术的报酬递减的数据。第二个方面包括所有关于农业创业者追求利润过程中利润报酬递减的数据，可能叫做企业家或者货币报酬会更好些。第三个方面的数据是关于非宗教报酬递减。"（p. 13）

费特教授说："这里至少有三个不同的问题：（1）技术部分，最好的机械和自然的组合；（2）有利可图的部分，创业者的最好组合；（3）与人口资源相关的社会经济问题。"（Economic Principles，p. 440，footnote.）

效率递减一说。首先，他指出，利润下降并不能说明农业从业人员的效率降低。利润下降有可能是由于工资的上升造成的。在此，琼斯认为真实工资是可变的，并且它们的变化影响了利润率。这一点与李嘉图的观点完全相反。李嘉图假定真实工资恒定不变，认为利润下降主要是因为农业效率递减。李嘉图的主张非常符合逻辑，因为三种生产要素中一种要素固定不变，其余两种之间必然相互影响。他主张，利润下降一定是因为地租增加，地租增加受限于劣等土地的耕种情况，而这又是农业生产力递减导致的。[①]相反，琼斯认为在气候、土地情况类似，甚至由一个政府统治的国家中，真实工资率也不相同。同一个国家的饮食、衣着、习惯和人们的平均素养总是在代代交替中变化。当产业生产能力保持不变，工资率的变化足够引起利润率的变化。因此，利润下降从来都不是农业生产力递减的有力证据。[②]

其次，琼斯声称原产品相对价值的增加也不能证明农业效率递减。制造业技术相对于农业技术的大幅提升很可能导致原产品相对价值变动：

"从一国发展进程来看，制造业产能和技术的提升幅度总是比依靠人口增加的农业大。这是一个不争的事实。原产品相对价值的增加可以从国家的进步中体现出来，其原因与农业效率的递减完全不同。"（Distribution of Wealth, p. 249）

最后，琼斯强调了一点，相对于其他国家的价格，原产品现金价值的增加并不能证明农业生产率递减。其原因，有可能是支付了

---

① 李嘉图主张绝对有必要增加货币工资，因为商品价格是持续上升的。货币工资的上升趋势与谷物价格上升同步，所以工人将总是可以取得同样数量的面包，不多也不少。

② Distribution of Wealth, p. 247 – 248.

李嘉图似乎使用了相同的表达方式说："即使用食物和必需品来估算，劳动力的自然价格也不能理解为是绝对固定不变的。同一国家不同时期这一价格不同，不同国家就更加不同。"（McCulloch: The Works of David Ricardo, p. 52.）他的工资基本定律是劳动力自然价格即为工资，它必须可以使劳动力维持生存且固定于一个种族，不上升也不下降。如果工人比其父母有了更多的孩子，那么他们的工资将低于正常工资，直到增加的死亡率重新构建均衡。

更高的工资、赋税沉重或者稀有金属的价值存在差异。[①]他从制造业产品效率增加追溯到农产品相对价值的增加，发现原产品的现金价值增加是一个基于价格方程的货币问题，而不是货物方面出现问题。

讨论了报酬递减规律之后，琼斯又提出了经济和谐论，反对李嘉图提出的地主的经济利益与全社会的经济利益相互冲突的理论。经济利益最根本的问题是农业进步是否对地主阶级不利。依据李嘉图的观点：

"如果地主利益足以使得我们不利用低价进口谷物的机会获利，他们也应该能使我们拒绝所有农业进步和使用工具务农。因为可以肯定的是，这些农业进步和进口谷物一样会使得谷物价格下降，地租也会下降，至少在一段时间内，地主纳税能力会受到损害。"[②]

他还区分了两种不同的农业进步：一种是增加土地自身的生产能力，一种是改善机械装置、用更少的人力来进行生产。两种方法都会导致原产品价格下降，从而影响地租。[③]

另外，在批判马尔萨斯的地租观点时，李嘉图坚持认为：

"农业进步和土地肥沃都会使土地在未来某个时期的地租增加，因为在食物价格不变的前提下，产量将会大幅提高。当然，如果人口增加了相同比例，或者人们

---

① 这里琼斯追随了马尔萨斯的观点。马尔萨斯认为很容易观测到不同国家的谷物价格是不同的，这可能是由于不同国家在不同环境下稀有金属价值不同。孟加拉和英格兰谷物价格不同，超过四分之三的原因是两个货币价值不同。（Principles of Political Economy, p. 193.）李嘉图自己也表达了相同的观点，他说当一个特定国家在制造业具有优势，那么其他国家货币会大量流入。相对其他国家来说，这个国家货币价值就会变低，而谷物价格和劳动力工资就会相对上升。（Principles of Political Economy and Taxation, p. 163.）

② Ricardo："Essay on the Influence of a Low Price of Corn on the Profits of Stock" in the Works of David Ricardo, ed. by McCulloch, p. 390.

③ McCulloch：The Works of David Ricardo, p. 42.

不需要这些超额产品，地租也会降低或者不会提高。"①

他总结说："与这些改进无关，社会得到即期利益，地主得到远期利益。地主的利益总是与消费者和制造商相对立。"②从他的表述中，我们可以观察到，他假定人口数量是固定的，突如其来的改进会使原产品价格下降、地租降低。然而，琼斯认为人口数量并非固定不变，并引荐了马尔萨斯食物创造自身需求的观点。③琼斯说："当人口递增导致食物供给增加时，并没有出现供需的巨大断层。"④随着人口数量的缓慢增加，累进的需求压力刺激农业进行改良，试图通过觉察不到的供给增加来养活民众。在这个过程中，每一次生产的增加都需要投入更多的资本，根据土壤肥力的不同而增加地租。原产品产量的增加不仅能增加土地所有者的报酬，还有利于人民的福利提高，所以地主阶级的利益绝不会与农业进步对立。他进一步指出，有必要牢记农业提升过程的研发、完善、实践、传播各环节平缓性过渡的方法。罗杰斯也同意此观点，他说农业的特点之一是农业的进步总是渐进的，以至于几乎觉察不到。⑤农业知识不可能一夜之间得到。

此外，在琼斯的经济和谐论里，他还指出了地主阶级短暂性繁荣和永久性繁荣的区别。具体如下：

---

① Ibid, p. 251.

李嘉图在他的地租一章里也主张："毫无疑问，由于农业进步而不是由于劳动力减少带来的产量增加使得原产品相对价格下降，自然会导致增加积累。因为，存货的利润会大量增加。这一积累会导致劳动力需求的增加、工资增加、耕作增加。只有人口增加之后，也就是说，在 3 号地也用于耕作之后，地租将会和以前一样高。相当长的时期内，地租是减少的。"（Ibid, p. 42.）

② McCulloch：The Works of David Ricardo, p. 202.

③ 马尔萨斯说，缴纳地租的原因是：（1）土地生产的数量比维持耕种的数量要多；（2）生活必需品的特质是可以创造自身的需求，按照必需品生产数量成比例增加需求数量；（3）最为肥沃的土地相当稀少。（Malthus：Principles of Political Economy, 1820, p. 139.）

④ Distribution of Wealth, p. 200.

⑤ Rogers：Six Centuries of Work and Wages, p. 469.

"地主在获取有限利益的时候，有可能会剥削人民群众的财富。但是其永久性繁荣必须发源于更多健康的、丰富的其他来源。""任何一个阶级收入的增加只可能有两种途径：一是侵蚀其他阶级的收入，社会总收入不变；二是从增加的产品中获利，其他阶级的收入不变，社会总收入净增加。""细心观察之后我们会发现，最终最有利的方式就是各阶级的收入同社会进步一起逐步稳步增加。""事实上，任何一个阶级能从其他阶级剥夺的收入都是有限的、无保障的。从能促使全体财富增加，或至少不会损害其他阶级利益的途径获取的财富是有保障的，并且其增长程度将完全超出我们的经验或计算范围。"（Distribution of Wealth, p. 270）

琼斯随后总结道，地主阶级通过减少生产阶级所得而获利是可能的，然而该部分利益是有限的且非常少。促进社会各阶级的财富共同增加，地主阶级增收的途径才是健康的、更加丰富的。最有利于地主阶级持续繁荣的环境同样也最易于刺激全社会的财富和力量的增长。地主们只是偶尔有些利益与社会其他阶级对立，所以认为地主地位非常特别的观点是错误的。①

琼斯认为第二种增加农场主地租的来源是增加资本效率。第一种来源是数量的积累，而后一种则是提升资本运作的质量。耕种过程中资本效率体现于两个方面：其一，在同一处土地上投入更少的资本来生产特定数量的产品；其二，在同一处土地上利用与之前相等的资本量产出更多的产品。不论是哪种结果，都表现为资本运作效率的提升，进而带来地租的增加。除非农业进步的程度超过了人口增加的比例，产品供大于求，地租才会永久性增长。琼斯认为，资本效率提升带来的地租增长一般都会伴随农业财富、人口、国家

---

① 这里，琼斯紧紧追随马尔萨斯的观点。马尔萨斯在他的著作《政治经济学原理》中用三个部分阐述了地主和国家之间严谨且必要的关系，而不考虑一个国家是增加自己的食物供给还是进口大部分食物。马尔萨斯确信地租的进步是社会进步的标志。

实力和资源的扩张。①同时，即使没有劣等土地存在，地租增长也可能会随人口的无限增加而持续增长。琼斯进一步指出，资本效率的增加使得贫瘠土地得到耕种，这也是地租增加的一个源泉。

"同样的农业资本生产力的增加引起了旧土地上地租的上涨，通常使人们可能把耕作扩充到自然肥力较差的土地，而获得和以前在旧土地上可以获得的同样多的收益。"②

在这一点上，琼斯与李嘉图的观点相互冲突。后者将劣等土地的耕种作为地租增长的原因。然而，前者坚持凡是地租上涨发生于对农产物的需求增多时，耕种扩大到劣等土地是对于地租上涨的实践性限制。③琼斯的观点可以简单概括如下：我们可以清楚地看到，随着人口的增加，如果仅仅依赖原有土地提供新的供给，那么原产品的相对价值、剩余利润或者地租的增长都不存在可指定的极限。但是当耕种劣等土地可以获得额外数量的产品时，原产品的价格永远不会超出生产的成本。如果能提高农业资本的效率，在劣等土地耕种的成本将少于原有土地上的成本，原产品的价格也不会上升。

---

① 琼斯指出，资本效率增高而引起地租上涨时，虽然国家财富和资源是增加的，但是这种增加不像由于农业资本积累引起的增加那么大。"当 100 英镑生产出（价格相同）价值 120 英镑的谷物（而不是价值 110 英镑的谷物）时，国家的财富只增加价值 10 英镑的谷物。当 90 英镑会生产出以前 100 英镑曾生产的同样数量的谷物时，国家的财富以另一种形式增多同样的数目，因为 10 英镑可以从农业中退出而农业的产量不减少，国家由于取得这 10 英镑资本可以用来生产任何其他商品而财富有所增加。国家财富的增多，无论在哪种情况下，都以 10 英镑的数目为限，和地租增长的数目相同。"（Distribution of Wealth, p. 224.）这里，我们可以观察到琼斯思想的指向，他总是更加关注增长的总量而不是增长率。

② Distribution of Wealth, p. 225.

③ Distribution of Wealth, p. 228.

在《社会经济学》一书中，卡塞尔教授表达了相同的观点："片面强调微分因素则会倾向于认为劣等土地的存在是地租上涨的重要原因。但是事实上，地租的存在决不依赖于劣等土地的耕种；相反，劣等土地的耕种会使得地租减少。"（p. 227.）

在讨论第三种引起农场主地租增加的来源时，琼斯还断言生产阶级所得份额减少、地租相应的增加和劣等土地的耕种或者说存在完全没有关系。"如果一个国家在已经耕种的土地以外没有其他的土地可以使用，需求可能经常领先于慢慢增加的供给，原产品的相对价值的增加和由其导致的地租上涨都将是不确定的。"（Distribution of Wealth, p. 231.）

劣等土地的耕种虽然不是地租上涨的重要因素，但是却限制了地租上涨的幅度。它们的存在既不会干扰土地所有者，同时又保护了消费者的利益。总而言之，劣等土地的存在抑制了地租的增长。①

在讨论资本效率时，琼斯也运用了类似于均衡规律的现代观点分析所有生产要素。因为农业知识有所改进，农业生产运用了更多的机械而减少了人力。农业的进步需要通过各种试验来检测这两个因素的效率。琼斯相信，在一些资本丰富的国家，资本所有者在追求自身利益的驱使下使用各种要素，他们会更多地使用辅助资本，而较少使用劳动力。②

琼斯认为第三种增加农场主地租的来源是在保持总产量不变的前提下减少生产阶级的所得份额。这种情况下，琼斯假定总产量一定，且农场主的正常利润不变，由于需求增加而供给没有相应的增加，导致原产品价格上升，生产阶级所得的产量份额减少。

"不论何种原因导致的原产品相对价值上升，总是会引起生产阶级所得产量份额的减少，这是相对于他们所使用的劳动和资本来说的，同时缴纳给地主的产品地租也会相应上涨。"③

这种情形下的地租增长不会增加国家财富。琼斯察觉到，原有土地租金的增加仅仅只是财富从生产阶级转移到地主阶级。他仍然拒绝接受李嘉图描绘的悲观情形，即随着地租上涨，利润必然下跌，而工资保持不变。他说：

---

① 阿尔弗雷德·马歇尔也指出，劣等土地的存在没有提升反而降低了优等土地的地租。"在这一关系中，我们应该注意到认为劣等土地或者其他生产作用物的存在会提升优等土地的地租的观点不是仅有一点点不对。这是对于真理的逆转。因为，如果劣等土地被洪水淹没或者被荒废而无法生产，那么其他土地的生产必须更加集中，产品价格会升高，地租也会比以前使用劣等土地时要高。"（Principle of Economics, p. 424）.

② Distribution of Wealth, p. 227. "各种情形"准确表达了琼斯的观点，他认为现代农业试验和均衡规律适用于所有产业。

③ Distribution of Wealth, p. 231.

"虽然农业的产能可能下降，但很少发生在富人身上。我甚至怀疑它是否会发生。如果真的出现农业产能下降，我们决不能草率地给出结论，因为掌握在生产阶级手中的谷物数量变少，利润和工资必然都会下降。与减少生产所得份额之前相比，生产阶级将要么消费更少的谷物，要么消费更少的其他商品。"①

人类产业不仅仅只生产原产品，其他产业的提升将会平衡农业产能的下降。在社会中，某一个产业产能下降的影响都将由另一个产业的产能增加来弥补。产量减少将导致该产品交换价值上升，而产量增多的产品价值则会下降。产品相对价值的变化将会对不同产业的产能产生同等的正负面影响。尽管农业资本效率的递减不一定会带来事实上的贫穷，但它仍然是不利的。②琼斯关于经济问题的观点一直都很乐观、振奋人心：农业效率增长可以支撑其他非农产业，而农业效率降低则可以由制造业劳动效率的提升来弥补。

他总结道，错误的观点总是来源于粗心的观察和草率的推理。他指责李嘉图学派没有充分考察其他国家土地的情况。

"作为英国人，我们有时候不知不觉地比较容易犯这些错误。我们太容易轻率地认为其他社会都与我们生活的社会状态相同，这种狭隘和错误的假设必然导致疏忽和错误。事实上，英格兰处于许多国家经济历程的极端和边缘。"③

他认为自己的理论是全新的，但他也非常谨慎地避免使这个理

---

① Distribution of Wealth, p. 233.

② "生产阶级所得份额减少，也就是说要么工资率减少要么利润率减少，这从来就不是人类哪个产业生产能力下降所导致的。"（Distribution of Wealth, p. 241.）但是李嘉图的观点却是："利润下降只是因为没有获得适合生产食物的土地；而利润下降的幅度和地租上升的幅度都完全依赖于生产支出的增加。"（McCulloch: The Works of David Ricardo, p. 375.）

③ Distribution of Wealth, p. 286.

论无所不能，总是考虑到经济理论的相对性。[①]

目前，我们已经研究了琼斯反对李嘉图的论点，那么我们现在来表述一下二者在地租理论上的观点的差异。[②]差异产生的根本原因是琼斯和李嘉图对级差地租和稀缺性地租认识上的差异。他们对于地租的概念是不一样的。对于李嘉图来说，在使用适当器具进行相似劳作的情况下，很容易通过对比劣等代理的产出来估计特定代理的地租。而琼斯则认为，最好能直接找到生产那些产品的稀缺或者丰富的方法带来的需求基本关系，正是这种生产使得代理是有用的。[③]在他的农民地租理论里，琼斯将地租的发源归咎于居民对必需品势不可挡的需求。一国所有的土地都要求被用于耕种。地租源于需求的增加，而不是"二号土地"或劣等土地的耕种，因为劣等土地的耕种只发生在地租上涨之后。任何一个国家，耕种最后一种土地之后，对于需求来说产品仍然相对稀缺，那么地租便会产生。特定等级的地租由土地的先天条件——稀缺价格决定。这是为了取得边际土地使用权的一种支付。[④]边际地租或稀缺性地租都否认了在不收地租的土地上耕种的可能性。经调查显示，同一块土地的多种用途使得贫瘠土地也可以收取地租。支付地租的土地产生了边际产品，

---

① "最小的但是对于我们来说是最有趣的一种佃农阶级——农业资本家或者农场主——所缴纳的地租，我曾和马尔萨斯先生以及其他人简单地把它作为剩余利润来处理。然而，这里所采取的关于这些剩余利润可以在土地上增加和积累的看法，我认为是新颖的。确实这使人高兴，并立即剥去了人们近来那样费力地给这种地租增加的原因与来源加上的虚伪外衣。"（Distribution of Wealth, p. 286.）"同时，既然我意识到我已经作出的提纲以及我所引用的那些细节是可靠的和公正的，那么我不能怀疑也不会怀疑详细资料的提供会证实我曾指出的那些原则，尽管这种逐渐补充的资料或许可能在某种范围内修改和纠正这些原则的局部应用。"（Distribution of Wealth, p. 306.）

② 参见附录 B。

③ Marshall：Principles of Economics, 8th edition, p. 423.

④ 假设土地只有一种生产用途，由此可能有免费或者不收地租的土地提供，那么地租不计入正常成本是正确的。在现代产业情形下，土地有一系列的用途。最为贫瘠的土地被用作其他用途，所得会高于地租。为了土地的第一用途，边际地租必须要与土地用于第二用途的收获相等。

在一定程度上，地租计入边际产品的成本。这说明地租理论与报酬递减规律和土地边际生产力无关。[①]对于农场主来说，土地肥力并不比适量的雨水和阳光更为重要，虽然他因为使用土地而负担成本，而使用阳光和雨水却是免费的。这种比较可以解释土地供给与地租的基本关系。[②]

现在我们可以说，一般地，贫瘠土地用于任意特殊用途，它自己能缴纳地租，因为特定用途下的土地比其他用途下产生的边际产出更多。所以，地租总是由级差地租和边际地租组成。级差地租是指，人们利用优等土地达到某个特定目的而产生的产品支出；边际地租是指，所有参与了某个特定生产的人都必须支付的正常产品支出的一部分。因此，李嘉图的地租观点应该得到进一步扩展，而不能因为琼斯的攻击而动摇。关注土地多种用途的竞争使得一些理论家认为地租是成本；而那些认为地租是土地使用过程中的分配份额的理论家则认为地租不是成本。对于李嘉图来说，后一种观点占主导地位。

李嘉图试图从地租理论中找寻一条可以解决所有土地问题的普遍规律。但是，这样的理论绝不存在。除了级差分析以外，我们需要其他原理：首先，稀缺性原理反映了影响价格的一种因素；其次，替代原理主导土地用途的转换；最后，均衡原理意味着经济上的土地供给与需求完全匹配。

自从琼斯开始批判李嘉图学派，地租理论所有的假设都受到了质疑。土地权利是天生的、不是由人类制造的观点受到攻击。土地权利无法被摧毁的假设被否定了，并且地租作为收入的一种形式，

---

① 如果地租不是成本，如果它也不计入价格，那么将地租描述为级差回报在理论研究中就非常重要。直到证明地租不是成本，基于比较不同单位生产能力的级差分析无法将地租与工资、利益区分开来。

② 对于农场主地租而言，琼斯认为地租就是剩余利润。所需要证明的就是强烈的需求永远无法与供给相等，所以价格高于生产成本。

与其他收入形式完全不同的假设也被修改了。①资本与劳动力报酬不等的现象绝不仅仅出现在农业领域。资本同样存在生产率不等和收益不均的问题。类似地，一个工人生产的产品经常与另一个工人生产的产品不同。工业收入的差异与农业收入的差异类似。进一步分析，我们从两个角度观察土地供给：实际供给和经济供给。一个是常数，另一个总是变化。李嘉图的历史地租理论——耕种顺序依次从优等土地到劣等土地——一直备受各种美国农业实验的质疑。他的静态理论认为经济状况决定目前的地租，也被修改而延展至所有其他的生产因素。动态理论认为地租增长的原因是财富和人口的增加，然而随后这种观点被历史上的经济事实推翻。

因此，琼斯发动的针对李嘉图地租理论的"起义"最终成功了。琼斯对经济体制的研究被证实是有用的，他指出了李嘉图政治经济学体系的局限性和非适用性。②他反对报酬递减规律、土地肥力不同产生原始地租、地主与其他阶级的经济利益相冲突的观点是有道理的，并得到后来学者们的支持。

---

① 1831 年，J. 克雷格已经表述了土地和资本回报的相似之处。"这些资源的收入极其相似，即使用普通语言表述，当不同人提供必要的循环资本时，固定资本的回报总是被称为地租。"（Remarks on Some Fundamental Doctrines in Political Economy, p. 138.）

1825 年，S. 贝利也指出了土地地租和劳动力租金的相似之处。"地租带来的额外利润与灵巧的工匠获得的超过一般工人工资的额外利润是相似的。一种独占权受限于劣等土地，另外一种独占权受限于劣等技能。"（A Critical Dissertation on Value, p. 185.）

J. S. 穆勒扩大了地租的含义。"一个竞争者的所有优势，无论是天生的还是后天取得的，也无论是个人的还是社会安排的结果，都会使其获得地租。"（Principles, Book Ⅲ, chapter 5.）

随后 J. B. 克拉克明确指出："决定靠土地获得收入的原理实际上也可以决定靠资本或者劳动力获得的收入。"（"Distribution as Determined by a Law of Rent", Quarterly Journal of Economics, 1890, p. 289.）

所有这些学者都试图将"地租"这一术语扩展到不同的所得中去。我们有大量不同的收入与地租完全相似。

② "然而，李嘉图先生完全忽视了这些原则可以真正适用的那些有限的范围，仅仅根据这些原则就推断那些支配各处土地在各种情况下产生的收入的性质和数目；并且，他不满足于这些，就根据同一狭隘的和有限的资料，着手创立一种全面的财富分配理论体系并说明世界上利润率或者工资数目所以发生变动的原因。"（Distribution of Wealth, Preface, p. 8.）

第五章　工资理论

第一节　劳动力的分类以及工资基金学说

根据琼斯的政治经济学体系，工资理论应该遵循地租理论。他认为，每年产品的下一次也是更重要的一次分配会被作为劳动力工资所消耗，不过这还是次要的，因为只有在调查了全世界大多数劳动者们所付的各种地租的形式和状况之后，才能对那些影响他们所获得报酬的因素有一个清晰的认识。[①]在论述工资理论时，他采用了和地租理论一样的方法，运用过去的经验来检验当今的实践。他将地租理论的论述重点放在了农民地租上，而这一点曾经被李嘉图完全忽视了；同样，在论述工资理论时，琼斯将他的注意力主要放在了劳动者群体上，这也是李嘉图学派未曾考虑过的。他对于这一问题的探究主要由两个问题组成：是什么基金支持着全球的劳动人口？是什么规律决定了分享该项基金的人数？他从生产和分配这两个角度出发来研究这些问题。

19 世纪早期的经济学家们认为工资包涵了所有的劳动报酬；然而，他们狭义地认为通常只有赚取"工资"的人才能被称为劳动力。他们认为所有的劳动者都是被资本家雇佣的。在英格兰，当古典经

---

① Distribution of wealth, Perface, XXVI.

济学家们正在发展他们的体系时，更大比例的手工劳动者正处在前所未有的境况之中。因此，这些学者们作出了这种简单假设，他们易于接受工资基金学说。为了驳斥当时的工资理论，琼斯首先提出"劳动者的三级分类"思想。首先，"未被雇佣的劳动者"，是指那些耕种自己占用的土地并以自己生产出的工资为生的农民。其次，"有报酬的扈从"（paid dependents），是指那些从他们雇主的收入中获得报酬的人们。再次，"被雇佣的劳动者"，是指那些从他们雇主的资本中获得报酬的人们。①这种对于劳动者的三级分类是完全根据劳动者们本质上的差异以及提供他们工资基金的构造而创立的。第一类劳动者是自给型的，他们的工资和地租之间有着紧密的联系。第二类和第三类之间的差别在于第二类劳动者的工资来源并不是一个以盈利为目的而积累和储存的基金，而是其收入的支出。然而，第三类劳动者则是由资本家们以盈利为目的而雇佣的。是否有谋利的动机是二者之间的区别所在。

琼斯用包容性的观点看待在不同社会、不同时期中机械生产与分配的巨大变化。他提出了三种工资基金，而非单一的一种。第一部分是劳动者作为土地的占有者自己生产的财富数量。这一劳动基金的分支养活了地球上绝大部分的劳动者阶级。在社会初期，人们完全依靠自身的能力生产，首先采集地球上自然生成的产品，随后以他们能够获得的方式耕作。随着社会文明的进步，土地的所有权开始萌芽。土地归于那些能够代表社会的人们。国家或许是最大的土地所有者，而占用者们在国家的强制下进行耕作。世袭的土地占用者出现了。渐渐地，有一群土地所有者处于占用者和国家之间，他们利用占用者的耕作，而这些耕作者被称作佃户。世袭的占用者

---

① "英国学者们仅仅看到了由资本来支付报酬的第三类被雇佣的劳动者，这导致他们错误理解了世界劳动人口基金支付的性质、程度以及构成，犯了一些严重且不幸的错误。他们通常误解了国外情形。"（Literary Remains, p. 14）.

和佃户占了世界所有耕作者的大多数。他们被利用的程度决定了他们的工资。在土地的耕作过程中，一部分是留给占有者的，这构成了他的工资；一部分交给土地所有者，这是他的地租。如果生产保持稳定，二者只能此消彼长。然而，在土地所有者的要求之外还有一条特定的限制。劳动者必须拥有足够的报酬来维持自己和家庭的生计，以此来保护下一代劳动者。如果说佃农需要土地的话，那么土地所有者就需要佃农。于是，耕作者的最低工资得以确立。通过观察和试验，琼斯总结道，用于维持这类可能是世界上数量最大的劳动者群体生计的基金，并不能储存或积累国家资本，但却是劳动者自己从土地生产中所得的收益。土地产量被认为是一个给定的值，这就决定了他们要交的地租，同时也决定了留给他们的工资数额。①

　　工资基金的第二部分来自于为维持劳动力所花费的上层阶级的收入。在资本家们成为工资的垫付者之前，有很长一段时间，收益所有者为了支持那些生产自己想要的商品的工人，必须将自己的收入支付给劳动力。工匠们早期一直直接依赖于消费者的收益。当资本或者资本家都不存在的时候，他们无法从增值的存储中获益。在亚洲，琼斯假定我们观察到有一个特定的基金通过完整和持续的作用与优势来维持非农业劳动者的稳定。他说必须要铭记两条事实：这种工人群体只可能存在于同收益分配者的雇佣关系中；而在亚洲，最大的分配者便是政府。在亚洲，君王的官员们主要将剩余农产品分配给非农业人口，而这非农业人口拥护的是东方君主制。这些经常进行文明建设和军事建设的东方国家，在历史上常常发现自己拥有剩余的所有权，便将它们用于宏伟的工程。在建设的过程中，君王的命令使得非农业人口用自己的双手和血汗建造了伟大的丰碑，比如中国的万里长城。

———————————

　　① Literary Remains pp. 433 – 434.

琼斯提到，在研究工资基金特定部分的功能时最好谨记几个观点。农业生产剩余由所有耕作期间没有被耕作者消耗或者使用的产品组成。它限制了全球的非农业人口。通过它的分配方式，农业生产剩余决定了非农业劳动者的工作以及其生产的商品作为财富的性质。很明显，农业生产剩余可能将落入不同人或者不同阶级的手中，而这些差异必将影响到不论是非农业者的工作还是他们所生产商品的性质。国家、土地所有者、耕作者或者三者按比例来分配这些生产剩余。

工资基金的第三部分是财富所有者为谋取利润提前支付给劳动者的积累或者储蓄而来的财富。英格兰在这方面发展得比其他任何地方都好。琼斯称，有两种重要的影响劳动力地位和财富的情形将被雇佣的劳动者同未被雇佣的劳动者和被雇佣的扈从截然分开。[1]第一种情况，这个基金应该出于盈利的目的而经历一个积累的过程才得以储蓄。同时，随着劳动者数量的增加，有必要通过使社会以不低于劳动者数量增加的速度储蓄并积累资本来确保持续的繁荣。而未被雇佣的劳动者和被雇佣的扈从的工资基金不是这样的。未被雇佣的劳动者的工资只是以即时消耗特定存货的形式存在；他的福利独立于社会中的任何一种储蓄。同样，被雇佣的扈从赖以为生的基金也没有任何储蓄，他的生存并不依赖于雇佣他的阶级的节约或者积累，而是依赖于雇佣阶级用于及时行乐的支出。第二种情况，长期雇佣劳动力可能会依赖劳动所生产商品的需求，而不是依赖当前雇主的需求。这就意味着，劳动者生产的商品必须有市场。他的生活水平会受到世界遥远地方消费偏好波动的影响。这类劳动者的工资由资本和人口的相对增长决定。琼斯留下了继续研究这一阶层劳动者的余地。他指出，资本家雇佣劳动力这一产业组织形式代表了

---

① Literary Remains, p. 173.

先进的生产方式，劳动力的工作连续而有效率。

琼斯指出，现代先进社会和旧社会在产业组织上有着本质的区别，这比它们所取得的成就更应引起人们的注意。当时的英国经济学家们眼光狭隘，他们只考虑其在英国所见的现象，并且在概括总结时对这一缺失置之不理。他们将工资描述成对于即期努力的任何报酬，而不论这报酬的形式。在对工资进行深入讨论时，被雇佣劳动者和雇佣者支付报酬的多少占据了主导地位。有大量以不同方式获得劳动报酬的人们没有被特别地指出。琼斯反对这种不加区别的轻率，而他们却认为自己的学说是研究这一问题的重大贡献。

琼斯也提到了资本主义制度对于劳动者的有利之处，因为这为他的服务带来了竞争。

"随着不断地积累，资本与劳动者数量的关系越来越密切，这时在劳动力市场上，人们在投资一些新资本时必将出现工资上的竞争——这是资本所有者所无法摆脱的。没有劳动的参与，任何机械都无法生产或运作。在辅助资本拥有相对优势时，这种竞争一直在提升工资率。并且，由于它是从所有其他原因中抽象出来的，这一进步保护了劳动者的利益，同时趋向于将劳动者的工资提升到资本家能够支付的最高点，即资本家用他的资本能够获得一个合理收益时的状况。"①

但琼斯还是很严谨地补充声明："然而，必须注意，只有当资本的增长快于人口增长时这才成立。如果资本增长等同或者慢于人口增长的话，那么就会出现其他结果。"②

第二节　人口理论

这一节我们将研究琼斯的人口理论。琼斯认为，人口问题与政

---

① Literary Remains, p. 460.
② Literary Remains, p. 460.

治经济密切相关，主要因为我们对人口问题的理解有助于我们解读工资率和利润波动的原因。① 琼斯将人口问题分为三类，即影响人口发展的一般因素、影响劳动阶级发展的特别因素、决定劳动阶级消费商品最终税收归宿的因素。②不过，最后一个因素同人口问题没有直接的关系，我们将在之后的税收章节再进行讨论。

琼斯明确地表示，恶习、苦难以及道德抑制（由马尔萨斯提出）并不代表所有的人口制约。总的来说，如果我们要彻底摆脱制约的三分法，我们必须弄清楚人口问题的概念并避免夸大，同时将它们分成两类：增加死亡人口数量的因素；减少出生人口数量的因素。③换言之，这些制约必须同时包括以上两个条件。他首先试着解释一些会增加死亡率却并不算堕落或者苦难的习惯：

"的确，如果我们涵盖了增加死亡率的罪恶下所有自愿的习惯，不仅仅只是指道德败坏，如果我们涵盖了苦难之下所有缺乏充分作用的引起死亡率增加的因素，尽管不用遭受良心的谴责，我们仍会在某种不确定的程度上扩展罪恶与苦难的影响。像律师、学生这类至死都在争论或者学习着的人们，无疑是他们自己恶习的受害者。一个死于无法负担从意大利到马德拉船票的人，是苦难的受害者。我们将从一个新的视角，在实践中探讨罪恶和苦难，并为人类敲响未知的警钟，因为这些弊病的影响已经控制了人口数量的增长。"④

随后，琼斯反驳了马尔萨斯对于道德抑制的狭隘分类。其缺陷在于没有包括相当一部分抑制因素，并将微弱的过失与别有用心且

---

① Lecture on Population, p. 153.（收录于《文献存稿》之中）在《论财富分配》的前言中，他也提到，马尔萨斯提出的人口问题必须一直在"对决定社会进步和国家状况因素的调查和对决定工资率原理的调查"中占据一个突出的地位。（Preface p. 9.）

② 他将一般的人口问题研究附属于他的最后两个调查。他的第三次调查将讨论人口问题同他的税收理论之间的关系。

③ Lecture on Population, p. 162.

④ Literary Remains, p. 95.

常见的罪恶混淆了。①

琼斯提出了"自愿抑制"一词来代替"道德抑制"。根据他的个人远见以及人们沉迷于次要需求的习惯，自愿抑制的范畴基于人们理性和道德这两点。为了检验在晚婚想法的影响下人口确切的增长方式，他发现可以便利地将人类的需求分为两类。社会中任何阶层都用各种办法满足他们自己的需求和偏好，他们认为他们应受到的尊重或享受是至关重要的，而这被称作"维护的方式"。他们将仅能满足健康存在的需求称为"生存的方式"。因此，维护的方式包含生存的方式，且生存的方式远远不能包含维护的方式。家庭生存的方式在数量上是有限且稳定的，而维护的方式可能会随着同一个国家不同阶层的偏好和习惯的变化而变化。在其他地方，琼斯用"根本需求"和"二级需求"来代替生存的方式和维护的方式。

> "人类的需求分为根本需求和二级需求。根本需求有一个给定的数值，包括了所有生活和健康的必需品。二级需求的数量没有限制，包括所有带来舒适和享受的事物。"②

注意到这两种需求在遏制人口增长上的相对影响后，琼斯认为，警告人们将面临无法满足自身根本需求危险的预见往往影响力有限，因为需求本身是有限的，当人们找到了自我满足的方式时，这一影

---

① "为了使遏制的错误分类观点显得更加突出，让我们来看看一个男性的专业人才，假定他在 35 岁前保持单身，并一直有建立家庭、生儿育女的预期，那么他的职业生涯会是怎样的？这样假设并不过分，鉴于他为了达到最终目标，在这段时期内，他的事业是光荣而有用的；他很小心地维护自己的自尊、过于看重他的荣耀、热心于他的努力，就是这样一群人在为社会服务。但是，在他的职业生涯中一旦他被天性的脆弱所击倒，那么，根据马尔萨斯先生的说法，对于由这个阶层所建立的快速增长的所有遏制会马上转化成大量纯粹的罪恶。"（Literary Remains, p. 154）.

② Literary Remains, p. 467.

在人类需求问题上，杰文斯指出 T. E. 班菲尔德是讨论根本需求和二级需求最为重要的学者。但事实上，班菲尔德的著作《论产业组织》出版于 1844 年，而琼斯的著作《地租》出版于 1831 年，比班菲尔德的早很多年。1833 年，琼斯在国王学院的就职演说中也讨论了这一问题。

响最先消失。但二级需求和根本需求不同，它是不确定的。二级需求的增长永无止境，它们使得人们谨慎的习惯几乎是随着需求数量的增加而与日俱增。①二级需求随着人类在社会层面的扩大而增长。纵观人类社会，琼斯断言，正是舒适和享受方式的增加极大且有效地促使人们用自身可能的力量最大程度地自愿抑制人口数量的增长，使其与财富的增长和分配成比例。这种自愿的抑制需要在人口增长问题上有更强的影响力。②二级需求遏制人口增长的作用不应被高估；正是不断增加的对舒适以及奢侈品的需求形成了人口增长的阻碍，而不是仅仅由于食物和必需品。

根据这些关系，琼斯研究了性和所有其他冲动的相对力度。他认为前者较稳定而后者是发展的。

"毫无疑问，性冲动创造了人类种族发展的稳定，直到到达地球可承载的人口极限……但是，在我们开始用这一角度审视人类之前，我们必须考虑到一部分人类天性所带来的趋势，绝不是整个人类天性的趋势。由于总的冲动起了相反方向的作用，这趋势可能被改变、相抵或者失衡。在这里，我们必须指出，性冲动充其量会继续保持稳定。我之所以这样说，是因为我们并没有需求的事实或者争论来表明性冲动会由于人们关注其他事物而减弱……但是，各种冲动并不稳定——随着人们欲望的增长，同时也随着他们大量的所谓二级需求的增长，这些冲动在数量和共同作用力上也不断攀升。"③

琼斯重点强调了这一事实：随着社会不同阶级中二级需求的增长，人们对于婚姻更加谨慎；一部分比重在增加而另一些保持稳定；在结婚的动机保持不变时，每一个新增需求都会创造出一个新增的延缓婚姻的动机。

琼斯关于二级需求的学说是以他的消费理论为基础的，而在他

---

① Literary Remains, p. 102.
② Literary Remains, p. 165.
③ Literary Remains, pp. 469 – 470.

的消费理论中，他将模仿作为消费进程中的一个重要因素。服装的潮流、贵族的家俱以及已经远去的一个时代的名流，却引领了小农阶级中成功的一代人。①他指出模仿在消费中的累积性影响，因此抢先论证了凡勃伦关于有闲阶级的理论。诉诸于历史，他还指出，在他的那个时代，他们并没有比先辈们吃得更差，英国也没有比以前雇佣更多的劳动力来生产食物。

在研究过马尔萨斯人口遏制分配理论的缺陷之后，琼斯采纳了算术和几何比率的理论，但他称这是不正确的。"让一个人口保持稳定或者缓慢增长的国家人口翻倍；二十年后，有生育能力的女性在年轻人口中的比重会减少，在生育年龄之下的女性比重会增加。而在一定时期内，人口数量不会像上一次那样正好翻一番。"②琼斯还拒绝接受算术比率观点，他说，尽管这在个别案例中可能是正确的，但对于所有时期所有案例来说，这是错误的。然而，琼斯反对马尔萨斯的论据并不充分，甚至常常回避一些问题。他并没有指出马尔萨斯似乎高估了一点人口增长速度：人口以几何比率增长并非等同于每二十五年翻一番。他也没有用重大事实在算术比率上攻击马尔萨斯：北美殖民地的人口长时间以几何比率增长，而这些人口必须进餐，所以最终年均食物产量肯定也会以一个几何比率增长。③

关于工资增长和人口增长之间的关系，在琼斯那个时代的经济学家们时而争论不休，时而主观臆断。在这些间歇之后，劳动者为消费品支付的价格通过劳动力供给的变化决定了劳动力工资。即，消费品价格通过劳动力市场上供求关系的变化，最终反过来决定了任一给定时间劳动力的工资。这些古典经济学家们认为，无论是由于工资数额的偶然增长或是劳动力消费品价格的下降，真实工资的

---

① Literary Remains, p. 236.

② Literary Remains, p. 150.

③ Edwin Cannan: History of the Theories of Distribution and Production, p. 140.

上涨都将是人口的推动力，刺激其快速增长，直到劳动力数量大于相对的需求量，从而将真实工资拉低到以前的水平。琼斯认为这样的推测是错误的。他基于社会基础以及其他考虑驳斥了这条与人口相关的"工资铁律"。

> "当谈到人口的发展时，人口变化常常被解释为似乎完全依赖于工资率的变化。这并不正确，因为原因是多种多样的，除了工资率之外，人们精神上和生理上的变化也会对不同时期人口的增长或是减少、加速或是放缓的趋势有很大影响。"①

随后，琼斯提出了他的一般原理：真实工资的每一次上涨会加速或减缓人口的发展，同时，每一次下降也会加速或减缓人口的发展。对于这一原理，他很谨慎地增加了一项例外，即人口已经位于生存底线的同时工资率下降的情况。此时的下降，必定减缓而绝不可能加速人口的发展。除此之外，工资的上涨会导致人口的增加，很明显它提供了维持更大数量人口的方法；但它也会帮助满足人们的二级需求，从而阻碍人口的增长。工资的下降会遏制人口的增长；但这种影响也会因为人们放弃满足其二级需求而被阻碍，这就会遏制人们的谋生手段在数量上的减少。

于是我们看到，当人们没有生活在生存底线时，工资率相同的变化会根据情况不同导致人口增长或者减少这两种截然相反方向的变化。这一共有四种可能性：

A. 工资上涨：

1. 会增加人为需求和高端消费，使得人口增长率保持稳定；

2. 会扩大根本需求，并加速人口增长。

B. 工资下降：

1. 会减少人为需求的物品消费，使得人口增长率保持稳定或加速增长；

---

① Literary Remains, p. 167.

2. 会减少根本需求的消费，并阻碍人口增长。

琼斯试图指出那些有助于决定工资率的变化是否影响人口数量和习惯的情况。他首先研究了那些导致工资率上涨的因素。根据重要性排名，工资到达劳动者手中的"形式"位居首位。如果工资是以实物形式支付，工资的上涨会加速人口的增长，工资的下降会阻碍人口的增长。但如果工资是以货币形式支付的话，以上结论就不成立了。以产品形式支付的工资上涨不太可能创造更多的二级需求来满足多余人口的根本需求。如果一个劳动力家庭获得了一个原产品形式的新增收入，以及另一个货币形式的新增收入，很明显货币形式比原产品形式的收入更有可能让他感到快乐。这个默默无闻的个体自然会增加他在根本需求上的消费，直接增加了他生存的方式。他手中获得的货币很可能被用来扩大他的生活费用。在各种情况下，获得货币工资的人比获得实物工资的人可以更加灵活地购买舒适和奢侈的产品和服务。琼斯总结道，马尔萨斯的观点是错误的。由于根本需求的一大缺陷就是遏制人口增长，而根本需求的大变动必然刺激人口的增长。

第二种情况是工资变化所需的时间长短。工资的突然上涨容易导致人口的正向变化（即增长）。工资逐渐上涨会引起人们对二级需求的渴望。影响工资率变化所需的时间十分关键，因为无论工资是以何种形式发放的，如果人们的习惯会跟随任意上涨而改变，那么上涨的过程必将是渐进式的，人口会有充足的时间来接受新的偏好和需求，并且我们认为使他们得到满足的习惯必然带给他们舒适和被尊重。方式的突然增加通常被用于满足更多人们已经熟悉的偏好和需求。

第三个影响工资率上涨与人口数量关系的因素是满足二级需求的商品是充足的还是稀缺的。对于人们在工资上涨时创造的消费习惯，有几项要求是必要的。人们必须对自己的偏好有相应的认识。

廉价是地位低下的人们主要的享受方法。商品必须是以一个合理的价格呈现在人们面前，人们才可能持续增加消费。在一个国内没有制造业的国家中，首先，要让熟悉商品的人们承认最好、最便宜的商品产自国外。接着，扫清一切阻碍国内产品生产的障碍，让产品适应人们新的、增长的需求。

第四种情况是，存在或没有存在的许多阶级是相似的，但不能相互混淆，位于社会最高和最低阶层间所有的中间阶级，很大程度上决定着工资上涨对人口规模的影响。现存人口的众多阶层很容易在消费上相互模仿。社会上的所有阶级都将形成一个长链条，以确定而渐进的交流方式传递着从最上层一直到最下层阶级的一些感受和习惯。在工资上涨的过程中，这对劳动阶级习惯的影响必然会更加剧烈，因为他们会有更多的途径来获得舒适和奢侈的满足。

第五种情况是，公民享有的自由程度和步入上层社会的企盼会强有力地刺激人们选择晚婚，从而抑制人口增长。如果有法律阻碍家庭职业的变化，抑或不同阶级在习惯的延续和执行上有差异，那么，国家并不鼓励人们相互模仿和深谋远虑。

第六种情况是，父母对于他们孩子结婚年龄的影响。除此之外，劳动阶级储蓄的投资功能在工资上涨阶段很大程度上影响着他们人口数量的增长。最重要的因素是劳动阶级受教育的程度和性质。教育问题与促使人们深谋远虑和自我尊重的各种原因都有密切关联。

从另一方面来看，劳动力工资下降对人口规模的影响是有条件的。根据琼斯的说法，这同工资上涨的情况是一样的。因此，如果工资的下降是突然的，那么它会对人们的健康不利；如果是渐进的，它的危害会小一些。至于其他情况，可以参考我们之前论述的工资上涨过程中的情形，它们可以充分解释工资下降过程中的变化趋势以及影响。

总而言之，琼斯在他的工资理论中研究了两个问题：工资基金学说和人口原理。他并没有提出一个普遍适用的工资理论。在他所说的第一类劳动者中，即世袭的占用者和佃户，他将工资看做"流量"的形式，而不是一个"基金"。它们由食物和必需品组成，而它们的固定数量由和土地所有者所签的租赁合同决定。第二类劳动者的工资，即被雇佣的扈从的工资也是由当前的收入派生的，而不是来自于资本。这些工资将会以实物或者货币的形式支付。只有第三类劳动者的工资来自于资本。在这里，他提出了工资的供求理论。①琼斯反对工资基金的刚性和先决性，他认为工资是多种多样并且相互区别的。因此，他更加质疑古典学说的范畴，而不是被假设情形的有效性。②

他那个时代的经济学家们常常将人口问题和报酬递减规律联系在一起进行研究。但琼斯感兴趣的是工资波动和人口规模之间的关系。他提出的二级需求学说可以看做是人口增长的一大阻碍。他研究了文明进程中人类冲动之间的相对力量，并强调了模仿的本能是消费过程中的一个重要因素。

---

① 他说劳动的价格就像其他商品的价格一样，每时每刻都由市场上劳动力的需求和供给相互作用所决定。（Literary Remains，p. 146.）

② E. W. Taussig：Wages and Capital，p. 210.

第六章 利润理论

第一节 资本的来源

我们已经提到过，虽然琼斯的地租理论和工资的理论出现在《论财富分配》一书中，但都是从生产的角度来进行讨论的。类似的，他的利润理论很大程度上也是关于生产的理论，而不是对利润决定因素的分析。

在琼斯的利润理论中，我们注意到三个重要而不同的特点。首先，与他同时期的经济学家们都把流动资金看作是资本最重要的一个部分，把劳动力维护基金作为流动资金唯一的组成部分。有时候固定资本会被彻底忽略，以至于"资本"常被用来单指劳动力的维护基金，而机器则另当别论。李嘉图在他著作的前言中说，机器是除了资本之外的又一生产的必需要素。[①]正是琼斯强调了辅助资本在财富生产中的重要性。

再者，琼斯坚持主张资本的积累不仅仅来源于存货的利润，而且不一定利润率高资本积累就多，利润率低资本积累就少。他对于

---

① "世界生产（从表面上看来源于劳动力、机器和资本的综合运用）被分配给社会的三个阶层，即土地的所有者，资本的所有者和劳动者。"（Ricardo：Principles of Political Economy and Taxation，p. 1.（Gonner's Edition））

这些同时代的资本积累理论的批判受到了之后一些学者的关注和支持。①

琼斯在利润理论中讨论了三个问题，即资本的来源、资本的积累和资本的作用。在他的设想中，资本包括所有用于生产财富或是预付劳务费的商品。资本从收益中被保留下来，用于生产财富，或者说用于获取利润。琼斯更强调财富的生产，而不是财富的分配。

资本作为从收益中保留下来用于辅助生产的部分，它来自于世界上所有国家人口的全部收入，也就是说，这些收入中任何一个部分都可能作为资本的来源。所以，收入的任一来源都可作为资本的来源。收入的这个特殊部分，在资本增长的不同阶段对一国资本增长变化的贡献都是最大的；并且在不同的国家，它对资本增长所贡献的份额也是完全不同的。因为在不同国家资本增长的不同阶段，不同的收入对资本积累的贡献率不同，利润从来就不是资本积累的唯一来源。而且，只有在很少的情况下，利润才是资本积累的主要来源。②对资本的最初贡献应来源于工资。最初，人除了劳力之外一无所有，他所获得的任何收入都是他个人努力的回报。这个对个人努力的回报就是工资，所以工资就必然是资本积累的最初来源。在不发达国家，工资是资本积累的一个相当可观的来源。即使在英格兰，存入英格兰银行的最初存款也是这一丰富的资本来源的例证。所以，工资很显然是资本积累的重要来源，当计算一国增加资本积累的能力时，我们决不能忽略工资的作用。③

---

① 在资本积累的问题上，尼科尔森教授说："琼斯对以前学者观点的批判应该得到特别的关注。"（Dictionary of Political Economy，Vol. 1，p. 7.）

② 他说，认为资本积累仅仅来源于存货利润的错误观点是由于仅把目光局限于英格兰造成的。在英格兰，资本积累主要来自于利润，但世界其他地方在很大程度上来说不是这样的。（Literary Remains，p. 226.）

③ 鲍利教授已经对此作出过估计。在战争之前的很长一段时间里，大约62.5%的英国收入来源于工人的工作，大约37.5%来源于地产。（pigou：A Study in Public Finance，p. 145.）

资本的第二个来源是地租。从表面来看，它几乎是和工资同时起作用的。琼斯认为，在土地被私有化并耕作过之后，土地的产出超过了维持土地耕作所需的部分。这部分多创造出来的价值就是生产剩余，也就是原始地租的来源。从全球绝大部分地区来看，这些原始地租其实是农业生产资本的一个重要来源。即使是在一个经济组织较为先进的国家，比如说英格兰，地租仍然是国家资本积累的相当重要的来源。琼斯说，认识到一国生产力的发展需要一个很长的过程是非常重要的。在这个过程中，与来自于工资和地租的资本积累相比，来自于利润的资本积累只占了很小的一部分，这是因为和来源于工资或地租的收入相比，来源于存货利润的这部分收入是微不足道的。①

当国家工业力量有明显增长时，利润作为资本的一个来源就上升到了相对重要的地位。对于作为资本积累来源的利润，琼斯大胆主张，国家从利润中获得积累资本的能力不会随着利润率的变化而变化。也就是说，当利润率较低的时候，资本积累量较大；当利润率较高时，资本积累量较少。

"如果回顾一下英格兰的历史，我们会发现，在英格兰的财富和资本增长最快的时期，利润率却在逐渐地降低。如果其他国家要想从当前的水平发展到英格兰的水平，那么他们国家资本也必然会像英格兰那样在累积增加的过程中伴随着利润率的下降。"②

他区分了利润率和利润量的概念，③并且否认了国家资本积累的能力取决于利润率的说法。他说，我们可以设想两个拥有相同人口

---

① 琼斯的观点被马歇尔的《经济学原理》一书采用。（p. 229）

② *Literary Remains*, p. 370.

历史上利率的下降是资本相对人口增加的结果，而不是新的有利可图的资本应用使得其他力量失衡。

③ 他说利润率是所有者资本的收入与资本的比例；而利润量是人口所拥有的资本收入，或者说是收入的其他表述。（*Literary Remains*, p. 52.）

的国家，每一个国家的资本（来源于利润）积累的能力取决于相对的利润量，但利润量不单独取决于一个国家的利润率，而是取决于各种相关资本综合后的利润率。在这里，琼斯只强调资本量的概念，他甚至没有把利润率当作促进资本积累的一个因素。对于他而言，总量的概念比平均量的概念更重要。所以，他坚决不赞同下降的利润率必然预示着资本（来源于利润）积累能力减弱的说法。

到目前为止，说到资本积累的来源，琼斯详细叙述了收入的三个主要分类。但他同时说，据估计，这些收入所有者的资本积累不能解释引起国家资本增加的所有收入来源。为了核算国家从不同来源积累资本的能力，我们需要将这些收益追溯到那些最终有能力储蓄或消费它们的人。无论是乞丐得到的施舍品还是国王的国民收入清单，所有的收入都会对国家的资本积累作出贡献。①

第二节　资本的积累

储蓄能力很显然要受到每一个人口分支的收入剩余的制约。总体看来，如果收入高，国家积累资本的能力就较强；反过来说，如果收入低，国家积累资本的能力就相应较弱。但是，即使资本积累能力一定，储蓄意愿在不同的人之间也会是不同的。琼斯提出了五种积累意愿的决定因素。

第一种因素是人们性格和气质的不同。为了未来的利益放弃今天的消费，很显然需要谨慎的态度、远见和自我否定的勇气等品质。不同国家的人群被赋予了不同的品质。但是琼斯坚持主张，人在不同环境下会有不同表现，而不是一直都保持你初次看到他时的模样。

---

① Literary Remains, p. 38.

如果从其他角度来看，不同国家的人群被置于一个相同的环境下，他们资本积累的不同是否可以表明不同道德品质和社会体制会产生较大影响呢？这点我们不能确定。而即使这些差异存在，它们也不能被精确地认知，除非不同人群都被置于一个完全相同的环境之下。①

第二种决定积累意愿的因素是不同阶层的收入在国家收入中所占比重不同。我们会发现，用于提高产业产出的资本积累很大程度上取决于社会形成初期的制度，因为它会影响人们财富的分配，同时也决定了生产阶层之间的关系和财富。这里，琼斯陈述了三个观点。当每个个体的收入都很微小时，很显然积累资本的能力就较弱；而当等量的总收入只分摊到很小一部分人，即每个人的收益都较为可观时，相应地积累资本的能力就较强。再者，如果想要有积蓄，那么个人平均收入就必须超过足够维持这些收入在社会上起作用的量；而如果需要有更为可观的积蓄，那么个人的收入就必须大大超出这个量。最后一点是，等量的收入在不同的国家内会以不同的比例在不同的社会阶层和消费者之间分配，这会使得资本积累的趋势有很大不同。

第三种决定资本积累能力的因素是对由资本积累产生的愉悦感的保障程度不同。任何一种暴力，无论是因为政府不力产生的，还是由于社会组织混乱产生的，它们都是资本积累的极大障碍。这种保障的缺乏在各个国家的发展过程中都长久地存在，它导致世界大部分地区生产能力停滞。封建时期的欧洲，封建贵族缺乏法律约束的暴力专政就彻底地导致了这种保障的缺失。在亚洲，财产保障的缺失是由特殊类型的政治体制所导致，它是这种社会危害的一个来源，而且影响更为持久深远。但是，暴力存在并不是造成资本积累

---

① Literary Remains, p. 375.

所衍生的愉悦感缺乏保障的唯一因素，不良的税收体制也会产生同样的危害。

第四，用于投资的储蓄能力的不同也可能影响资本的积累。假设每个人的资本积累都有安全保障，不会受到来自暴力或财政失误的威胁，我们可以发现不同国家为投资提供资金的能力是很不一样的。比如，储蓄银行的建立促进了资本的积累。其他条件不变，仅仅是用于投资的储蓄能力的差异就可以在一定时期内对资本的积累量产生较大影响。

最后一种决定储蓄能力的因素是资本积累者社会地位提高的影响。当从资本积累中获得的愉悦感得到保障后，有很多的设备可以用于投资，且有明确的促进资本积累的方法来提高储蓄者的社会地位时，所有因素都结合在一起来增强各个社会阶层储蓄意愿。但是，在国家的发展过程中，对人民大众社会地位变化的阻碍都是实际且有效的对资本积累意识普及的阻碍。大多数国家的经济体系和政治制度都是反对社会地位变化的。琼斯指出欧洲有三种这类的阻碍：种族血统的差异；非农职业的稀少；恶性的立法和管制，比如从事某职业所获得的特权等。

在讨论了决定资本积累的这些因素之后，琼斯把资本的积累看做是一国经济发展早期阶段社会进步的结果。由于社会的进步是促进资本积累的一个很重要的因素，所以，与外来的资本输入相比，我们应该给予它更高的重视。在这种情况下，琼斯看起来不太赞成利用外国借款，虽然那些借款或许可以用来改善国内的社会现状。

"有人评论说，最初，资本的积累是社会进步的结果，而不是社会进步的原因。之后它们进入了一个循环，互相促进。所以，外国资本的输入并不能像土地自身产生的资本积累那样广泛持久地提高劳动力的效率。"①

---

① Literary Remains, pp. 12, 30.

第三节　资本的作用

当讨论资本的作用时，琼斯首先区分了两种不同的资本。第一种是支持性资本，用于维持劳动力的生产；第二种是辅助性资本，用于提高劳动力的效率。他用这样的分类来讨论资本的不同影响，这与他的地租理论是一脉相承的。资本在工业生产中有不同的运用形式，它可以用于支持增加的劳动者的生产劳动，也可以以工具形式或是以前劳动所产生的产品形式来辅助劳动者的生产。这两者的区别是：在第一种情况中，劳动力数量总是在不断增长的；而在第二种情况中，与所用的资本相比，劳动力数量几乎是不变的。假设一定资本用来雇佣三个劳动力耕作土地，如果资本量翻倍，那么将雇佣六个劳动力，也就是说在生产中的劳动力数量翻倍了，但由于后雇佣的三个劳动者的效率不一定会比之前的高，所以产量应该不会超过原来的两倍。但是如果不是用资本来维持新增加的三个劳动者的生产，而是把它作为辅助性资本来提高最先雇佣的三个劳动者的生产能力，也就是让这三个劳动者的效率得到提升，那么这三个人就拥有了第一种情况下的六个人无法拥有的生产能力。[1]我们必须承认的是，在农业生产中辅助性资本对提高劳动效率的作用没有工业生产中的那么明显。

辅助性资本和直接用于支持增加的劳动者生产的资本的第二个区别是，如果一定量的附加资本以前劳动成果的形式被用于辅助劳动者的生产，与这些新的资本被用于支持增加的劳动者生产的情况相比，只需要更少的年收入就足够使这些资本发挥作用，从而长久

---

① Distribution of Wealth, p. 207.

地有效。换句话说，支持性资本与辅助性资本的区别体现在再生产的过程中。①琼斯断言，支持性资本的直接作用在于使得一项工作得以持续，但是它会受到人口数量和工资率的制约，所以它只在一些不发达国家比较常见。他强调说，辅助性资本的积累对国家财富的增长是很重要的。辅助性资本的积累不仅有助于提高直接或间接被雇佣耕作的人们对土地的掌控能力，同时还会减少年收入量，使得给定的新的资本量有利可图。

在关于一国生产力的讨论中，琼斯提出了三个影响劳动效率的因素，即劳动力应用的持续性，指导劳动生产的技术和对劳动的辅助力量。这些因素都由资本所决定。首先，稳定持续的劳动力比散漫的劳动力更具生产力，这是不言而喻的。劳动的不连续性使时间白白浪费，而时间总是在一项劳动转向另一项劳动的间断处被浪费的。资本，或者说是过去的劳动力劳动成果，使得劳动的连续性成为可能。②其次，劳动力的效率受到认知程度和技术水平的制约，并在它们的指导下进一步去影响生产者的目的。一个无知的未开化的人可能花费一天的时间去捶打一块冷铁，而依然不能把它锻造成任何有用的东西，因为他不知道热量对金属延展性的影响。如果劳动的持续性是资本在生产中运用的实际结果，那么生产中所用到的技术也有同样的效果。指导工业生产的思想可能来自于资本家，也可能来自于资本家雇佣的技术工人。由于劳动的连续性和劳动中所用

---

① 琼斯的计算如下："让我们假设 100 英镑用在土地上作为 3 名工人的生活费，生产出他们自己的工资和 10% 的利润，或者说 110 英镑。让用在这块土地上的资本增加一倍，并首先假定这新资本养活额外的 3 名工人。在这种情况下，增加的产量一定包含他们的全部工资以及通常的利润。因此，必须包括全部 100 英镑以及这 100 英镑上面的利润，或者说 110 英镑。下一步，让这同样的额外资本 100 英镑以农具、肥料或者过去劳动的任何结果的形式应用在土地上，而实际工人的数目没有变动。假设这项辅助资本平均耐用 5 年。用来偿还资本家的每年收入，现在就必须包括他的利润 10 英镑和资本的每年损坏折旧 20 英镑，或者共计 30 英镑，这是每年需要的收入，以便继续使用那第二个 100 英镑，可以获得利润，而不是像在使用直接劳动那样需要 110 英镑。"（Distribution of Wealth, p. 211.）

② Literary Remains, pp. 12, 30.

的技术都取决于过去劳动成果的积累，所以第三个影响效率的因素就是生产能力，它对资本的依赖性比前两个因素更强。但是国家辅助性资本的增长是不确定的，而且伴随它的每一次增长，都会有一次机器生产能力的提升。

琼斯提到了辅助性资本对一国生产力的两个重要影响。第一个是扩大了非农业阶层。也可以说，在土地耕作的过程中，更多资本的应用使劳动力得到解放。当然，辅助性资本的积累不是影响农民阶层和非农阶层比例的唯一因素。①任何能提高农民实际耕作效率的因素都可能产生这样的影响。但是，在文明国家的发展进程中，辅助性资本的积累是唯一我们可以确定的在这方面产生正向推动作用的因素。

辅助性资本的第二个影响是，它的积累可以增加中产阶级的收入。资本家的财富、影响和数量会随着辅助性资本的积累同比例增加。琼斯说，我们可以看到资本家的增加，开始时我们并不能将他们从劳动者中区别开来，接着因为他们在国家的工业生产中占有越来越大的份额，他们开始慢慢地从大量的劳动者和地主中凸显出来，最后他们变得不仅能够影响生产力的发展，还能影响到整个社会和国家的政治，这就使他们完全地以资本家的身份显露出来了。在研究经济的发展和分析各国的不同实力时，他发现，资本是财富的一个特别的部分，资本在修正连接社会各阶层之间的纽带和决定各阶层的力量这两方面都起着重要作用。②非农业人口数量的增加和中产阶级人数及收入的相对增加是社会进步的两个重大变化。

---

① 琼斯认为农业剩余是最为重要的；它的数量限制了地球上非农人口的数量，它的分配决定了那些非农人口的职业。在资本主义社会得到发展之前，这一观点可能是正确的。在不同于现代的早期时代，大部分消费标准是明确的。所生产的食物剩余粗略地暗示了非农人口可能的数量。但是在现代社会，相反的，需求非常复杂，对象也变幻莫测，所以除了预测最为显著的收入变化之外，其他的所有预测都是冒险的。

② Literary Remains, p. 556.

辅助资本的使用也是显示不同国家文明程度的一个标志。拥有更多财富的国家在辅助性资本上的投入多于用于支付劳动者工资的投入。

"在英格兰，用于支付劳动者工资的投入仅为对辅助性资本投入的五分之一；但是在俄罗斯，这一比例近乎为一比一。"[1]

总的来说，琼斯的利润理论包括了对资本来源、资本积累和资本作用的讨论。他将这些问题与财富的生产理论紧密地联系起来了。他并没有明确地说明利润的来源，也没有给出利润分配理论的确定形式。关于资本提高财富生产效率的主张似乎暗示着资本家获得的份额取决于资本的生产能力，这应该是一个关注利润的生产理论。在探索资本的来源时，他仅仅触及到了取决于资本总量和利息率的总利润量思想，这也就是说，他的利润分配理论其实在某种程度上不能说是利润理论，而应该说是一个决定总利润量在不同的资本家中分配比例的理论。

---

① Literary Remains, p. 229.

第七章　琼斯的其他理论贡献

第一节　契约平衡体系

　　为了更好地理解琼斯的整个政治经济学体系，除了地租、工资和利润理论以外，研究他在契约平衡以及包含什一折合偿付问题在内的税收方面的历史性贡献也是十分必要的。这些理论不像先前讨论的那些理论那样地位突出，但它们的重要性不可忽视。没有关于这些方面的介绍，琼斯的研究成果不可能得到全面的阐述。

　　琼斯的制度经济学引导他去探讨英格兰早期的政治经济状况。他是第一个提出"契约平衡体系"这个说法的人。① 他也是第一个将注意力放在整个重商主义阶段的人。虽然他的相关文章最早发表在1847年4月的《爱丁堡评论》上，但是，1833年他在国王学院做演讲时就已经讨论了这一问题。"在这崇高的境界里至少世界金银储备得到公平分配，不同时期内盛行着两种体系。虽然这些体系有共同的目标，但是它们在方法、原理和效果上有很大区别。在出现得较晚且没有持续超过一个世纪的重商主义制度下，这两个体系虽然经常被混淆，但是我们决不能任其混淆。旧体系的各个部分可能在成文法和古老文件中有着准确的描述，但是作为一个整体系统，我认

---

　　① 他很谦虚地说，如果我们想给它起一个名字，这个体系也许可以被称为"契约平衡体系"。（Literary Remain, p. 547.）

为它没有被历史学家所关注。"①

亚当·斯密已经在《国富论》（第4册）中讨论了重商主义制度的目标，但他没有具体研究重商主义者实现其目标的方法。琼斯第一个阐明了重商主义制度下的管制方法和各种措施。为了批评重商主义学派，学者们频繁强调贵金属与国民财富的混淆是错误的根源。但是琼斯选择从另外一个更加富有洞察力的角度来进行驳斥。他把缺乏军事征服和经济帝国主义视做早期英国立法的逻辑结果，此立法采用了限制性的获得贵金属的方法。那是和平的方法，它有自己的理由。"允许我们自己的矿产为零，排除征服和破坏，那么，这一结论是非常合理的。"②

契约平衡体系的条款将其自身分成两个部分：建设性方案包含那些将金银带进国家的方法；保护性方案用来保护金银免于流出国家。第一个方案必须先于第二个，问题在于先得到金银，然后再将其保留在国内。

有两个组织用于建设性目标——主要城镇和镇长警员组成的市政当局。前者在欧洲大陆是普遍的，后者只针对英格兰。主要城镇的命名可能来自德语 Stapelen（堆放），因为在永续的集市上商品成年被堆放在一起。这个制度包含了集市和市场建设的一部分原理，对于商人建立公司后相互保护、交易和价格管制都是必要的。对于

---

① Literary Remain, p. 54.
② Literary Remain, p. 295.

国王来说也是有利可图的，因为既增加了税收收入又便于征收。①对琼斯来说，实施保护方案的方法有 4 个，即建立铸币厂、税收官员、国王的外币兑换交易所和雇佣的法令制度。依据保护性方法的逻辑顺序，国王的外币兑换交易人和税收官员应当居于首位。当代人会认为，国王的外币兑换交易人是贸易监管人，在国家的货币交易中拥有无限的权力。他的首要任务是决定外国货币在英国货币体系中的价值，带着外国货币到来的外国商人一定要到汇兑官员那里兑换英镑。除此之外，汇兑交易人被授权进行外国货币的交换磋商。税收官员是财政代理人，职责是征收税款。

铸币厂的建立有两个目的：第一，铸币厂可以使得流入英格兰的外国货币再出口；第二，在确定英国货币价值时，铸币厂可以估计出不同于国王宣称的真实价值的价值。前者是一种经济错觉，后者涉及合法的货币理论。在那段时间，确定货币的价值是国王最珍贵的特权之一，没有人有权干涉这一特权。根据这个原则，除了在国外铸币厂或者汇兑官员那里兑换成英镑之外，没有任何外国货币可以在英格兰流通。最高统治者经常将自己的价值赋予自己的货币，外国人不可以干涉他的决定。在决定交换等价之后，国外货币被估

---

① 爱德华一世统治之前，英格兰的出口贸易主要由外国人操作，其中最主要的是汉萨商人。1313 年，一项包含了国内外主要产品的计划首次被英格兰采用。英格兰的特产是羊毛、皮、皮革、铅和锡，其中羊毛尤其被关注，它是英格兰最高统治者的珍宝，被认为可以温暖整个世界。镇长和警员被授权选择一些城镇，对城镇里那些将羊毛贩卖到其他地方的经销商处以罚款，并且在考虑周全的情况下可以暂时改变所选的城镇。爱德华三世的统治展现出比其他人更加引人注目的影响，这个计划促进了国家财政的繁荣。他在英格兰和爱尔兰的不同城镇建立了主要产品法庭，主要产品法律和主要产品特权。他与法国战争的额外开支几乎全部来自羊毛出口的税收。羊毛出口的重量由镇长核实，并在港口再次称量以在镇长和税收官员之间签订契约。

出口贸易在消亡的痛苦下对外国人进行限制（正是这一年出台了主要产品条例）。在 1353 年，英格兰有 10 个主要城镇。国内主要产品的指定被认为对英格兰是有利的，因为它打破了弗兰德斯的垄断，随之而来的竞争将提高羊毛的价格。外国商人从其他地方带来了金银，而税收增多，且税收对外国人比对英国人征收得更多，从而刺激英格兰提供更多的供给。但是，高额税收和大规模走私限制了国内主要产品条例的成功。从 1363 年在加来地区出台以后，直到 1558 年这一条例都被认为是固定的甚至唯一的英格兰主要产品条例。

值或被重铸，国王的特权被充分地维护，下一步必然是阻止货币出口。在外国商人离开之前，他们必须给出令人满意的证据证明他们进口货物所得的货币已经全部用于购买英国商品，所以没有货币可以被他们带走。为了加强这一原则发布的各种法案各种条例被称为"雇佣的法令制度"。对这类交易进行审查的最有效机构叫做"主办人"。①

　　一个更独特的经济现象是对于旅行者消费清单的管制。如果旅行者自行保管消费清单，那么他们会设法走私货币。因此政府下令不论何时签订了这样的契约，这个外国人应该把清单交给财政部门，他将可以在一个给定时间内运输与契约价值等价的英国货物至欧洲大陆。

　　但这些管制措施很难持续，情况一旦发生改变，管制就不再能维持。英格兰经济增长和状况改变是对这一体系的首次冲击。根据是否是经济力量和政治政策，这些因素被分为四种：投机商人的出现，这被认为是最主要的导致契约平衡体系失常的因素；国外交换清单的应用；通货的退化；法国攻占加来地区。在契约平衡体系受挫之后，取而代之的是贸易平衡体系。

　　贸易平衡体系重要的特点是在贸易过程中不断加入大量新的金银。它完全抛弃和拒绝了最早的契约平衡体系创建者为了实现其目标而采用的手段和机构。托马斯·蒙恩是第一个批评契约平衡体系的人，琼斯对他的赞誉绝不少于使得重商主义学说最小化的亚当·斯密。他评论说要消除契约平衡体系的谬误需要几个世纪，正如否定重商主义政策需要几百年一样。他所采用的方法通常是去发现一

---

　　①　雇佣的法令制度规定，到达英格兰港口的所有陌生商人都应该处于"主办人"的监督之下，而"主办人"授权于城镇的政府官员，必须是可信任的贸易专家。"主办人"不会公开陌生人签订的所有契约，他只是准确记录外国人签订的每一个契约。如果任何一个外国商人忽视了向"主办人"报告或没有服从"主办人"，他将被投入监狱。这些措施不仅阻止了货币出口，还刺激了国内产业并开放了市场。

个体系的起源，而后去追寻其衰落的轨迹。他对待经济制度从原始到现在的历史观中透露出经济思想的连续性和经济状况的动态性。

第二节　税收理论和什一税

对于琼斯来说，税收是国家收入中政府分红的一部分，来源于工资、地租和利润。[①]他反对任何单独的税收体系，认为没有哪部分生产和分配的财富会被标记上带给国家零税收的特性。"我们应该努力去观察各阶层的收入局限，来决定这样一个点，当对于一个单独的分配收取更多的税收时，结果会导致一方或者双方严重超出负荷。"[②]

他指出单一土地税收制度的两个错误。[③]第一，地租由利润剩余组成的情况仅存在于资本家的资本被赋予尊贵地位的国家，比如英格兰。而在爱尔兰，资本家的资本是固定不变的，情况就不是这样了。同样，像印度这样没有资本家阶层的国家的情况也不是这样的。事实上，在全球更广泛的地方，地租就是利润剩余的定义是不适用的。即使在地租真正是利润剩余的国家，通过税收占用地租也是很不明智的。因为地租的一部分通常被地主用于修建排水、沟渠来优化土地，增加了土地的价值。第二，被说成构成了全世界地租的利润剩余不只是主要归功于优质土壤。毫无疑问，土壤肥力的不同是决定产量不同的因素之一。但是，相比于工业、技术和辅助资本的增加，这一因素只是一个无关紧要的潜在可能性。

---

① "再次追寻社会的多种形式和多个阶段，我们应该尽力逐一指出被政府收取的来自于劳动者、土地所有者或者资本家的收入。"（Distribution of Wealth, Preface, p. 28）

② Distribution of Wealth, Preface, p. 28

③ Literary Remains, p. 273.

　　当从利润的角度来考察税收，琼斯认为利润是可收税的，直到资本家将资产移出本国而不愿为其交税为止。[①]对利润征税将会减少资本，反之，资本的减少将造成对劳动力需求的减少，结果是工资下降。琼斯坦承，何时会出现这种情况是不确定的。

　　更重要的是对工资征税这一问题。在他的人口理论中，琼斯提出三个问题，最后一个问题关注了对劳动阶级消费的商品征税的最终税收归宿。他主张，预先告知对工资征税的税收归宿是不可能的，因为这取决于税收对人口增长的影响。[②]由于对工资征税几乎与工资率下降完全相同，而废除对工资征税就等同于工资率上升，相同的规律决定了税收的影响也同时调整了工资率变化对于人口规模的影响。琼斯在人口理论的讨论中提及，排除特殊情况，任何在工资率方面的改变都会增加或阻碍人口的增长。现在，假设工资率以税收的形式降低，在人口增长被阻碍的情况下，人口数量的减少当然会增加工资率。在这种情况下，税收负担将从劳动者转嫁到雇佣者，从工资转嫁到利润。假设同样的情况发生在工资上，在它不影响人口增长的情况下，只是牺牲了二级需求，税收负担不会发生移动。

　　琼斯也讨论到直接税、间接税和混合税。直接税是不能逃脱的税，比如人头税，它出现在社会的早期阶段。间接税是任何人可以去选择承担或不承担的税。混合税形式上是间接税而实质上是直接税，或者形式上是直接税而实质上是间接税。

　　在国家历史中，地租是税收的最早对象，间接税的增加标志着国家财富的增加。从整体上看税收体系，琼斯认为国家财富的三个主要部分都是可收税的。"由于将税收负担全部施加在地租和利润上是不合理的也是愚蠢的，所以对全部工资免于征税也是错误的慈善和虚假的智慧。每一位社会成员都有能力为国家总财富的积累作出贡献，这

---

　　① Literary Remains, p. 276.
　　② Literary Remains, p. 277.

是制度充满活力、国家健康发展的确切的标志。"①他也论及税收扩散理论："所有关于不用纳税的阶级或者收入的观点完全都是虚妄的。那些强迫别人缴税的人通常不缴税；税收的最终归宿和表面上的归宿不一样；但是没有哪个社会阶级能够不承担公共负担。"②

正如前文提到过，琼斯在什一税的折合偿付运动中显示出了他的管理才能和理论上的真知灼见。什一税最初是自愿缴纳，但是逐渐变成了义务的，首先是教会的法规，随后成为了法令。它们是第十个部分，免去了耕作和每年土地增加的成本。农民和牧师都很讨厌这个体系。③在 1831 年之前，琼斯就对这个问题产生了兴趣，并在他的地租理论中加以评论。在讨论谷物法时，他持有这样的观点："我们假设什一税可以折合现金偿付，并且取消济贫税或将其减为很少的数目，那么，农场主在估算他们特有的负担时就不会感到不明确的压力，并减少许多对风险损失较为模糊的忧虑。而现阶段这些压力和忧虑都一直存在，要缴纳款项的存在使他们不悦。直到假设实现之前，恐怕没有真正公平的谷物法会给予农场主充分的保护，而非农阶级却会很容易相信谷物法过分地和不公平地提升了物价。"④

关于什一税的折合偿付，琼斯提出了三个论点：⑤ 首先，折合偿付是合意的；第二，代替了什一税未来支付的款项应该被用做相同的目的，并支付给相同的人，就像什一税从前那样；第三，此过程的第一步应该是将责任转移到未来的支付中，并从佃户转移到地主。他还提及了三个政府实施什一税折合偿付的目的来为政府议案辩护。第一个目的是完全解放国家的资本和工业，用最好的方式从土地上

① Literary Remains, p. 280.
② Literary Remains, p. 567.
③ 这种不便使牧师被迫接受实物税，并自己把它们收集到教会区不同的农场什一税仓库。这经常在什一税主和纳税人，即牧师和会众之间产生不合意的对立。
④ Distribution of Wealth, p. 299.
⑤ Remarks on the Government Bill, 1836.

获取最高的可能产量；第二个目的是同时除去现实的征税模式所产生的障碍；第三个目的是提升宗教命令的效率。

地主，这个什一税折合偿付的第二个团体直接受到这些措施的影响。土地所有者通常急切地要求永久地解决什一税问题。去除资本自由雇佣障碍和促进地租总体增长的期盼为这一要求提供了充足的理由。但是，什一税问题的第三方——牧师有着天生相反的兴趣。他们不能通过影响折合偿付直接达到获利的目的。他们认为这仅仅是一个损益问题，很显然，他们将通过延迟或逃避什一税折合偿付而获利。

琼斯也谈到从这一来源得到的牧师收入不受欢迎的原因。什一税呈现给缴纳者的形式是餐税，而餐税会提高耕作成本。随着土地产量的提高，地租和什一税也提高了。但它们以不同的速度增长：地租增长很慢，什一税则很快。当更多资本投入获得更多农业产出时，经验证明全部产品的绝大部分将会被耕作者保留而替代了这一进步，为此减少了耕作者的利润。地租虽然在数量上逐渐增多，但是占总产量的相对比例逐渐变小。由越来越少的原始品组成的租金比什一税增长得慢，但是，通常由相同部分组成的产量将会大幅增长。因此，虽然什一税保留现状，但是摆脱各种愤怒源头的希望很小。

为了使未来缴纳的什一税成为地租的一部分，琼斯提出了两个可替代的方案，一个是普遍的，一个是特殊的。第一个计划目标是在所有的王国土地上建立未来什一税占未来地租的一般比例；第二个计划目标是在每一个个别的情形中确定什一税占地租的实际比例，并永久执行。琼斯反对第一个计划。如果在个案中什一税占地租的比例差别很小，在不违背缴纳者和收款者权利的条件下，建立一个一般比例是可能的。但对于不同土地，这一比例的差别很大。不同质量的土地会用不同的花费获得相同的产量；劣等土地比优等土地的花费要更多一些。再者，相同产量的土地的租金将会随着生产花费的不同而不同，当花费大时，地租会相对较少，而花费小时，地租会相对较多。然而，什一税的缴纳原理是同产同税；也就是说，不同的地租将有相同的什一税。因此，由于劳动力投入和花费不同使得地球上不同质量的土地产量相同时，什一税与地租之间将不会有一个一般的比例。如果所有土地的什一税占地租的比例相同，将会使一些地主发现自己的什一税变为原来的双倍，而他们邻居的却大大减少，这显然是不公平的。什一税的所有者也会遭受不公平。个别牧师的收入将会变化莫测，而且通常处于一种最不理想的变化方向。贫困地区牧师的收入已经很低的情况下收入会变得更低，因为在那里什一税与低地租的实际比例本应很高；而富有地区的牧师收入将成比例地增加，因为这些地方什一税对租金的实际比例本来是较低的。后者将在一般比例制度下受益，而更为贫困的前者则受损。

关于什一税折合偿付的第二个计划是以不同土地不同的什一税地租比例为基础。琼斯认为这是个伟大的国家计划，可以使得运用到土地上的新资本完全自由，以发挥其最大效应。和实际地租相比，琼斯建议确定合理的什一税价值，宣布一个大概的未来的地租替代什一税计划。在这一计划下，直到资本家盈利得到保障，或者说直到资本能收回利润，新资本获得的产品不需要交什一税。地主将也有相同的安全保障，当地租下降时，他的什一税也将成比例下降。同时，专用于宗教命令的资金也随着地租上升和耕作改进而增加，还会随着人口的增加逐步增加，但不是大幅度的。事实上，当什一税是总产出固定的一部分时，在某种程度上也会满足宗教命令扩张的需求。在这样的安排下，佃户的资本将会自由地流向土地，不受什一税的约束。但对地主来说不是这样的。地主的支出总是要考虑地租，而什一税所有者将继续分享这一地租。

这一计划实践上的成功彰显了构思者的聪明才智，表现出人文关怀的同时实现了公平公正的目标。

第八章　琼斯的批判及其影响

　　琼斯对于经济学发展的理论性贡献在于比古典学派更广泛地界定了政治经济学范畴，并且对于经济发展持有更为乐观的观点。当他研究经济制度时，他总是会考虑到政治条件和社会因素。虽然正如他所说，他不想界定"地租"这一个概念，但是他的地租理论实际上就是关于土地收入的理论。因此，他的工资理论也把工资视做劳动收入，而不是一项基金。他的利润理论对资本积累进行了彻底的研究，这部分研究后来被尼科尔森和埃德温·坎南所采纳。他的人口理论比他之前的人口理论更加客观和科学，没有道义上的因素，因为自愿约束比道义上的约束更能够令人愉悦。他的二级需求学说对于财富分配理论的研究确实是一大贡献。

　　距离琼斯 1831 年出版他的第一部著作《论财富的分配和赋税的来源》已经快有一个世纪了。在评价这一个世纪以来琼斯对于政治经济学发展的贡献时，总结过去和现在的伟大的经济学家们对琼斯理论体系的不同评价是一件很有趣的事情。

　　琼斯的书一出版，麦克库洛奇就在《爱丁堡评论》上发表文章加以批判。内容如下：

　　"我们不能说琼斯先生在他研究的领域是很成功的。他的观点广泛但却很肤浅。事实上，他从未进行深入挖掘。他得出的结论尽管有一些是正确的，但大多数都与他书中的主题无关。"①

　　麦克库洛奇在他的《政治经济学文献》一书中用最不令人愉快的评论再次谴责琼斯的书是不适用的："几乎没有必要去关注这部主要由一系列不相关不实用的对李嘉图现实地租理论的批判组成的书。"当然，我们知道，麦克库洛奇是李嘉图热切的追随者，因此他的观点过于极端，不太公平。况且杰文斯认为，他的《政治经济学文献》一书中的观点并不都是正确的。

　　另一方面，《文献存稿》的编辑惠威尔博士给出了很多琼斯对于经济理论作出贡献的例证。他信赖琼斯首创的地租分类方法和政治经济学归纳推理方法。琼斯"去看看"的哲学也被他的朋友高度赞扬。②

　　就像上面我们提到的，J. S. 穆勒采用了琼斯关于地租分类的理论。在《政治经济学原理》一书中，他认为琼斯的著作《论财富分配》是"关于不同国家土地占有形式的有价值的大量事实的汇总"。③杰文斯也说：

---

　　①　麦克库洛奇的批判具体如下：
　　（a）"对于土地在不同年代不同国家被如何占用的思考将会是一件重要的有价值的工作。但是从琼斯先生的才智来看，我们并不认为他是可以填补这一空白的适当人选。"
　　（b）"琼斯先生长期研究分成制佃农制度下土地的占用情况。这一制度下佃户将产出的一定比例作为地租缴付给地主。但是，他书中这部分是特别肤浅的。他以为分成制佃农的耕种技术直到哥伦梅拉时代才传入意大利。而事实上，分成制佃农制度在 200 年前就在意大利闻名遐迩了。"
　　（c）"琼斯先生指出了对土地生产能力递减规律进行改善的影响，这是无可厚非的。但是，他书中对于其中原理冗长的论述中有很大一部分都是别人已经充分阐述过的。"
　　（d）"琼斯先生对于利润的论述不像其对于地租的论述那样新颖而有价值。他勤劳地去证明在社会发展进程中利润不会有减少的自然趋势。但是，当土地生产能力递减规律成立时，利润自然而然就减少了。"
　　（e）"总之，我们不能说我们从琼斯的书中获益很多。很显然，他推翻地租理论的努力失败了。"
　　②　显然，"去看看"的做法得到当今统计学家们的高度赞扬。塞克里斯特在《统计方法介绍》一书中说："经济科学的方法已变成统计方法了，琼斯'去看看'的建议被完全采纳。"
　　③　J. S. Mil: Principles of Political Economy, Book I, p. 317.

"琼斯关于不同国家财富分配和土地占有形式的书是一本值得欣赏的著作，他细致地调查了过去及现在人们的基本情况。"①

也许琼斯最无保留的崇拜者是 J. K. 英格拉姆教授：

"琼斯是李嘉图体系早期的最系统的最彻底的批判家。他的后继者没有给予他充分的评价。J. S. 穆勒采用了琼斯的观点，承认了琼斯的功绩，却鲜有赞赏。琼斯使用的研究方法是归纳性的，他的结论是建立在对当前事实的广泛观察和对历史的不懈探索之上的，他的杰出在于他的结论既无夸大又不偏颇。"②

埃奇渥斯教授把琼斯看做"历史哲学家而不仅仅是一个年代记编者。他理应是英国历史学派的奠基人。"③其实英国历史学派的其他人也在努力对他作出公平的评价。汤因比在他的《工业革命》一书中断言："全世界政治经济学家都已经拥护李嘉图学派，反对马尔萨斯及其后继者。理查德·琼斯已经被喧嚣的掌声所淹没。"④

艾希里教授也认为，"琼斯一直强调要认清现实就必须调查历史，但是他的呼吁无人理会。唯一能证明他的研究产生过影响的是 J. S. 穆勒在农民土地保有权的研究中提及到他的观点。"⑤

坎南教授认为琼斯的历史研究具有重大价值：

"1831 年，理查德·琼斯给了李嘉图狠狠一击。相比李嘉图而言，琼斯的视野更为广阔，他对整个历史都有研究，而不是仅仅盯着战时的英格兰。显然，事实已经证明，农业生产力较低既不是唯一可能的也不是最重要的引起地租上涨的原因。尽管农业生产力并不比早期更低，但是在过去的 300 年里，英格兰的地租却有着巨幅的增长。"⑥

马歇尔对琼斯的态度是公平公正的：

---

① Jevons：Principles of Economics，p. 193.
② Ingram：History of Political Economy，p. 139.
③ Dictionary of Political Economy，Vol. Ⅱ，p. 491.
④ Toynbee，Industrial Revolution，p. 9.
⑤ Dictionary of Political Economy，Vol. Ⅱ，p. 310.
⑥ Cannan：History of the Theories of Production and Distribution，p. 333.

"琼斯没有完全掌握学说、教条的一般性和分析性观点的一般性之间的区别。他有他自己的缺点。虽然他那时想要做的以及他想要影响的不被外界所认可，但是自从惠威尔博士在 1859 年出版了他的著作后，他就支配着大部分认真研究经济的英国人。"①

马歇尔的《经济学原理》中采纳了琼斯关于储蓄来源的观点：

"即使在现代英格兰，专职人员和受雇工人所得的地租和收入是积累的重要来源，它们也是在所有文明社会早期阶段积累的首要来源。"②

J. N. 凯恩斯在他的经典著作《政治经济学的范围与方法》中对琼斯关于时间空间和经济学说的相对性的强调给予了较高评价。③而陶西格教授在他的著作《工资和资本》中则提到琼斯是批判工资基金学说的重要人物。④

当提到"契约平衡体系"这一术语的运用和首创，两位著名经济学家给予琼斯高度评价。科萨认为是琼斯创造了这个恰当的短语。⑤而在尼科尔森那里也得到同样的评价。⑥

---

① Marshall："The Old Generation of Economists and the New"，Quarterly Journal of Economics，1897.

琼斯的影响是非常微小的，在 J. B. 威廉姆斯最新的《英国社会和经济史读物指南》（A Guide to the Printed Materials for English Social and Economic History）一书中根本都没有提到琼斯。

② Marshall：Principles of Economics，8th Edition，p. 229.

③ "琼斯坚信，如果考虑时间地域因素，李嘉图地租理论的适用性是有限的。他指出，一个基于个人所有权和自由竞争假设的理论并不适用于东方社会，因为东方社会产权共有且地租由习惯所规制。更不用提那些毗邻英格兰的土地上的一般的土地占有制度，例如分成制佃农制度。同样，他指出，由于时间的限制，李嘉图地租理论不能很好地适用于一些情况，诸如中世纪经济。在中世纪，土地在很大程度上共同拥有，所有者和耕种者之间不存在自由竞争。"（Scope and Method of Political Economy，p. 298，4th Edition，1917.）

④ "相比西尼尔、马尔萨斯或者查尔姆斯来说，琼斯对于流行的一般学说的反对最为有力。他是一名有能力的学者型的思想家，他精通历史因而视野开阔，并从历史中总结经验教训。他关于工资基金学说的观点有着重大意义。"（Wages and Capital，p. 208）

⑤ An Introduction to Political Econmy，p. 198.

⑥ 尼科尔森说："琼斯恰当地设计了契约平衡体系。"（Dictionary of Political Economy，Vol I，p. 84.）

关于赋税，琼斯的贡献较少。但塞利格曼教授却认为："琼斯是最早否定李嘉图税收归宿理论的人之一，他是驳斥李嘉图分配理论的第一人。"①

最后，琼斯的制度经济学渐渐被大家接受。计量经济学的首席经济学家米歇尔教授认为琼斯在经济史中占有重要位置。

"和李嘉图同时代的理查德·琼斯，一个英格兰教堂的牧师，他精通英国历史，并熟悉同时期英国以外各地方的状况。他指出李嘉图整个体系只适用于近期发展的制度状况，在运用范围上是有限的。琼斯通过对其他时间地域财富分配理论的研究，拓宽了经济理论的研究基础……"②

研究了很多经济学家对于琼斯政治经济学体系的认可观点以后，你可能会问，琼斯对当代和以后的学者会产生影响吗？事实上，我们不得不承认他的影响是微小的。③除了 J. S. 穆勒和福西特采用了他关于农民财产的分类外，没有同时代或后来的经济学家可以被称为他的信徒。他可能对于经济概念的改变有些间接的影响。但对于英格兰经济学研究的总体进程来说，没有直接的影响。这里有三个主要原因：一是他写书拖延，二是他的实践活动过多，三是他的经济理论不适用于那个时代的英国。

我们必须承认他的书写得很慢。惠威尔博士的信清楚地表明琼斯头脑不是很灵活。他的信是 1928 年 9 月 9 日写的，具体如下：

"你找到地租、利润和工资的真正涵义了吗？你一定一直在做这件事情，因为它们在召唤你。我现在一直在读一本小册子，可能你也知道这本小册子。我读的是

---

① Seligman：The Shifting and Incidence of Taxation，p. 195.

② Mitchell："Prospects of Economics" in the Trend of Economics，edited by Tugwell，1924.（p. 17）

③ 普莱斯教授在他的《英国政治经学简史》中对琼斯如此评价：理查德·琼斯，在哈利伯瑞继任马尔萨斯的职位。在他的《论财富的分配和赋税的来源》一书中，对李嘉图的地租理论提出多处质疑。但是李嘉图对于英国经济观念的影响不可动摇。（Short History of Political Economy，p. 64.）

第三版，汤普森的《真实地租理论》。如果你还没有读过，建议你立刻去读。这本小册子表明，你的推测其实早已被成熟论证，而你的拖延会使得这些观点不再引人注目也不再新颖。这里，你想研究地租来源于富饶土地的多余产量是错误的，证明来源于一些没有富饶土地的国家地租的案例、不同案例中税收的归宿、道义上因素和国家习惯的影响。毫无疑问，所有这些问题都只是稍有触及，而无意探讨更深层次的一般原理，但是仍然显示了清晰的主导观点和研究趋向。基于这一考虑，你正是那个拥有可以将这些零散观点相互联系起来并系统化成为普遍观点的恰当人选，你还可以提供所搜集的众多例证来进行说明，所以你不能再徘徊了。同样，从季刊上我对于桑德勒先生的理解是，他可能很愚蠢地将人口增长的事实和一些预防性的阻碍结合在了一起。不久，所有这些骚动的学说必须汇聚统一于一个体系。政治经济学家并不都是相互斗争的。如果他们不明白常识，他们拥有过多的理论，他们就会被践踏、被忽视。如果在最值得称赞的过程中，你允许其他人插足你的领域，将会导致好逸恶劳和管理不善的出现。"①

琼斯的确是一个喜欢拖拉的作家。要不是他的朋友的诚挚鼓励，我们怀疑琼斯是否能够出版他的著作。在另一封信中，日期标注为1829年7月31号，惠威尔博士写到："我一直对你的政治经济研究寄予厚望，并且从现在开始，我希望它的进展不会停止。"②两周以后，惠威尔寄给他另一封鼓舞人心的信，信中表现了一个密友的最珍贵和最友好的鼓励。这封信如下：

"尽管现在乌云密布，但是透过云层我仍然可以看见你。你正满意地看着你关于政治经济研究的半张草稿并且刚刚发现其优点和恰当分类的困难。你身边堆满了非常糟糕的稿子，这些也是你校稿时想要再看看的东西。琼斯太太正在徒劳地询问你大喊大叫的意义。作为一个好孩子，你努力做着你的任务中那些基础并机械的部分，但并不像我做的那样，你的不耐心让你做得一点也不好，直到第二个版本才能使你纠正自己的错误。"③

---

① Dr. Whewell：Writings and Letters，Vol. Ⅱ，p. 93.
② Dr. Whewell：Writings and Letters，Vol. Ⅱ，p. 101.
③ Dr. Whewell：Writings and Letters，Vol. Ⅱ，p. 102.

　　从这些信中我们发现，琼斯很懒惰并且很慢才写完他关于地租理论的部分。虽然他多次以演讲大纲的形式提供关于他的一些观点的简要陈述，但是他没有再出版任何关于他的《论财富分配》的更实质性的内容。而且，正如我们先前提到的，这些都收集并出版在他的《文献存稿》里。他没有留下许多或者系统的关于他的学说发展历程的资料，这当然也是为什么琼斯的影响如此微弱的主要原因之一。

　　另一个解释他默默无闻的原因就是当他被任命为哈利伯瑞学院的政治经济学和历史学教授的同时，他也在负责什一税折合偿付问题；他把他的兴趣从理论研究转向应用政治经济研究。就在他被任命为什一税委员的时候，他收到了东印度学院主管关于保留他教授职位的许可。他在演讲中继续着自己的思考，为此他经常以不同的形式改写书稿。由于这个习惯，他留下的论文包括许多副本。

　　琼斯一直希望他的国家政治经济研究体系完整系统，但是所有这些计划都被他的现实生活和社交嗜好打乱，这些都在第二章有所提及。另外，他创立一个系统学说的另一个大障碍就是他工作的不耐心，而耐心是他进行写作所必需的。

　　最重要的是，他之所以影响力不大是因为他的经济论述都是基于其他国家的经济制度，而不是英国的。他主要的兴趣所在也不是当时英国的经济问题。由于当时的生活成本很高，经济学家们开始把劳工的生活维持基金作为资本的最重要的组成部分。与之相反，琼斯更注重辅助资本的重要性而不是流动资本。为了写作地租理论，琼斯依附于地主的支持，而那个地主因为1846年谷物法的废除而受挫。在他的工资理论中，他把更多的研究空间留给了未被雇佣的劳动者和有报酬的扈从，而不是英国类型的被资本雇佣的劳动者。任何一种经济理论，如果它与当时的经济问题相分离，就不会得到公众的认可。琼斯也不可能例外。

　　所有这些原因——他的慢节奏和不耐心、日常活动还有关于国家政治经济研究的特别体系，都不符合当时英国的情况——组合起来最小化了琼斯在英国古典经济学家们心目中的影响。①然而，他清楚地看到远处值得他辛苦工作的目标；他肩负起探索知识的重任，尽管他的职业生涯非常短暂。在通往真理的道路上，通过观察和归纳，他指出，人类进步只能是缓慢的和艰涩的。如果是这样的，琼斯的做法至少是一部分人的特权，他们一路走过来已经展望到令人振奋的最终胜利。从他的著作出版到现在已经有一百年了，而且最终一个显赫的学派——制度经济学派已经成长起来，一个世纪以前琼斯强调的归纳研究方法、统计方法和历史方法得到了重视。也许在不久的将来，琼斯会在经济思想史中占有他应得的地位。

---

　　①　琼斯没有得到英国经济学家们的认可。应该指出的是，作为历史学派的重要人物，他也无法与德国历史学派的施穆勒和罗雪尔相媲美。

附 A

　　对琼斯的三级分类法进行深入研究有助于我们认清他的思想指向和经济学说。下面的条例展示了他的分类思想：

　　1. 李嘉图学派存在三个错误：[①]

　　A. 假定在国家繁荣和文明进步的进程中，农业生产能力持续下降。

　　B. 世界劳动阶级仅仅依靠收入留存的基金来维持生存。

　　C. 随着国家的繁荣富强，利润率逐渐减少，这说明积累新资源的能力在逐渐下降。

　　2. 琼斯提到爱尔兰小农地租的三个缺点：[②]

　　A. 没有任何外部控制有助于约束农民人口，使它不超过容易养活的限度。

　　B. 对农民的利益没有任何保护，使其在决定他们应付的数目方面不受惯例和规定的影响。

　　C. 土地所有者和使用者之间没有直接的共同利益。

　　3. 农场主地租的增长可能有三种不同的途径：[③]

　　A. 耕作中更多资本的投入促进了总产量的增加。

　　B. 资本运用更加有效率。

　　C. 生产阶级拥有的份额减少，相应地，地主阶级的份额增加。

　　4. 关于假定农业劳动效率递减的三个谬误：[④]

[①] Distribution of Wealth, Preface.
[②] Distribution of Wealth, p. 139. Also Literary Reminds, p. 209.
[③] Distribution of Wealth, p. 178.
[④] Distribution of Wealth, p. 241.

143

A. 利润率下降。

B. 与国内其他商品相比，原产品的相对价值上升。

C. 与其他国家的价格相比，原产品的货币价值上升。

5. 有三个事实表明英格兰地租的上升是由于农业生产的增加：①

A. 农业耕作传播过程中国内的整体地租都有所上升。

B. 农业耕作雇佣的人口比例减少。

C. 地主占有产量的比例减少。

6. 劳动基金大体上可分为三部分：②

A. 劳动者创造并消费的收入，这部分收入不属于其他任何人。

B. 不同于劳动者阶级所拥有的收入，这部分收入直接用于维持劳动力生存。

C. 用来谋取利润的有限且适当的通过财富存储或者积累得到的资本。

7. 劳动耕作者可以被分为三类：③

A. 世袭的使用人。

B. 所有者。

C. 承租人。

8. 承租人又可以分为三种：④

A. 农奴。

B. 分成制佃农。

C. 爱尔兰小农。

9. 李嘉图学派的资本或利润率积累理论有三个错误：⑤

A. 当利润率低时，利润的积累会变慢；当利润率高时，利润的积累会变快。

---

① Distribution of Wealth, p. 264.

② A syllabus of a Course of Lectures on the Wages of Labor to be Delivered at King's College, 1833.

③ Syllabus, p. 46.

④ Syllabus, p. 48.

⑤ Syllabus, p. 51.

B. 利润是资本积累的唯一来源。

C. 世界上所有劳动者的生存依靠收入的积累和储存，而不依靠收入本身。

10. 决定劳动效率的三个原因：①

A. 劳动力劳动的持续性。

B. 劳动力的技术。

C. 劳动力的辅助力量。

11. 全世界的劳动者可以被分成三大不同的类别：②

A. 未被雇佣的劳动者，耕种自己的农田，靠自己生产所得的工资生活。

B. 有报酬的扈从，由他们的雇主从总收入中拿出一部分支付其工资。

C. 被雇佣的劳动者，由他们的雇主从总资本中拿出一部分支付其工资。

12. 控制辅助资产增加的三种情形：③

A. 磨损必须要带来利润。

B. 必须以新的形式出现。

C. 必须比已知资产更好使用。

13. 人口研究中的三个主要问题：④

A. 影响人口增长的一般因素。

B. 影响人口增长的特殊因素，包含工资率波动对于人口的影响。

C. 在不同条件下，决定劳动阶级消费商品最终税收归宿的因素。

14. 决定农业劳动者工资的三个条件：⑤

A. 劳动者耕种规模。

B. 土地的肥沃程度。

---

① Literary Remains, pp. 9, 347, 189, 402.
② Literary Remains, p. 13.
③ Literary Remains, p. 70.
④ Literary Remains, pp. 94, 471.
⑤ Literary Remains, pp. 124, 218.

C. 劳动力的效率。

15. 决定资本积累的三个要素：①

A. 资本积累来源。

B. 资本积累倾向。

C. 所处环境是否利于资本积累。

16. 提高社会地位的三个制约因素：②

A. 血统和种族的区别。

B. 非农职业很少。

C. 恶性立法和条例使得从事这些非农职业变为特权。

17. 财富增加的过程中，人们要建立新的消费习惯必须同时满足三个条件：③

A. 人们知晓并熟悉一个新的符合他们偏好的商品清单。

B. 这些商品价格必须合理，且是他们的财富增加可以达到的。

C. 一定不能存在无法克服的物质上和道德上的障碍，比如说距离、财政或其他管理条例等会对新商品的获得设置障碍。

18. 琼斯提出了关于"什一税折合偿付"的三个观点：④

A. 这种折合偿付是令人满意的。

B. 代替了什一税未来支付的款项应该被用做相同的目的，并支付给相同的人，就像什一税从前那样。

C. 此进程的第一步是将责任转移到未来的支付中，从承租人转移到地主。

19. 琼斯提到了有关"什一税折合偿付"的三个团体：⑤

A. 政府部门，代表了全国人民和所有的国家利益。

B. 地主。

---

① Literary Remains, pp 53，316，390.

② Literary Remains, p. 383.

③ Literary Remains, p. 480.

④ Remarks on the Government Bill for the Commutation of Tithes, 1836.

⑤ Ibid.

C. 什一税所有者。

20. 琼斯提出了政府在"什一税折合偿付"计划中的三个目标：[1]

A. 完全解放国家的资本和工业，用最好的方式从土地上获取最高的可能产量。

B. 同时除去现实的征税模式所产生的障碍。

C. 提升宗教命令的效率。

---

[1] Ibid.

附 B

李嘉图和琼斯关于地租理论的不同观点

琼斯	李嘉图
1. 地租来源于增加的劳动力或资本，报酬随着投入量增加等比增加。	1. 地租来源于增加的劳动力或资本，报酬随着投入增加而递减。
2. 产量增加，地租增加。	2. 产量增加，地租减少。
3. 农业发展对地主有利。	3. 农业发展对地主不利。
4. 地租的上升是财富的创造。	4. 地租的上升只是现有财富的转移。
5. 地租上升，国民产值上升。	5. 地租上升，国民产值固定不变。
6. 劣等土地限制地租增加。	6. 劣等土地导致地租增加。
7. 最小化报酬递减规律的重要性。	7. 报酬递减规律是地租理论的基础。
8. 地租的增加与土地肥沃程度无关。	8. 地租的增加与土地肥沃程度有关。
9. 资本效率提升使人们开始耕作劣等土地，这导致了地租的上升。	9. 报酬递减规律起作用使人们开始耕作劣等土地，这导致了地租的上升。
10. 土地生产能力增加，地租上升。	10. 土地生产能力降低，地租上升。
11. 地主阶级的利益并不与其他阶级的利益相悖。（社会和谐理论）	11. 地主阶级的利益总是与其他阶级的利益相悖。（阶级斗争理论）
12. 地租增加来源于总产量增加，也就是地租总量增加。	12. 地租增加来源于不同种土地的边际产量增加，也就是边际产量越大，地租越高。

148

13. 在地租理论中强调了农业生产力。	13. 在地租理论中强调了利益分配。
14. 地租就是资本投资的剩余利润。	14. 地租与耕作获得的收入是不同的。
15. 可以使用加法或乘法来估计地租的总量。	15. 使用减法或除法来计算边际地租率。
16. 农民地租中工资与地租紧密相连：一方决定另一方。但是这种关系在农场主地租中不成立。	16. 利润与地租紧密相连：二者此消彼长。它们运动方向相反。
17. 强调人类制度。农场主地租的出现归因于资产阶级的兴起。（经济层面的解释）	17. 强调土地的物理构成。（物质层面的解释）

参考文献

一、原始资料

Jones, Richard, An Essay on the Distribution of Wealth and the Sources of Taxation, 1831. London, J. Murray.

——, An Introductory Lecture on Political Economy, Delivered at King's College, London, 1833.

——, Lectures on Capital and Labour.

——, Lectures on Population.

——, "Primitive Economy in England", Edinburgh Review, 1847.

——, A Short Tract on Political Economy, Including Some Account of the Anglo – Indian Revenue System.

——, Text Book of Lectures on Political Economy of Nations, Delivered at the East India College, Haileybury, in 1852.

——, Tract on the Incidence of Taxes on Commodities Consumed by the Labouring Class.

(The above – mentioned seven lectures were collected in one book, entitled Literary Remains, edited by Whewell). 1859. London.

——, Syllabus of a Course of Lectures on the Wages of Labour, Proposed to be Delivered at the East India College.

——, A Few Remarks on the Proposed Commutation of Tithes, with Suggestions of Some Additional Facilities, 1833.

——, A Letter to Sir R. Peel.

——, An Essay on he Law of Bailments.

——, Observations on the English Tithe Bill.

——, "Peasant's Rent" in Ashley's Economic Classics, 1895. New York and London, Macmillan & Co.

——, Remarks on the Government Bill for the Commutation of Tithes, 1836, London.

——, Remarks on the Manner in Which Tithes Should Be Assessed to the Poor's Rate, 1838. London, Shaw & Sons.

二、二手资料

（一）著作

Anderson, J., Enquiry into the Nature of Corn Laws, 1777.

Annual Register, 1855, Vol. 97.

Ashley, W. J., An Introduction to English Economic History and Theory. 4th edition, 1923, London, Longmans, Green & Co.

——, Economic Organization of England, 1915. London, Longmans, Green & Co.

Bagehot, W., Postulates of Political Economy in Economic Studies, 1880. London, Longmans, Green & Co.

Bailey, S., A Critical Dissertation on Value, 1825. London, Hunter.

Banfield, T. C., The Organization of Industry, 1844. London.

Bastable, C. F., Theory of International Trade, 4th ed., Rev. 1903, Macmillan.

Bonar, J., Malthus and His Work, 1924, N. Y., Macmillan.

Boucke, O. F., The Development of Economics, 1750 – 1900 – 1921. N. Y. Macmillan & Co.

Buckle, H. T. , History of Civilization, Vol. ii, 1868. D. Appleton & Co.

Bygone Sussex, W. E. A. Alon, 1897. M. Bygone Series, vol. 27.

Cairnes, J. E. , The Character of Logical Method of Political Economy, 1875, Harper & Brothers.

——, Leading Principles of Political Economy. 1879. London, Macmillian & Co.

Cannan, E. , History of the Theories of Production and Distribution, 1924. P. S. King & Son, London.

Cassel, G. , The Theory of Social Economy, 1924. Harcourst, translated by McCabe.

Cossa, L. , An Introduction to the Study of Political Economy, 1893. Macmillan.

Craig, J. , Remarks on Some Fundamental Doctrines in Political Economy, 1821. London.

Cunningham, W. , The Growth of English Industry and Commerce. 3 vol. , 5th edition, 1912. London.

Dictionary of National Biography, vol. 30. 1885. London, Elder, Smith & Co.

Davenport, H. J. , Value and Distribution, 1908. Chicago, University of Chicago Press.

Edgeworth, F. Y. , The Objects and Method of Political Economy, 1891.

Edgeworth, M. , Memoirs, 1820. London.

Edie, L. D. , Economic Principles and Problems, 1927. N. Y. , Thomas Y. Crowell Co.

Ely, R. T. , "Land Economics," in Economic Essays in Honor of J. B. Clark, 1927. N. Y. , Macmillan & Co.

Fetter, F. A. , Economic Principles, 1915. N. Y. , Century Company.

Gide, C. And Rist C. , History of Economic Doctrines, 1915. N. Y. , D. C. Heath & Co.

Haney, L. H. , History of Economic Thought, 1920. N. Y. , Macmillan.

Hare, A. J. C. , The Life and Letters of Maria Edgeworth, 1895. Boston.

Hollander, J. H. , David Ricardo, 1910. Baltimore, Johns Hopkins Press.

——, Ricardo's Notes on Malthus' Principles of Political Economy, Introduction, 1928. Baltimore, Johns Hopkins Press.

Ingram, J. K. , History of Political Economy, 1915. London.

Jevons, W. S. , Principles of Economics, 1905. N. Y. and London, Macmillam.

——, Principles of Science, 1874. London.

——, Theory of Political Economy, 1911. London, Macmillan.

Johnson, A. S. , Rent in Modern Economic Theory, 1903. N. Y. , Columbia University.

Keynes, J. N. , Scope and Method of Political Economy, 4th edition, 1917, Macmillan.

List, F. , The National System of Political Economy, 1904. Longmans, Green & Co. , London.

Malthus, T. R. , An Essay on the Principle of Population, 1890. London.

——, An Inquiry into the Nature and Progress of Rent and the Principles by Which It Is Regulated, 1815. London, J. Murray.

——, Principles of Political Economy, 1820. London, Murray.

Marshall, A. , Principles of Economics, 8th edition, Macmillan.

Mayo – Smith, R. , "Methods of Investigation in Political Economy," Science Economic Discussion, 1886.

McCulloch, John R. , Literature of Political Economy, 1845. London.

Mill, J. S. , Early Essays, 1897. London, Y. Bell & Sons.

——, Logic, vol. ii.

——, On the Definition of Political Economy, In the Essay on Some Unsettled Question, 1877. 3rd edition.

——, Principles of Political Economy, 1920. London, Longmans, Green &

Co.

Nicholson, J. S. , Tenant's Gain Not Landlord's Loss, 1883. Edinburgh D. Douglas.

Patten, S. N. , The Premises of Political Economy, 1885.

Patton, F. L. , Diminishing Returns in Agriculture, 1926. N. Y. , Columbia University.

Price, L. L. , A Short History of English Political Economy, 12th ed. , Methuen & Co. , 1924.

Ricardo, D. , Principles of Political Economy and Taxation, Gonner's Ed. 1908. London, George Bell & Sons.

Rogers, J. E. T. , Economic Interpretation of History, 1888. N. Y. , Y. P. Putnam's Sons.

——, Six Centures of Work and Wages, 1884. N. Y. , Putnam's Sons.

Roscher. W. , Principles of Political Economy, 1878. N. Y. , Holt (2 vols) .

Secrist, H. , Introduction to Statistical Methods, 1925. N. Y. , Macmillan.

Seligman, E. R. A. , Economic Interpretation of History, 1902. Columbia University Press.

——, Essays in Economics, 1929, N. Y. , Macmillan.

——, Principles of Economics, 10th edition, N. Y. , Longman's, Green & Co.

——, The Shifting and Incidence of Taxation, 1910. Columbia University Press, 3rd edtion.

Sidgwick, H. , Scope and Method of Political Economy, 1904. Macmillan.

Taussig, F. W. , Wages and Capital, 1896. N. Y. , D. Appleton & Co.

Thompson, T. P. , The True Theory of Rent in Opposition to Ricardo and others, 1826.

Torrens, R. , Essay on the Production of wealth, 1821. London.

Toynbee, A. , Industrial Revolution, 5th edition, 1905.

Tugwell, R. G. , The Trend of Economics, 1924. N. Y. , Knopf.

Veblen, T. , Theory of the Leisure Class, 1917. N. Y. , Macmillan.

——, "Peasant's Rent" is Ashley's Economic Classics, 1895. New York

Ward, T. H. , Men of the Reigh, 1885. London, and N. Y. , Routledge & Sons.

Weber, M. , General Economic History, translated by F. H. Knight, 1927. Greenberg.

West, S. E. , The Application of Capital and Labor to Land, 1815.

Whewell, W. , Writings and Letters, ed. By Todhunter. 2 vols. , 1876. London.

Young, A. , Travels, vol. ii. 1793. Dublin.

（二）论文

Ashley, W. J. , "The Enlargement of Economics," Economic Journal, vol. 18.

——, "The Historical School of Political Economy. " Dictionary of Political Economy, vol. ii.

——, "On the Study of Economic History," Quarterly Journal of Economics, 1893.

——, "Place of Economic History in University Studies. " Economic History Review, vol. i.

Böhm – Bawerk, "The Historical vs. the Deductive Method in Political Economy. " American Academy of Political and Social Science, Annals, 1890.

Camp, W. R. , "The Limitations of the Ricardian Theory of Rent. " Political Science Quarterly, vol. 33.

Cannan, E. , "The Origin of the Law of Diminishing Returns. " Economic Journal, 1892.

Carlton, F. T. , "The Rent Concept, Narrowed and Broadened. " Quarterly

Journal of Economics, 1907.

Clark, J. B. , "Distribution as Determined by a Law of Rent. " Quarterly Journal of Economics, 1890.

Cohn, C. G. , "A History of Political Economy. " American Academy of Political and Social Science, Annals, 1894.

Edgeworth, E. Y. , "Richard Jones," Dictionary of Political Economy, vol. ii, p. 491.

Edie, L. D. , "Some Positive Contributions of the Institutional Concept. " Quarterly Journal of Economics, 1927.

Ely, R. T. , "Land Income. " Political Science quarterly, 1928.

——, "Landed Property. " American Economic Review, 1917.

Fetter, F. A. , "Price Economics vs. Welfare Economics. " American Economic Review, 1920.

Froment, P. , "The Law of Non-proportional Returns; Its Evolution and Improvements. " Review of Political Economy, 1928.

Gentlemen's Magazine, March 1855.

Giddings, F. H. , "The Sociological Character of Political Economy. " American Economic Association Publication, 1888.

Gonner, E. C. K. , "Ricardo and His Critics. " Quarterly Journal of Economics, 1889.

Gras, N. S. B. , "The Rise and Development of Economic History. " American History Review, vol. i.

Hamilton, W. H. , "The Institutional Approach to Economic Theory. " American Economic Review, 1918.

Hayes, H. G. , "Land Rent and the Price of Commodities. " American Economic History Review, 1927.

Hobson, J. A. , "The Law of Three Rents. " Quarterly Journal of Economics, 1890.

Hollander, J. H. , "The Present State of the Theory of Distribution. " American Economic Association Publication, 1906.

Hoxie, R. F., "The Historical Method vs. Historical Narrative." Journal of Political Economy, vol. 14.

Ingram, J. K., Presidential Address: Journal of the Statistical Society, 1878.

Jevons, W. S., "The Future of Political Economy." Fortnightly Review, 1878.

Leslie, T. E. C., "Economic Science and Statistics." Athenaeum, 1873.

——, "The Known and the Unknown in the Economic World." Fortnightly Review, 1879.

——, "On the Philosophical Method of Political Economy." Hermathena, 1876.

——, "Political Economy and Sociology." Fortnightly Review.

Loos, J. A., "The Historical Approach to Economics," American Economic Review, 1918.

Mackenzie, J. S., "Historical Method." Dictionary of Political Economy, vol. ii.

Marshall, A., "On Rent." Economic Journal, vol. iii.

——, "The Old Generation of Economists and the New." Quarterly Journal of Economics, 1897.

McCulloch, J., "Jones' Distribution of Wealth." Edinburgh Review, 1831.

Mitchell, W. C., "Quantative Analysis in Economic Theory." American Economic Review, 1925.

Nicholsen, J. S., "The Accumulation of Capital." Dictionary of Political Economy, vol. i.

——, "The Balance of Trade." Dictionary of Political Economy, vol. i.

Patten, S. N., "The Making of Economic Literature." Economic Bulletin, vol. i.

Price, L. L., "Some Aspects of the Theory of Rent." Economic Journal, vol. i.

——, "The Study of Economic History. " Economic Journal, vol. 16.

Seligman, E. R. A. , "On Some Neglected English Economists," Economic Journal, 1903.

Sommer, L. , " Theoretical and Historical Methods in Economics. " Schmoller's Jahrbuch, August, 1928.

Taussig, F. W. , "Exhaustion of the Soil and the Theory of Rent. " Quarterly Journal of Economics, vol. 31.

Turner, J. R. , "Henry C. Carey's Attitude toward the Ricardian Theory of Rent. " Quarterly Journal of Economics, vol. 26.

Veblen, T. , "The Preconception of Economic Science. " Quarterly Journal of Economics, 1899.

——, Why is Economics Not an Evolutionary Science?" Quarterly Journal of Economics, vol. 12.

Viner, J. , "Some Problems of Logical Method in Political Economy. " Journal of Political Economy, 1917.

Wagner, A. , "On the Present State of Political Economy. " Quarterly Journal of Economics, vol. i.

Young, A. A. , "Economics as a Field of Research. " Quarterly Journal of Economics, 1927.

——, "English Political Economy. " Economica, March, 1928.

索　引

RICHARD JONES:
AN EARLY ENGLISH INSTITUTIONALIST

BY
NAI-TUAN CHAO, Ph. D. 1897—

SUBMITTED IN PARTIAL FULFILLMENT OF THE REQUIREMENTS

FOR THE DEGREE OF DOCTOR OF PHILOSOPHY

IN THE

FACULTY OF POLITICAL SCIENCE

COLUMBIA UNIVERSITY

PREFACE

The following essay is an attempt to present the economic theories of Richard Jones, an English writer of the early Nineteenth Century. His institutional approach to economic problems attracted my attention for two reasons. In the first place, while I was working as a compiler in the National Bureau of Historical Research in Peking from 1920 to 1922 I was greatly impressed by the abundance of historical documents on Chinese economic history, but at the same time I was disappointed to find that the English Classical economics had nothing in common with Chinese economic conditions. Thus I became anxious to discover any English writer who emphasized the historical and institutional treatment of economics.

In the second place, after receiving instruction in economics from Professors Seligman, Seager, Mitchell and Simkhovitch at Columbia University I realized that the modern tendency of economic theory is to put great emphasis upon comparative, study, historical treatment and the institutional approach. My study under these teachers led me to inquire whether these modern ideas could be traced back to any writer of the period when the Classical School dominated economic thought.

I owe a special debt to Professor E. R. A. Seligman, who first suggested the subject of this dissertation to me, and without whose instruction the work could scarcely have been undertaken. For invaluable suggestions and supervision in the development of the study I am greatly indebted to Dr. E. M. Burns. Without her criticism and untiring guidance the work would not have been completed. I also wish to express my gratitude to Mr. R. W. Souter for his suggestions and my obligation to Miss Irma Rittenhouse for her aid in correcting the manuscript. I am particularly indebted to my friends Mr. and Mrs. S. S. Slaughter for their assistance in the course of the preparation of this study. Above all, my gratitude is extended to my wife for her warm sympathy and constant encouragement.

N. T. C

New York, April 30, 1930.

CONTENTS

CHAPTER I

INSTITUTIONAL ECONOMICS

I. *Chief Characteristics of Institutional Economics*

ECONOMIC theory moves through a cycle of criticism, reconstruction, and approbation of the institutional order. The laissez-faire theory was first formulated as an instrument of criticism and reconstruction of Mercantilism, the success of the laissez-faire doctrine laid the foundation of the Classical School, which emphasizes the rational and calculating nature of man and undertakes to interpret economic equilibrium. Classical political economy discusses the influence of competition as a check on human selfishness in the pursuit of profit. Its fundamental assumption throughout the analysis is the invariability and universality of economic forces.

But the economists of today are not so much interested in abstract economic theory. In recent years they have neglected the old deductive approach and have turned more and more to the finding of facts as a method of study. They have a strong inclination towards those fields of economic study which bear directly upon the economic welfare of the people. Many students of economics are convinced that the order of study should be a search for principles through analysis of existing situations. Most of our younger economists[1] hold that it is a mistake to differentiate economic theory from the study of economic institutions. They would maintain that while the theories of value and distribution will retain their place as the important subject-matter of economics, further development of such supplementary topics as those dealing with economic institutions is to be expected and desired.

Institutional economics claims to meet the demand for a generalized description of the economic order as a whole. It lays stress upon the process of habituation. It asserts that habits are formed mainly by the discipline of the daily world, and that such habits, shared by large numbers of the people, are called institutions. An institution is a type of usage which has become indispensable by its general acceptance. Institutional economics attempts to explain the character of the social order in conjunction with its economic phenomena. Its inquiry must go beyond sale and purchase to the peculiarities of the economic system which allows these things to take place upon particular terms. It must not stop short of a study of the conventions, customs, habits and thinking and mode of doing which make up the scheme of arrangements which we call the economic order. It must set forth the relations, one to another, of the institutions which together comprise the organization of modern industrial society.

There are four chief features of institutional economics. In the first place, this approach to economics is based upon an acceptable theory of human behavior. Institutions are merely conventional methods of behavior

---

[1]　Important recent contributions to institutional economics are as follows: Mitchell: "The Prospects of Economics," in *The Trend of Economics* , 1924, edited by Tugwell; Hamilton: "The Institutional Approach to Economic Theory" in *American Economic Review* , 1918; Edie: "Some Positive Contributions of the Institutional Concept" in the *Quarterly Journal of Economics* , 1927; Thorpe: *Economic Institutions* , 1928.

of the group and the economist had a good use for the study of institutions because they are those habits which are shared by large portions of the people; they are mass phenomena. If we want to understand the behavior of people in the large, the important task is the study of institutions.

In the social sciences we are concerned with changes that have occurred in human behavior in the past, and we are interested in the further improvements which can be made in the future. Changes in social life have been due primarily to changes in behavior. If the life of the large mass of people in this country is now widely different from that of their ancestors, it is not because men are born nowadays with better brains. Our reflexes, instincts and capacity to learn are believed to be substantially the same as those of our cave-dwelling forefathers. The reason that we have managed to achieve a much higher level of economic well-being and comfort must be ascribed to the fact that we have acquired mass habits of thought and activities quite unlike the habits of thought and activities of the caveman. We have developed, through a long process of cumulative change, more effective ways of training our native capacities. It is these widely prevalent social habits. learned afresh with modifications by each generation, that make our behavior so different from that of our ancestors and that will make the behavior of our descendants different from ours.

So far as we are interested in social change we must center our attention upon the development and cumulative changes of human behavior in our institutions. Custom plays an important part in our economic activity as well as in every other department of social life. To-day much of our personal expenditure is controlled by what custom has declared to be proper, rather than by any act of our own individual reason. "Custom, convention, prestige—all are names indicating the influence which a group exerts

173

over the choices of acts of its members through mere social approval and public opinion, or uncompelled deference to superior competence. " [1]

The individual is a social product. He is not self-contained, with natural and stable wants, for he is constantly shifting his likes and dislikes with the social mind of his crowd. The larger part of our behavior in detail is imitative; it takes advantage of what other people have invented the great characteristic of modern civilization is that it embalms discoveries in print, producing a cumulative stock of other people's experience. The institution of money economy stamps its pattern upon human nature, makes us all react in standard ways to the standard stimuli, and affects our very ideas of what is good, beautiful and true. "Institution" is really a convenient term for the most important among the highly standardized social habits. Hence, it seems that the behavioristic point of view will make economic theory more and more a study of economic institutions.

Secondly, economic theory should be relevant to the modern problem of control. A shift in problems and a general demand for control have made institutional economics an appropriate method of attack. The shift in problems has been due partly to a discovery that institutions are social arrangements capable of change, partly to a consciousness that economic activity, once thought voluntary, is controlled by subtle conventions and habits of thought. In economics as in other sciences, we desire knowledge mainly as an instrument of control. Control means the shaping of the evolution of economic life to fit the developing purposes of our race. Economic life is too intricate and conditions in different industries too diverse for a single form or organization to work equally well everywhere. Competition is not always

---

[1] Z. C. Dickinson: *Economic Motives*, 1924. p. 216.

satisfactory as a protective force, assuring to buyers honest goods and reasonable prices and to sellers a fair return for their labor and capital.

Under our present economic organization, there are several disadvantages. ①One of the outstanding features in our industrial society is uncertainty as to the demand for goods caused by the fickleness of consumers'
desires and the business cycles. Our existing economic organization makes
demand abnormally variable and production in anticipation of orders extremely dangerous. One other equally important feature of modern. industry
is the existence of waste. The fundamental eause of waste is the fact that
conditions under free enterprise require that managers of great concerns
give their attention primarily to the problems of general business policy and
strategy rather than to those of internal plant management. But the most
striking aspect of modern industry is the failure of business enterprises to
procure the active cooperation of employees in increasing output. It is indeed evident that the need for better methods of controlling economic activities is more urgent to-day than a century ago.

Institutional economics deals with the problem of control from the
standpoint of historical development. ②The primitive human clan was an
enlarged family, bound together by ties of blood, and the system of control
was correspondingly close and complete, producing much communism in
primitive institutions. The Roman Empire, which is famous for its system
of control, extended military control nntil it embraced the entire Western
world. During the Middle Ages the chief organs of control in the towns were
the guild merchant and, later, the craft guild, while at the same time, the

---

① S. H. Slichter: "The Organization and Control of Economic Activity," p. 328, in *The Trend of Economics*, edited by Tugwell.

② J. M. Clark: *Social Control of Business*, Chap. Ⅱ.

Church was insisting upon the doctrine of the "just price." The Mercantile doctrine of a later era used to be called "the system of restriction." The presumption of this school of control was that any especially useful branch of production should receive artificial support, and the most useful branches were thought to be foreign trade, shipping, and manufacturing. Against the perverted restraints of Mercantilism arose the doctrine of individualism, which stated that individuals should work in what places and at what trades they chose, that business should determine for itself what branches of production to develop, that the control of quality and workmanship should be left to the consumer and his power of choice. But even such a real individualist as Adam Smith did not claim perfection for the system of free enterprises, for he justified some sorts of control on the grounds that national defense is more important than national wealth.

Present-day industry is essentially a matter of public concern and the stake which the public has in its processes is not adequately protected by the safeguards which individualism affords. The community has ample grounds to devise effective methods to protect or promote its interests, and control must be exercised by modifying the arrangements which make up our scheme of economic life in such a way as better to satisfy our needs. Control of particular fields of economic life, however, requires a knowledge of particular institutions. If we want to deal intelligently with the problem of inflation, we must understand the financal organization of society. For this purpose the economist's business is to analyze the workings of existing institutions. We can accept as scientific only those theorists who make the cumulative changes of institutions their chief concern.

Thirdly, economic theory should unify the whole economic order, and only institutional economics can meet this test. In describing economic organization in general terms it makes clear the kind of institutional world within which each particular factor, such as banking, the money market and the corporation, has its existence. It shows the nature of each by pointing out the parts they play in the larger whole. For many years there has been a notable difference between the way in which economists have handled economic theory on the one hand and the way in which they have handled such problems as insurance, tariff, public finance, trusts, and labor on the other. The monographs have made little use of the theoretical treatises, and the treatises have drawn upon the monographs only for illustration. If we make economics an account of the cumulative changes in economic behavior, all studies of special institutions become organic parts of a single whole.

Lastly, institutional economics is concerned with matters of process. It is a dynamic concept, considering economic phenomena in the process of change. It deals with the evolutionary process as well as with wave-like fluctuations. The former term applies to those changes which, in the absence of great disturbing causes, develop in a certain definite direction without being subject to repetition, such as the growth of population. The latter refers to variatons which are changing their directions in the course of time and are subject to repetition, such as the fluctuations of price levels.

In studying the processes of change, institutional economics takes into consideration both qualitative and quantitative variations. In certain cases, such as economic organization, the technique of production, and the effect on demand of changes in fashion, qualitative changes are not less important than quantitaive variations for the seemingly eternal features of the social structure are gone in a few generations. For instance, land is now free to all, now parcelied out with well-nigh absolute right of individual possession. In other cases, such as prices. rates of interest and the distribution of income, quantitative variations are of fundamental importance and their study is promoted by the extension and improvement of statistical compilations.

One must not forget in the study of economics that the phenomena with which it deals are pervaded by the spirit of life, moving forward and backward, progressing or decaying, under those influences which control the rise and fall of social institutions. The price structure, the wage system, and like institutions, refuse to retain a definite content. Not only are things happening to them, but things are going on within them. An evolutionary economics must contain a theory of a process of cultural growth as this process is determined by the economic interest, a theory of the cumulative sequence of economic institutions' stated in terms of the process itself. The science is biological rather than mechanical. In a word, we are in the incipient stage of a reconstructed institutional economics, responsive to the method of science grounded in a modern psychology of human behavior, and unified by the principle of intelligent control of economic life through additional knowledge of economic experience.

II. *The Institutional Approach of Richard Jones*

It is very interesting to notice that there are but few recent developments in economic doctrine for which we cannot find a forerunner in an earlier period.

"British economists during the twenties and thirties of the Nineteenth Century," Professor Seligman remarks, "far from presenting the dull level of uniformity and agreement which is really associated with the name Classical School, abound in writers, many of them of considerable ability, who did not scruple to attack the premises as well as many of the conclusions of the dominant sect, and who struck out for themselves new paths which have had to be re-discovered by modern thinkers. "①

This statement is true even of a single writer like Richard Jones, the man who should be regarded as the first imporfant writer to attack the doctrines of the Ricardian School, and who also should be considered as the founder of modern institutional economics. His theory of the distribution of wealth is wholly based upon his concept of existing customs. In his opinion, it would be a great misconception of the actual course of human affairs to suppose that competition exercises unlimited sway over distribution. When the division of the national produce is a matter of fixed usage, political economy has no definite law of distribution to investigate. It has only to consider the different institutions of various nations. In discussing the theory of rent, for example, Jones presented many different economic organizations in various nations. He always traced the development of the social and national character back to economic habits and traditions.

"We may be prepared," he says, "therefore, to see without surprise the different systems of rents which in this state of things have arisen out of the peculiar circumstances of different people, forming the main ties which hold society together, determining the nature of the community and the governed, and stamping on a very large portion of the population of the whole globe their most striking features, social, political and moral. "②

In his discussion of almost every economic problem, terms such as "economic habits," "economic custom," and "economic tradition" appear frequently. His article on the system of the balance of trade is regar-

---

① Seligman: "On Some Neglected British Economists," *Economic Journal*, 1903.
② Richard Jones: *Distribution of Wealth*, 1831, p. 4.

ded as an original contribution to the study of early English economic institutions. The immobility of labor and the accumulation of capital are also treated from the standpoint of economic institutions.

Jones' inductive philosophy is to "look and see. " He believed that the economic principles which determine the position and progress of man and govern his economic conduct under various circumstances can be learned ony by an appeal to experience. He also pointed out the relativity of economic forces and offered a realistic study of economic phenomena. He suggested a physical, social and political interpretation of economic motives. He asserted that those scholars must be shallow reasoners who by mere effect of consciousness, by consulting their own views, feelings and motives, and the narrow sphere of their personal observations, and reasoning *a priori*, think that from them they will be able to anticipate the conduct, progress and fortunes of large bodies of men, differing from themselves in moral or physical temperament, and induenced by differences, varying in extent and variously combined, in climate, soil, religion, education and government. ①

Jones' method of induction led him to compare conditions in developed and undeveloped countries. From labor conditions, rent payments, capital accumulation, to the wealth of a nation at large, he emphasized throughout all his works the method of comparison. In discussing the productive power of the people and the inequality of distribution of income, he always took into consideration the social and national character of different countries. He insisted that "if we want to understand the subject of wages or rent, for instance, and take the trouble to observe how the various nations of the

---

① *Distribution of Wealth*, *Preface*; *Literary Remains*, edited by Whewell, 1859, p. 188.

earth employ and pay their laborers or distribute to the landowners their share of the produce of the soil, we shall gain much information in our progress. " Such comparison of the economic factors operating in different countries might yield inductive principles and so make it possible for backward nations to be brought into better alignment with modern economic progress.

Jones did not make any distinction between economic principles and economic problems. He said that theory and practice are often presented as opposed one to the other. but, strictly speaking, theory is the result of an examination into facts, and is never opposed to facts. Since he put great emphasis upon experience and observation, he was naturally inclined to minimize the importance of the deductive method.

The different opinions of the champions of the inductive and deductive methods are, however, due to the fact that there are minds that tend to deductive reasoning to systematic exposition, to generalizing and dogmatizing; while there are other minds of a more historical bent, that turn to induction, to historical and statistical investigation. [1] The latter lean to special study, even to microscopic study; the former lean to systematic arrangement. Each tendency has its strength and its weakness, its merits and its defects. Which method is to be used depends on the nature of the particular problems and on the turn of mind and very probably on the accidents of training and education, of the individual investigator. The principle of proportion in the employment of the factors of production in industry may be equally well employed in dealing with scientific methods, As the producer of wealth will push his investment in the different agents of produc-

---

[1]   Wagner: "On the Present State of Political Economy," *Quarterly Journal of Economics*, Vol. I, 1886.

tion up to a certain point, which has been called the margin of profitableness so, in the manufacture of economic wisdom, each of us should expend his little fund of energy, partly on the fixed capital of the deductive organon and partly on the materials of historial experience. The margin of profitableness in the intellectual as in the external world will differ with the personality of individuals. ①

The use of the inductive method tends to broaden our views of the relations of society. It carefully observes the limits of time and place, and abstains from asserting its principles to be either universal or perpetual. It emphasizes the importance of history for the purpose of discovering what blunders men and nations have made in their economic experience and how these blunders may be avoided in the future. The inductive method is also comparative; that is, it compares the economic institutions which perform the same function in different nations. The method is, finally, statistical; that is, it collects statistical data as a basis for its knowledge, in order to measure economic forces and gauge the results of economic action. ②

Between Jones' *Political Economy of Nations and List's National System of Political Economy* there is close resemblance. In his Lectures Jones made an introductory remark:

"I shall attempt to trace from history and observation, in what manner and by what agencies different populations now produce and deal with, or in other days have produced and dealt with, their respective amounts of national wealth. I believe that we shall find such a survey the safest method of deciding on what causes have determined the relative wealth of

---

① Edgeworth: "The Scope and Method of Political Economy," Inaugural Lecture delivered in 1891 at tha University of Oxford.

② R. M. Smith: "Methods of Investigation." *Science Economic Discussion*, 1886, The Science Company, New York.

different communities in past times, or determine it in our own. " ①

Jones also emphasizes the human factor in dealing with the problem of national wealth, which he believes depends upon human skillfulness and not material riches. And the same expression was echoed in Germany a few years later by F. List, who made a bold attack on the Classical School.

"That book of actual life I have earnestly and diligently studied, and compared with the results of my previous studies, experience and reflections. And the results have been the founding of a system which, however defective it may as yet appear, is not founded on bottomless cosmopolitanism, but on the nature of things, on the lessons of history, and on the requirements of the nations. " ②

From these two instances we are in a position to say that the German historical school adopted the same method of scientific research as Jones pursued.

The principle that economic doctrines, true for any givenepoch, are relative to the particular circumstances of that epoch and cannot be regarded as permanent or true for all time, is an essential element in the teaching of the historical school as well as in modern institutional economics. Economic doctrine concerning the actual world we live in is built up as a branch of empirical knowledge; it has no universality. ③ Our positive knowledge of economic conditions and changes is merely empirical and we may be misled if we constantly formulate the results as laws which hold generally.

Jones put much emphasis upon the elements of time and place, as well as stressing analytical investigation and practical application.

---

① *Literary Remains*, p. 340.

② List: *The National System of Political Economy. Preface.*

③ Cunningham: "The Relativity of Economic Doctrine ," *Economic Journal*, March, 1892.

"A teacher of political economy has first to examine the phenomena presented by the conditions of differnt nations, that he may ground his principles securely. This is the analytical or investigating portion of his labor. Then he must be prepared to show how these principles may be used to account for the exact condition of any particular class in any given nation. This is part of the pratical application of his subject to human affairs. If he neglects either branch of his labor, he performs his office imperfectly. "①

On these grounds Jones insisted on the limited applicability of the Ricardian theory of rent as regards both place and time. A theory based on the assumption of individual ownership and freedom of competition could not, he pointed out, be applied to Oriental states of society in which joint ownership is the rule and rents are regulated by custom, nor even to those instances in which land is held on a customary tenure, as in the métayer system. Similarly, as regards limitations of time, he showed that she Ricardian law of rent could not hold good in a condition of affairs such as existed in medieval economy, when land was to a great extent held in common and the relations between the owners and the tillers of the soil were not controlled by free competition.

"We must get comprehensive views of facts, that we may arrive at principles which are truly comprehensive," said Jones. "If we take a different method, if we snatch at general principles, and content ourselves with confined observations, two things will happen to us: first, what we call general principles will often be found to have no generality; we shall set out with declaring propositions to be universally true which at every step of our further progress we shall be obliged to confess are frequently false; and, secondly, we shall miss a great mass of useful knowledge. " ②

The sphere of economics has changed and is changing as history is

---

① *Literary Remains*, p. 575.
② *Literary Remains*, p. 569.

made, and since the motive forces acting upon human nature are not mere-ly mechanical powers, they too have assumed different modifications at different times. It is doubtless true that our older economists often had an insufficient appreciation of the historical variations in economic conditions, and in particular did not adequately recognize the great extent to which competition was limited or repressed by law or custom in states of society economically less advanced than industrialized nations. We should fully recognize that the elaborate and careful study of economic facts in all de-partments, which the historical school has encouraged and carried out, is an indispensable aid to the development of general economic theory. [1] The followers of the historical method will not, however, be quick to cast all responsibility upon any economic institution, as they recognize that there have been few institutions that have been wholesome or harmful for all peo-ples or in all stages of civilization.

But inferences based on historical research, as distinguished from ob-servation of the present order of events, labor under special disadvanta-ges. Often there is more or less uncertainty concerning the facts them-selves. On this point Jones himself frankly admitted that history has suffered to drop from her pages, perhaps has never recorded there, much of the in-formation which would now be most precious to us. [2] An imperfect, incom-plete record may be even worse than no information at all, so far as affor-

---

[1] Sidgwick: An Address delivered in 1885.

In the Science Economic Discussion, 1886, Professor Seligman submitted a paper on the Continu-ity of Economic Thought, in which considering, first, the relativity of economic doctrines, second, the continuity of political economy, he reached two conclusions, Under the first conception he de-nounces the absolutism of the Classical School and under the second he depicts the historical or evolu-tionary approach of economic science.

[2] *Literary Remains*, p. 570.

ding a basis for theoretical conclusions is concerned. We see the past, as it were, through a mist, and we cannot crossexamine its facts as we often can the facts of the present time. [1]These are the defects of the historical method in the narrow sense.

Statistics has been mentioned as the second source of knowledge. Jones not only was an advocate of the statistical method, but he suggested in 1833 that a statistical society be organized.

"Statistics, unlike history, presents all the facts essential to our reasonings in inexhaustible detail and abundance, but leaves us to speculate upon causes, and to guess at effects as we can. It is not pleasant to reflent how little has been done in England to systematize statistical inquiries, or to preserve and spread the information which statistics can give us. In this respect, as in many others, the cultivators of physical science have set a brilliant and useful example. There is hardly a department in their province which has not the advantage of being pursued by societies of men animated·by a common object and collecting and recording facts under the guidance of philosophical views. We may hope surely that mankind and their concerns will soon attract interest enough to receive similar attention; and that a statistical society will be added to the number of those which are advancing the scientific knowledge of England. "[2]

We find in the Jubilee volume, 1885 of the Statistical Society of London the following interesting statement which reveals Jones as a member of the permanent Committee of the Statistical Section of the British Association for the Advancement of Sciences:

"In 1832 a Statistical section was added to the British Association for the Advancement of Sciences. In the following year this Association then in its the third year of its existence, met at Cambridge and appointed a permanent committee of the section to regulate its

---

[1] J. N. Keynes: *Scope and Method of Political Economy*, p. 326.
[2] *Literary Remains*, p. 571.

affairs, The chairman of this committee of the section was Mr. Babbage, the secretary Mr. D. W. Bethune, and among the members were Hallan, the historian, Professors Malthus, Simpson and the Rev. Richard Jones, all distinguished economists, the late Sir John Lubbock and M. Inctelet. " (Jubilee Volume of the Statistical Society of London, 1885, p. 15) .

He further observed that if a spirit of statistical inquiry were fully spread over the world, if the same phenomena were noted simultaneously in all the more civilized countries. with a common perception of their bearing on political questions, no very long period would elapse before such observations could afford the grounds for safe and useful conclusions. [1]By means of this statistical method, then, the historical study of economic institutions and the comparative investigation of the different economic structures of nations will become easy and more useful. The formal incorporation of economic science and statistics has great advantages. It tends to correct the errors to which economists and statisticians are especially prone. [2]If the latter have been apt to think only of facts, it has been the besetting sin of the former to neglect facts altogether; if statisticians have often been content to collect phenomena without heed to their laws, economists more often still have jumped to the laws without heed to the phenomena; if statisticians have confined themselves chiefly to the region of dry figures and numerical tables, economists have dwelt chiefly in regions of assumptions, conjecture and provincial generalizations.

It is interesting to note that economists express today the same opinion of the importance of statistics as Jones did a century ago. Since the days of Jevons it has been more clearly seen that the deductive science of econom-

---

[1] *Literary Remains*, p. 181.

[2] Leslie: "Economic Science and Statistics," *The Athenaeum*, 1873.

ics must be verified and rendered useful by the purely empirical science of statistics, [1] Political economy, being concerned pre-eminently with quantities, and with groups as distinguished from individuals, has a special tendency to become on its inductive side statistical, just as on its deductive side it tends to become mathematical. [2] Statistics is of paramount importance in the descriptive function of economic inquiries, For example, statistics of production, wages and prices are essential elements in any complete description of the social condition of a community. The functions of statistics in economic theory are, first, to suggest empirical laws which may not be capable of subsequent deductive explanation; and second, to supplement deductive reasoning by checking its results, and submitting them to the test of experience.

Furthermore, statistics plays a still more important part in the applications of economic science to the elucidation and interpretation of particular concrete phenomena. Jones had some insight into this idea, when he predicted the recent development of quantitative and statistical economics. He suggested, for instance, that the population problem be studied by means of statistical inquiries.

In statistics, the method of classfication plays an important role. Classification is a contrivance for the best possible ordering of ideas of objects in our minds, for causing the ideas to accompany or succeed one another in such a way as shall give us the greatest command over the knowledge already acquired, and lead most directly to the acquisition of more knowledge. [3]We can classify things correctly only in so far as we can

---

[1] Jevons: *Theory of Political Economy*, Introduction, p. 22.

[2] J. N. Keynes: *Scope and Method of Political Economy*, p. 341.

[3] J. S. Mill: *Logic*, Vol. II, p. 258.

see them in their true relations, and to see them in their true relations is nothing less than to know their true nature. The value of classification is co-extensive with the value of science and general reasoning. Science can extend only so far as the power of accurate classification extends. ①

Jones' economic doctrines are based upon his threefold classification. He always employed this method of approach in his study on the theory of rent, the principles of wages, the function of capital, and in his discussion of current problems, such as the commutation of the tithes. ②

Jones was, no doubt, one of the most important writers who studied economic institutions. His concept of human nature was based upon habit and culture. He studied human behavior as a phenomenon of the mass, and his attention was focussed upon the role played in human behavior by institutional factors. He knew something of economic history and contemporary conditions outside of England, and always kept in view the elements of time and place in discussing economic problems. He was not searching for levels of equilibrium, but was interested in the cumulative changes of economic institutions. He encouraged the use of the statistical method for the advancement of knowledge and information. Above all, he took a broader view of economics in its relationship to other sciences than was common in his time.

---

① Jevons: *Principles of Science*, Vol. II, p. 345.

② For details, see Appendix A.

CHAPTER II
LIFE AND GENERAL BACKGROUND

I. *Social Background—Contemporay Thought*

IF we are to appreciate the doctrines ot an individual writer we must not lose sight of the social conditions of his times. Jones' economic theory may, perhaps, seem commonplace today, but, at the time when he wrote, it was unusual to find such ideas as he expressed. The class which was rising to power in the two generations following Ricardo's death accepted his (Ricardo's) political economy as established truth, a safe guide to public policy. Never, in fact, has Classical political economy enjoyed such popular favor and intellectual prestige; never has it exercised such practical authority as in the two decades that followed Ricardo. [1]Miss Martineau's *Illustration of Political Economy* popularized in a fresh form the Ricardian doctrines. Within a few years the circulation of her book reached ten thousand copies. Cabinet ministers, newspaper editors and politicians appear to have vied for the privilege of having their proposals supported by her stories. When the political Economy Club was organized, the princip-

---

[1]   Mitchell, The Prospect of Economics, in *The Trend of Economics*, edited by Tugwell, p. 11.

ies of political economy were assumed to be already discovered; the members bound themselves to encourage their diffusion; and their duty was to watch carefully that no doctrines hostile to Ricardo's views were propagated. ①The period from 1821 to 1845 may be described as the age of principles or dogma. For example, as soon as Jones published his book on rent, McCulloch, the most faithful disciple of Ricardo, wrote a severe criticism of it in the Edinburgh Review,② denouncing Jones as a heretic. The members of the Political Economy Club were missionaries, trying to limit the influence of hurtful publications, ③ and the influence of the Ricardian School was dominant. That political economy was considered an established science is evident from the following statement made by Torrens in 1831:

"In the progress of the human mind, a period of controversy amongst the cultivators of any branch of science must necessarily precede the period of unanimity. With respect to political economy, the period of controversy is passing away, and that of unanimity rapidly approaching. Twenty years hence there will scarcely exist a doubt respecting any of its fundamental principles. ④"

DeQuincey admired Ricardo as a great revealer of truth. James Mill exhibited the system of Ricardo with thorough-going rigor. J. R. McCulloch criticized current economic legislation in the *Edinburgh Review* from the point of view of the Ricardian doctrine.

A sort of *Ricardian myth* existed in economic circles for some time. It

---

① Ashley: *Address to the British Association*, *Economic Section*, Leicester 1907.

② This will be discussed further in Chapter Ⅷ.

③ Although the subject of conversation at each meeting of the political Economy Club was to cover a doubt or question on some topic of political economy as revealed in the records of that club, yet there was the over-shadowing influence of three doctrines affecting almost all questions: those of Ricardo as to value and labor, and as to rent, and that of Malthus as to population.

④ Torrens: *Essays on the Production of Wealth*, p. 13.

cannot be doubted that the exaggerated estimate of his merits arose in part from a sense of the support his system gave to the manufacturers and other capitalists in their growing antagonism to the old aristocracy of landowners. [1] The age was one of revolution in industrial affairs; the population increased, manufactures developed and prosperity in agriculture was maintained through the operation of the Corn Laws. Such was the condition of the English industrial world when Ricardo published his *Principles of Political Economy and Taxation in* 1817. He appeared to arrange the seeming anarchy of affairs in intelligible order by means of so precise a theory of the action of free competition that the success of the book was immediate and complete.

Ricardo regarded man as a constant quantity and supposed that the world was made up of men who were influenced by environment only. All city dwellers hoped to obtain the cheap food and high profits which the Ricardian system promised, while the business men of England were already inclined to think that the influence of custom and sentiment in business affairs was harmful and were hence prepared to welcome a theory of free enterprise.

The growth of philosophical radicalism also influenced the tone of the rising school of English economists at the beginning of the nineteenth century. The philosophical radicals held that the whole theory of political government could be deduced from a few simple axioms of human nature. According to Bentham, the leader of the group, the problem of what ought to be is very easy to propound, but the account of what is, is hard to deal with. Thus many economists followed Bentham in discussing what

---

[1] Ingram: *A History of Political Economy*, p. 133.

ought to be rather than what is. The account of what is, is observation; the problem of what ought to be is speculation, and speculation leads to abstract study.

The Utilitarian philosophy re-enforced the dominant power of the Classical School of political economy. Both combined to stress the deliberate calculation of means to an end in human nature, as opposed to action from habit or instinct, to give a new lease of life to individualism, and to regard the individual judgment on matters of an economic character as the best. They had three preconceptions; the physical world is constant (as in the case of the law of diminishing returns); social organization is stable, without much change in the future; and human nature is a calculating machine. These three ideas permeated the current thought thoroughly. Orthodox political economy remained in 1848 substantially what Ricardo had made in 1817.

Into such a philosophical milieu came Richard Jones, who had been cultivating an unorthodox type of economics, a type of theory that deals with a range of problems undreamt of in the philosophy of free competition. He was interested in the cumulative changes of institutions rather than in abstract theory. In the midst of the growing success of the Ricardian group, he protested that its conclusions, especially those concerning rent, applied only to a very recent period and a very small area. ①He urged with great seriousness the need for historical investigation, but his plea fell on deaf ears because the world was not ready to receive his doctrines. In order to understand him thoroughly we must first trace his intellectual backgroud and the development of his economic theories.

---

① *Dictionary of Political Economy*, Vol. 11, p. 310.

II. *Personal Background and Friendships*

Richard Jones, the son of a solicitor at Tunbridge Wells, was born in 1790. His early life has not been adequately treated in any biographical records,[1] and we do not know much about his early education. He began his college life at Caius, Cambridge, in October, 1812, and had originally been intended for the law because of his mental acuteness and his natural eloquence. [2]But his health was unequal to such that career and the change of plans which resulted in his entering the University of Cambridge as a student of literature and philosophy made him acquainted with many of the friends whom he most valued, and who continued on the most intimate terms with him during the whole of his life.

In tracing the intellectual background of Jones' inductive approach to economic problems, we find it was developed at the time of his Cambridge

---

[1]   Some of the biographical records may be mentioned as follows:

Men of the Reigh, *by* T. H. Ward.

Gentlemen's Magazine, March, 1855, p. 360.

Annual Register, Vol. 97, 1855, p. 247.

Encyclopedia Britannica, Vol. 15, p. 500, 13th edition.

Dictionary of National Biography, Vol. 30, p. 157.

W. Whewell, edited by Todhunter.

Dictionary of Political Economy, edited by Palgrave and Higgs.

Peasant Rent, *Preface*, edited by Ashley.

Literary Remains, *Preface*, edited by Whewell.

Memorials of old Haileybury College.

Political Economy Club, 1821-1920, edited by Higgs, London.

[2]   The impression of a "full man" which Jones' writings conveys is confirmed by the genial picture of his personality which Miss Edgeworth gave in the memoirs (Vol. 3, p. 55): "such crowds of i-deas as he poured forth, uttering them so rapidly as to keep one quite on the stretch not to miss any of the good things."

undergraduateship and nourished by the sympathy of some of his college companions. Jones himself was always prompt in maintaining that all the best part of his mental habits had been acquired at college. [1] He possessed good humor and good spirits, and he naturally became a favorite with many circles in the university, especially the most intellectual. [2]When he entered the Caius College, there was at Trinity College an analytical society organized by J. Herschel, G. Peacock and C. Babbage. They had begun to hold "Sunday Morning Philosophical Breakfasts" in the year 1812; and Jones attended them. These university companionships influenced his mental development.

His most intimste friend was Dr. W. Whewell, who lated edited Jones' *Literary Remains*. Both were interested in the inductive method. Jones took his B. A. in 1816 and left the university to take holy orders and practice the ministry at various places in Sussex, a part of England for which he had a truly filial fondness.

Just as his intellectual background, especially the inductive method of thinking, was nourished by his college life, his economic theory had its foundation in the experience of those days when he resided in the rural district of Sussex. Just as social intercourse and intellectual friends helped him to his way of thinking, the natural scenery and sylvan beauty of Sussex must be counted as a kind of inspir ation to him to become a keen observer of physical and social phenomena. Jones always maintained that the love of natural scenery lasts undiminished, and is superior to most other pleasures, hence he had decided to live in Sussex, which was notable for

---

[1]   *Literary Remains Preface*, p. 20.

[2]   Such as the one composed of Herschel, E. Jacob, Alexander Darblay. Dr. Peacock, .Mr. Babbage, Sir Edward Ryan, John Musgrave and T. Greenwood.

the variety of its interests. [1] The breezy South Downs, the bold Hill of Chanctonbury, the wide extending weald, the ruined castles and monasteries, eloquent of bygone ages, and the mighty waters of the ocean forever washing its shores all combine to make Sussex a land of enchantment for those who have the salt of the sea in their blood, who delight in the beauty of hill and woodland or who care to muse upon the intricate movements of those forces. Jones was engaged in ministerial duties in various rural parishes of Sussex. He was, beginning in 1822, for a course of years curate at Brasted, and among his parishioners Jones was regarded with great affection for his kindness to his flock. He married Charlotte Attree at Brighton in 1823.

He was also well known to his county neighbors as a most sagaclous agriculturist and took great interest in agricultural problems. In Sussex the South Down breed of sheep has attained great fame, and the knowledge he had was by no means without its bearing upon his speculations in politlcal economy. He meditated for many years on the subject and was led to large and novel views which he hoped to develop and explain in the subsequent years of his life. In the vigor of his intellect and with his mind not yet drawn aside by the excitement of public life, he brought into shape his economic doctrines when he was at Brasted from 1822 onward. During the writing of his book on rent he was always encouraged by his intimate frievd Whewell, who made many suggestions which guided him in his work, and who also helped him by securing assistance from the University Press toward the expenses of publication.

---

[1] *Bygone Sussex*, p. 9.

III. *His Theoretical and Practical Activities*

The immediate success of the publication of his book on " Rent" in 1831 resulted in his being appointed professor of political economy at the then newly established King's College, London, in 1833. He delivered on the twentryseventh of February, 1833, his introductory lecture in that institution. Mallet has given us a vivid picture of Jones' entry into professional life :

"The Rev. R. Jones, professor of political economy at King's College, gave his introductory lecture six weeks ago; about three hundred persons were present, and it was spoken of in the highest terms. He was requested to print it, with which request he injudiciously complied, for the lecture does not read so well as when delivered. The next lecture about sixty persons attended; of whom three or four only paid for a course. It was then determined that no persons should be admitted without subscribing; and the consequence was that last Wednesday, when the third lecture was to be delivered, Mr. Jones was alone in the room with another professor, and no lecture took place. " ①

The reason for this lack of popularity, however, will be found in the fact that in King's College political economy was by no means a favored subject, The prdecessor of Jones was Nassau Senior, who had been obliged to resign his chair of political economy because of his publication of a pamphlet recommending a reform of the Irish Church and a new appropriation of Irish tithes. When Jones was appointed to succeed Senior, the authorities of King's College wanted the word " political economy" dropped

---

① *Political Economy Club*, edited by Higgs, p. 249.

and "political philosophy" substituted, but Jones insisted that if the latter title were adopted he would feel himself at liberty to treat of political institutions, which so alarmed the conservatives, after their experience with Senior, that they gave way to him.

In 1835 he succeeded Malthus as professor of political economy and history at East India College at Haileybury. His appointment to that position was made by Lord Lansdowne through the recommendation of Miss Maria Edge-worth. [1]The atmosphere was entirely different in the East India College from that of King's. Jones was admired and respected by all his students, was generally regarded by them as the cleverest of all the professors and was, perhaps, the most popular. [2]

From the first moment he opened his mouth in the lecture room all the students knew that he would exact the most complete silence and attention, and would be intolerant of the slightest interruption. And, indeed, to do him full justice; it must be admitted that he was one of those persons who delivers his lectures so well that it is difficult not to listen to every word he utters. His old pupil, J. W. Sherer, painted a lively description of him as follows:

"Who can forget the wonderful struggling out of the gown and out of the great coat, and then into the gown again, and the rolling and roaring, and the coughing and the choking and all the other marvellous accompaniments which, grievous as they were, could not conceal the clear apprehension, the lucid and unencumbered arrangements of the subject,

---

[1] Miss Edgeworth mentioned this fact in her letter to P. Edgeworth in 1835 in which she said: "You have seen in the papers the death of our admirable friend Mr. Malthus. How well he loved you! His lectureship on political economy has been filled by a very able and deserging friend of mine, Mr. Jones, whose book on Rent you have just been reading, and whose book and self I had the pleasure of first introducing to Lord Lansdowne, under whose administration this appointment was made. (*The Life and Letters of Maria Edgeworth*, edited by A. J. C. Hare, vol. II, p. 616).

[2] He never asked questions, nor did he expect the students to make preparations beforehand. His only way of testing the progress of the students was by examining their note books once a month.

and the sterling sense and mas – culine judgment, which made the lectures so highly valu-able and instructive Those on political economy, however, were infinitely superior to the others in "history"; the latter, indeed; were not deficient in vivid sketches of character and able general remarks, but they were. quite wanting in detail and completeness, and one may safely say that if a student had derived his only knowledge of Indian history from Jones' lectures, he might have passed a good examination, and yet have known exceeding-ly little about the subject. "①

Jones was not only an effective and attractive lecturer, but also was one of the well-known talkers of the day, especially as an after-dinner speaker. He would often sit perfectly silent and apparently in a state of great mental depression during the whole of dinner, but by slow degrees his imagination would be stirred into activity by more than one glass of the best wine which the college cellar could produce. Unhappily for his brother professors his conversation—however clever and amusing—was interlarded with stories and anecdotes which, quite unconsciously, he repeated over and over again. The stories all hung together, as it were, in strings, and his brother professors were so familiar with the sequence of each series, that when one story ended they all knew what would come next, and had to resign themselves to the inevitable with a composure and an exchange of smiles which, no doubt, Jones mistook for interested appreciation. Jones' clothes and waistcoat were generally well splashed with gravy spots after dinner; he was remarked by people to "carry his last week's bill of fare on his waistcoat. "

The vivid personality of Jones would be incompletely portrayed without some sidelights depicting his activities as a preacher. In this role he was certainly peculiar and quite unique. His sermons never lasted more than

---

① *Memorials of Old Haileybury College*, p. 173.

fifteen minutes. The following lively description of him, contributed by Sherer, touches on this point:

"The pulpit in the Chapel at Haileybury was in front of the altar, and stood facing the congregation, with its back to the communion rail. It had to be ascended with some agility, from behind, and the appearing of the minister was rather like that of the figure of those toy-boxes, whose lid you open and whose inmate starts at once into considerable stature. Oh ! who can depict the appearing of Jones ! First, an amazing rumbling of stools over which he invariably fell; then a panting for breath, a groaning and a muttering; and lastly, with a start, the elevation, in the sight of all men, of a huge torso, surmounted by a colossal red face, incarnadined beyond its wont by recent exertion, and this, again, wreathed with a little brown wig, somewhat disarranged by the troubles of the ascent. The temper, too, was a little exasperated by the inconvenience of the rostrum; and when, after a good deal of rocking and diving after spectacles, which would fall off the cushion, we were bid to prayers, it was with a voice such as a zealous sea captain would use in a storm to an inattentive sailor. Then followed a sermon, the chief peculiarity in the delivery of which consisted in this, that as soon as the preacher got hot and uncomfortable, the discourse was abruptly brought to a close, without any reference to its completeness or otherwise. "[1]

Any sketch of Jones would be lifeless and insipid, unless it were boldly colored with port wine, but it must not therefore be supposed that he was incapacitated by his habits for steady application. During his tenure of the Haileybury Professorship he was appointed Tithe Commissioner (in 1836) . Every morning, except on his lecture days, his carriage took him to the station of the Great Eastern Railway at Bronbourne. Regularly at the Shoreditch Terminus his portly figure might be seen emerging from the train at a particular hour to enter a cab and be conveyed to his office, where he was very popular among the clerks and other officials.

---

[1] *Memorials of Old Haileybury College*, p. 180.

Jones' administrative ability was shown during the period of commutation of tithes. In the carrying out of this scheme Jones had a large share in reconciling the clerical body to the measure. This was no easy task, for the bill commuting existing tithes on certain principles of valuation deprived the clergy of all prospective increase in the value of their tithes arising from an increase in the produce of the land. Jones' influence in the matter was due to the fact that when he was professor at King's College he was brought into contact with the Archbishop of Canterbury (Howley), the Bishop of London (Blomfield) and other dignitaries of the Church, and thus had the means of knowing their opinions on this question. The Act of 1836 entrusted the commissioners with the administration of a commutation, voluntary for two years and afterwards compulsory. They proceeded immediately to their task, and the success of the measure in practice must be regarded as a notable proof of the wisdom with which it was conceived, and the fairness with which it was carried into effect. The great bulk of the commutation was effected in a very short time. It was ascrided dy eminent persons in a great degree to jones' energy, promptness and clearness of view. A report was annually submitted by the Commissioners to the Home Secretary on the progress achieved in their task. Jones, who wrote these reports at first, made a point of confining them within the limits of a single page. The forms and the instructions for assistant commissioners and other subordinate officers were drawn up mainly by him. He was chiefly concerened in obtaining as a part of the machinery of the commutation maps of every parish, showing the parcels of land on which tithes were apportioned, and these maps, sanctioned by the seal of the commissioners, became legal authority for parochial and other assessments.

In 1851 the tithe commission ceased to exist separately. It was merged in a Copyhold Commission, of which Richard Jones was not a member. in leaving his office, he drew up a memorandum respecting the work connected with the tithe commission and that still remaining to be done, which he left for the instruction of his successors. [1]Jones was then made Secretary of the Capitalar Commission, and afterwards one of the Charity Commission for England and Wales. His executive Powers in public service were beyond doubt admirable and excellent.

Because he removed from speculative to practical economy he did not publish his lectures in a lasting form. His public service and the fascination of society absorbed his time. Thus he never effected what his friends had anticipated, and what he might have accomplished by a greater concentration of his powers. He died in the College at Haileybury in 1855. [2] Four years later his friend Whewell collected his published and unpublished lectures and occasional papers and published them in *Literary Remains*. [3]

---

[1]　In the annual report of 1851 Jones expressed the opinion that the powers connected with tithes and rent-charges must continue some time after he expiration of the present Titbe Commission; of these powers some must be permanent, some temporary; the final consummation of the commutation must be an act declaring tithes, after a reasonable period, to have ceased to exist, and forbidding courts of justice to entertain claims for them.

[2]　"On the 26th day of January, 1855, occurred the death of Prof. Jones. He was not very ill, and was not more than 65 yeas of age, but it was generally believed that he had tried his naturally vigovous constitution somewhat imprudently. . . Both St. , John Herschel and Dr. Whewell were present at his funeral. The interment took place at the village of Amwell about two miles distance from the college. " (*Memorials of Old Haileybury Collage*, p. 125) .

[3]　A reference to the publications of Jones may be mads as follows: *An Essay on the Distribution of Wealth*, *and on the Sources of Taxation*, 1831; *An Introductory Lecture on Political Economy*, *delivered at King's College*, *with a syllabus of a Course of Lectures on the Wages of Labor*, 1883; *A few Remarks on the Proposed Commutation of Tithes with Suggestions of some Additional Facilities*, 1833; *Remarks on the Manner in Which Tithes Should be Assessed to the Poor's Rate under the Existing Law*, 1838; *A Letter to Sir Robert Peel*, 1840; *and Text-Books of Lectures on the Political Economy of Nations delivered at the East India College*, Haileybury, 1852.

CHAPTER III
JONES' SYSTEM OF POLITICAL ECONOMY

I. *General Characteristics of his Theoretical Approach*

THE distinctive feature of Jones' theoretical approach to political economy is its recognition of development in economic life, with the consequent emphasis on the dynamic as distinguished from the purely static element in economic organization. Political economy is a science of organic phenomena. Human nature and social institutions are not fitxed products, but are still undergoing incessant modification by those modes of daily activity which varying circumstances involve. Different communities of different countries and the same community at different times will exhibit a great variety of economic processes. The economic structure of any given community, the direction taken by national energies. the occupations of different classes, and of sexes, the constituents and the partition of movable and immovable property, the progressive, stationary, or regressive condition in respect to productive power, and the quantity and quality of the necessities, comforts and luxuries of life are the results of forces political, moral, and intellectual as well as industrial. The adoption of the historical method necessarily brings economics into a close relation to these other departments of study. Jones' work is teeming with such ideas.

Jones, besides being an institutional economist, was interested in the treatment of economic welfare. He put less stress upon wealth and more upon welfare. By welfare was meant not merely an abundant supply of serviceable goods, but also a satisfactory working life filled with interesting activities.

"We see then that the laws which regulate the production and distribution of wealth thus viewed, have abundance of human interest and philosophical dignity. We view wealth no longer as a mass of dead matter; nor do we treat its princioal divisions, rent, wages, or profits, merely as data in arithmetical calculations; but, tracing the shifting forms of society so far as they are influenced by changing habits of production or modes of distribution, we survey a nation's riches always in close connection with the progress and fortunes of the human race; with alterations in the political element of nations, and in the capacities and opportunities of all orders of the people for improvement independence and happiness. "①

He also maintained with Adam Smith that the degradation and abject poverty of the lower classes can never be found in combination with growing national wealth and political strength In his summary of peasant rents he declared that the actual state of penury and misery which makes the cultivators helpless and keeps them destitute is the great obstacle to the commencement of national improvements, the heavy weight which keeps stationary the wealth and population and civilization of a very large part of the earth.

Jones set forth the doctrine of economic harmony which was later adopted by Bastiat in France and Carey in America. His doctrine of economic harmony was based upon his optimistic views concerning economic

---

① *Literary Remains*, p. 561.

problems:

"When we have advanced so far with our examination of phenomena which regulate or follow the distribution of the annual produce into rent, wages and profits, we shall at least have shown that the deep gloom which was thought to overhang much of the subject was an illusion; that no causes of inevitable decay haunt the fortunes of any class during the progressive development of the resources of a country; that the interests of no portion of society are ever permanently in opposition to those of any other; and that there is nothing either in the physical constitution of man or in that of the earth which he inhabits, that need enfeeble the hopes and exertions of those to whom the high, and, if properly understood, cheerful and animating task is committed of laboring through wise laws and honest governments, to secure the permanent harmony and common prosperity of all classes of society. "[1]

Throughout the whole analysis he emphasized three important things: firstly, he stated that agricultural improvements make productive power keep pace with the advance of civilization; secondly he claimed that there is no conflict of economic interest between the landlord and the capitalist, contrary to the belief held by the Ricardian School; thirdly, he advocated a theory of population which was more objective and scientific than that which was held by Malthus, and his doctrine of secondary wants proposed to clear up the dismal atmosphere of the Malthusian system of political economy.

II. *Jone's Theory of Distribution*

The struggle over the corn laws made the distribution of income the chief issue in English economic policy during Jones' lifetime. The practical

---

[1]   *Distribution of Wealth*, *Preface*, p. 35.

problem was whether the government should maintain the high incomes of the farmers and landlords, or whether the import duties should be reduced to increase the incomes of manufacturers and merchants. Similarly, economists of the day made distribution the center of economic theory. The theoretical question was: what determines the proportions in which the national dividend is shared between landlords, capitalists, and laborers?[1]

Jones' theory of distribution was very different from the current doctrine of his day. He treated the problem from an entirely new augle. His purpose in introducing the problem of distribution was not merely to determine the proportions in which the national dividend should be shared between different classes of the community, but chiefly to discover the existing differences in the productive powers of different nations from the standpoint of the various distributive institutions.

"Production must, of course, practically precede distribution: but, although some wealth must be produced before any can be distributed, lands and labor, adopted in the early stages of a people's progress, exercise an influence over the character and habits of communities which can be traced for ages; which in many cases is never effaced, and this influence must be understood and allowed for, before we can adequately explain existing differences in the productive powers and operations of different nations."[2]

While Karl Marx considered the productive processes as the important factor in molding society; Jones himself explained, on the contrary, the distributive processes as the essential elements in social conformation. "We may predict that, till different forms and modes of distributing the national revenue have superseded the old ones, all hope of rapid change in

---

[1] Mitchell W. C.: "The Prospects of Economics" in *The Trend of Economics*, edited by Tugwell, 1924.

[2] *Literary Remains*, p. 554.

the character of their population, or in the power and resoures of the community, will prove illusive"[1]

Jones also held that the labors of those who have treated of the principles which govern the distribution of wealth have as yet been rewarded by no such success as that which has crowned the efforts of those who have investigated the circumstances which influence the amount produced. [2]According to his view, the attempts to explain the laws of distribution have hitherto led to little besides contradictory opinions. Political economy has been distrusted. The facts on which its conclusions must be founded have been thought too variable and too capricious in their combinations to admit of their being accurately observed or truly analyzed, or, consequently, of their yielding any safe permanent general principles. Truth has been missed, because those who have been most prominent in the discssion of the distribution of wealth have confined the observations on which they founded their reasoning to the small portion of the earth's surface by which they were immediately surrounded, and have then proceeded at once to erect a superstructure of doctrines, either wholly false or limited in their application. [3]In this state of confusion in the concept of the theory of distribution, Jones took up the problem at issue with a very different plan and under the guidance of experience and wide observation.

Jones' *Distribution of Wealth*, consists of two parts. The first deals with peasants' rent, and the second with farmers' rent. These two parts together constitute Book I of his work. He intended to write four books on the distribution of wealth; however, the other three did not appear in book

---

[1]   *Literary Remains*, p. 555.

[2]   *Distribution of Wealth*, *Preface*, p. 5.

[3]   *Distribution of Wealth*, *Preface*, p. 22.

form but only in a mass of lecture notes left after his death. His system of political economy in the strict sense was incomplete. In order of discussion he took up "rent" first, because slight progress in this subject was sufficient to show that the greater part of the nations of the earth are still in the agricultural state, and because, in this state of society, the relation between the proprietors of the soil and its occupiers determines the details of the conditions of the majority of the people, and the spirit and forms of their political institutions. [1]Next came the problem of wages. It is put in second instead of first place simply because in his opinion a clear perception of the causes which affect the amount of remuneration received by the majority of the laborers in the world can only be attained after a survey of the forms and conditions of the various rents they pay. [2]As to the theory of profit, Jones' major inerest was in the accumulation of capital as a factor in production rather than in its distributive process. "In performing this task, I have not confined myself to those circumstances alone which affect the rate of profits as a point of equal or indeed superior importance." [3] Lastly, in dealing with taxation, he discussed the problem of incidence and the principle of justice, and, above all, made the point that the state should share in the joint wealth of its subjects, without causing production to be checked or to decline.

Throubout the whole analysis of his theory of the distribution of wealth, Jones gave chief attention to the economic institutions of other nations than England. He did not attempt to discuss the theory of value, except that on occasion he did try to impugn the validity of Ricardo's so-

---

[1] *Distribution of Wealth*, *Preface*, p. 23.

[2] *Distribution of Wealth*, *Preface*, p. 24.

[3] *Distribution of Wealth*, *Preface*, p. 26.

called labor theory of value. [①]He put great emphasis upon the production of serviceable goods; his study of distribution was, in fact, a step toward the study of production. [②]

III. *Jone's Theory of Production*

In spite of the title he chose for his book, *The Distribution of Wealth*, Jones was much interested in the theory of production. Thus, in discussing different kinds of land tenure and of laborers he always compared the relative productive powers of different nations under different institutions. Similarly his treatment of capital, although originally approached from a distributional angle, consists in fact of a discussion of the importance of auxiliary capital as compared to circulating capital in the process of production. Behind his theory of distribution there is always a theory of production.

The productive power of nations, declares Jones, depends on two circumstances: [③] first, on the fertility or barrenness of the original sources of the wealth they produce; second, on the effciency of the labor they apply in dealing with those sources, or in fashioning the commodities obtained from them. In the earliest stages of society the quality of the soil af-

---

[①]   "This theory it is not necessary for our present purpose to examine. I beg however, in passing to be unmbered among those who believe it defective, and who think that in comparing the exchangeable value of different commodities, other circumstances must be taken into consideration besides the quantity of labor bestowed directly or indirectly upon each. " (*Distribution of Wealth*, p. 206) .

[②]   Like most other writers of the historical school, Jones did not formulate any general principle of distribution.

[③]   But neither of the two circumstances led to the discussion in a theory of production of the amount of per capita produce.

fects the production of wealth, but in the later stages it affects it in a degree so small as to be inconsiderable. "In a majority of instances, the efficiency of the labor of nations is what determines their relative wealth, not differences in the fertility of their soil and waters. "[1] Jones was defending Adam Smith's system of political eonomy when he declared that political economists were well justified in confining that part of their science which relates to the production of wealth to the discovery of causes which affect the efficiency of labor, and have committed but an unimportant error in not dwelling on differences in the national fertility of countries. [2]

Following in the footsteps of Adam Smith, he proceeded to discuss the efficiency of labor as one of the most important factors in the progress of national wealth. He set forth three causes of the efficiency of labor, namely, the continuity with which it is applied; the skill by which it is directed; and the power by which it is aided. [3] Moreover, he discussed the circumstances which regulate the amount of per capita produce. He claimed that the wealth of a whole population obviously depends not merely on the fertility of the industry or of that portion of it employed in production, but on, the proportion which such productive labors bear to those factors which are

---

[1]   *Literary Remain*, p. 334.

[2]   The two following quotations show how much Jones appreciated Adam Smith's work on production:

"In the new path (production) Smith took the lead; and nothing which has been done since his time in this direction will bear a comparison with the results of his labors. " (*Distribution of Wealth*, *Preface*, p. 4).

"On the last branch of the subject (production) much knowledge bas becn accumulated, and principles have been established important both for theoretical and practical purposes, however difficult the application of them to particular circumstances may sometimes be. These constitute a body of political truths, in the solidity and permanence of which a majority of the enlightened and reflecting part of mankind may be said to have acquiesced…" (*Distribution of Wealth*, *Preface*, p. 5).

[3]   All these causes are conditioned by the employment of capital, which will be discussed in the next chapter.

not employed in producing wealth, "A nation, if three-fourths were soldiers or menial servants, would be poor, however fertile the labor of the other fourth might be. "[1] Jones also made a distinction between productive and non-productive labor, but he used these terms intelligently. He asserted that we should not commit the common error of supposing that that portion of the community which is not so employed is unproductive of anything useful, or that the epithet "unproductive" is degrading.

In comparing the efficiency of productive labor in different nations, he made a distinction between motive forces and mechanical advantages. He said:

"The distinction between the increase of contrivances and means to apply the same motive forces with greater mechanical advantage, becomes important when we are comparing the efficiency of labor in different nations. The relative number of horses in France and England will give us no information as to the productive powers of the two nations, as far as those powers are aided by horses, unless we know the relative merits of the implements which determine with what mechanical advantage a horse's power is applied in agriculture, and indeed in various otner occupations of the two countries. [2]

No contemporary writers paid so much attention to the problem of technology as did Jones. He insisted that it is available technique which determines the degree to which man can conquer and exploit nature and adapt it to its use, an achievement which produces material culture in its dynamic setting. The progress of economic science and institutions is directly related to the development of technology, inasmuch as our economic life is the product of the application of the existing technique to the problems of

---

[1]   *Literary Remains*, p. 346.

[2]   This statement of Jones was intended to demonstrate a fallacy on the part of M. Dupin, who considered the motive force alone in comparing the respective productive powers of England and France.

the exploitation of nature . Hence , in the discussion of production no one can neglect the problem of technology.

Jones employed the term "production" in a broad sense. An article is not considered by him to be completely produced until it is placed in the hands of the person who is to consume it. Thus , tea designed for English consumption is not said to be produced until it has been conveyed from China , through the mediation of different individuals and through the instrumentality of auxiliary capital in various shapes , to the English purchaser who means to consume it. [1]This kind of treatment , which includes the exchange phenomena in the process of production , was not common in his time. [2] According to Jones , production is not necessarily the production of material goods; its criterion is in this sense the creation of new utility. When an activity brings about an addition to the existing amount of utility , we have an act of production.

Jones emphasized the importance of the close relationship between the economic and social organization of nations and their powers of production. He first sketched out a standard of the continuity of labor and of technical knowledge and mechanical facilities by which to judge the perfection of productive powers of nations. Then he discussed the political, social, moral and intellectual changes which accompany changes in the economic organization of communities. He points out that the explanation of these influences is most distinctly a part of the proper and peculiar task of the political economists. Economic science can never be successfully pursued if such subjects be wholly eschewed by its promoters. He emphasized the

---

[1] *Literary Remains* , p. 192.

[2] English writers subsequent to James Mill have generally been inclined to follow Mill's example by keeping a consideration of exchange out of their treatment of production.

economic habits of nations as an important factor in the subject of national wealth. "Such an analysis of the economic habits of the various divisions of the human race must obviously have its interest and use in whatever mode we may think it best to approach a knowledge of systems of abstract truth on the subject of national wealth. "[1] But he further remarked that as communities change their powers of production, they necessarily change their habits too. During this change or progress, all the different classes of the community find that they are connected with other classes in new relationships, that they are assuming new positions, and are surrounded by new moral and social dangers and new conditions of social and political excellence. Jones always kept in mind his belief in the cumulative changes of institutions in dealing with the subject of production.

IV. *Other Features of His System of Political Economy*

In spite of the fact that Jones decried all attempts to frame accurate definitions, he was very fond of coining new terms. [2] In addition to the terins "Balance of Bargain" and "National Anatomy," Jones was also the first to use the term "dismal system" in, reference to political economy, which was later adopted by Carlyle, who slightly changed it to "dismal science. " Jones said: "The perception of this fact is of itself sufficient to in-

---

[1]   *Literary Remains*, p. 340.

[2]   "If any reader, during this inquiry, is really puzzled to know what we are observing together, I shall be very sorry; but I am quite sure that I should do him no real service by presenting him in the outset with a definition to reason from. " (*Distribution of Wealth*, *Preface*, p. 47) .

Attempts to give definitions are regarded by Jones as throwing dust in the eyes of the student, and as diverting his attention from more important points.

spire distrust in those dismal systems which teach that the whole human race is under the resistless domain of an impulse, forcing ever its aggregate numbers forward to the extreme limit of the subsistence they can produce. "[1]

Jones also formulated a theory of the economic interpretation of history.

"Those indeed who value what is called political economy chiefly because it leads to an insight into the manner in which the physical circumstances which surround man on earth develop or sway his moral character, will feel interested on yet higher grounds in tracing the effect of a system, springing out of common necessity, which, for a long period in the growth of nations, binds the majority of their populations to the earth they till; a system which has continued for a series of ages to stamp its peculiar impress on the political, the intellectual, and moral features of a large portion of the human race. "[2]

And in one of his lectures he mentioned the economic interpretation of politics:

"The fact that in the political progress of nations there is an inseparable connection between increased freedom and increased responsibilities; that freedom, in short, is a blessing which, from the very constitution of men and society, none can long enjoy who do not deserve it, is a truth which, vaguely seen by others, shines out in all its evidence and detail to the political economist, who, tracing changes in the modes of producing and distributing wealth, observes step by step the alterations which take place in the connections, mutual independence and all the cementing influences that hold together those human materials of which states are composed···"[3]

He also remarked that it is not our province to praise or blame this or that form of government, or code of laws, but to show in what cases the es-

---

[1] *Distribution of Wealth*, *Preface*, p. 17.
[2] *Distribution of Wealth*, p. 66.
[3] *Literary Remains*, p. 593.

tablishment of each is or is not possible, why institutions and laws which endure and flourish under one state of economic conformation wither and die away when transplanted to a place where society does not present the proper materials to give them life and support. "Our subject then is, to a great extent, the mother science on which the philosophy of constitutional legislation rests, as does in a great measure the philosophy of jurisprudence. The law-giver who would frame codes and institutions without such knowledge as we present, may be an eloquent dreamer, but can never be a practical statesman. "[1]

In summary, Jones' system of political economy was very different from contemporary theories. His theory of distribution was not chiefly adapted to the purpose of studying the English problem of distribution alone; moreover, it was discussed from the productive point of view rather than from a distributive angle. He paid a great deal of attention to the economic institutions of the less advanced countries in order to support his arguments against the current economic doctrine of the Ricardian School . In his theory of production he emphasized the importance of technology as a factor in the productive power of nations. He also discussed the influence of economic habits and other social conditions upon production. As to the other features of his theoretical approach, he set forth his optimistic views in the theory of harmony and in his economic interpretation of history.

---

[1]   *Literary Remains*, p. 576.

CHAPTER IV
THEORY OF RENT

JONES' system of political economy, as we know, was based upon a study of economic institutions. But we must ask further: why was Jones interested in economic institutions of other nations than England, and how did he develop his theory of rent? In answering these two questions let us first review the current theory of the distribution of wealth at that time.

According to the Ricardian doctrine of distribution of wealth, wages are fixed by the standard of living, which is supposed to be constant; profits will decrease as more and more labor is required to provide necessities for the mass of the working population; and the future belongs to the landlords who will grow richer while the laborers and capitalists grow poorer. Both the theory of wages and the theory of profits are intimately related to the theory of rent, which is regarded as the cornerstone of the Classical theory of distribution and is based upon the assumption of free competition, holding that landlord and tenant respectively are actuated by competition alone; that the landlord endeavors to obtain the highest rent he can, and the tenant the lowest; that both are independent, intelligent agents, able and willing to carry their goods and services to the best markets; and that the tenant, knowing all the advantages of different soils, places and trades, is able and willing to move, taking with him his improvement to any soil or place or trade where he will be more favorably situated. ①This system of landlord and tenant relationship is also assumed to be the universal form of tenure.

Since the Classical theory of distribution of wealth was centered on the theory of rent, Jones naturally took it as the target at which to aim. For, if he could prove that the Ricardian theory of rent was incorrect, the whole Classical theory of distribution would collapse, since it would be built upon unsound foundations. Again, as the Ricardian theory of rent assumed the English type of land system to be the universal form of tenure, Jones' next step was to disprove this by investigating the various economic institutions of other nations than England. He chose his battlefield on the theory of rent and employed the study of economic institutions as a kind of weapon for attack. Thus the main object of Jones' theory of peasant rent is not only a study of the peasant rent itself; but also the collecting of economic material to support his arguments against the principle of universality and the doctrine of free competion of the Ricardian school.

Jones set forth the chief fallacies of the Ricardian doctrine of rent as being: (1) that increasing rents proceed always, not from additional wealth created on the soil, but from a transfer of wealth which existed before into the hands of the landlords; (2) that rents invariably proceed from the application of additional capital to agriculture with a diminished return; (3) that nothing that does not alter the relative fertility of the land cultivated can increase rents; (4) that improvements in agriculture do not increase rents; (5) that such improvements in agriculture lower rents, at least for a time, and lessen the means of the landlords; (6) that increasing

---

① Price: *A Short History of Political Economy in England* , p. 80.

rents bring no addition to the resources of a country; (7) that every rise in rents is a mere transfer of value, advantageous only to the landlords, and proportionately injurious to the consumers; and (8) that the interests of the landlords are always opposed to those of other classes in the community. We shall discuss these points later.

I. *Peasant Rent*

Jones divided his theory of rent into two parts: peasant rent and farmer rent. He declines to give a definition of the term "rent," saying: "It has been mentioned to me, that I have given no regular definition of the word rent. The omission was not undesigned. On a subject like this, to attempt to draw conclusions from definitions is almost a sure step towards error."[1]

In his study of peasant rent there are four points which command our attention. In the first place, the economic law of free competition has been entirely abandoned. Custom and institutional inquiry occupy a prominent place. Secondly, historical research, instead of deductive reasoning, has been greatly emphasized. Thirdly, the close relationship between wages and rent has been clearly brought out. Fourthly, the importance of capital, production, and distribution has been given a great deal of consideration.

Historically, peasant rent came first in order of appearance in the progress of nations; therefore it may be called primary rent. Economically, peasant rent is used in referring to an occupier of the ground who extracts

---

[1] *Distribution of Wealth*, *Preface.*

Jones did not like to confine his concept of rent to a definition. As a matter of fact, his theory of rent is that of an income from land.

his own wages from the earth. The origin of rent arises from the soil—the appropriation of soil, not the superiority of soil. The appropriation of soil is a political and human institution, while the superiority of soil belongs to the physical and natural phenomena.

"When men begin to unite in the form of an agricultural. community, the political notion they seem constantlty to adopt first is that of an exclusive right to the soil of the country they inhabit. Their circumstances, their prejudices, their idea of justice or of expediency, lead them, almost universally, to vest that right in their general government, and in persons deriving their rights from it. " ①

This fact is true of old nations as well as of new countries. Throughout Asia, the sovereigns had ever been in the possession of an exclusive title to the soil of their dominions. In China the emperor was regarded as the "Son of the Heaven"; he was the sole proprietor. In America, land was considered to be the property of the federal government. It could be occupied only with the government's consent, in spots fixed upon and allotted to its people, and on condition of a previous money payment. But the United States Government does not convert the successive shoals of fresh applicants into a class of state tenantry; rather the formation of a race of proprietors takes place.

With the aid of experience and history Jones came to the conclusion that in the actual progress of human society rent has usually originated in the appropriation of the soil at a time when the bulk of the people must cultivate it on such terms as they can obtain, or starve. This necessity which compels them to pay a rent, he maintains, is wholly independent of any difference in the quality of the ground they occupy, and would not be re-

---

① *Distribution of Wealth*, p. 5.

moved were the soils all equal. Here Jones assumes that the form and amount of the rents they pay are determined by a direct contract. He is not discussing either differential or marginal rent.

He divided the peasant rents into four parts, namely: labor rents, metayer rents, ryot rents and cottier rents. It is worth noting that this type or classification of peasant rents was later adopted by J. S. Mill, who devoted four chapters to peasant proprietors immediately after his discussion of the significance of custom on the distribution of produce.

Labor rent may be called service rent; instead of money or produce payment the tenant must render a certain amount of labor to the proprietor. Jones' survey of labor rent covered Eastern Europe from Russia to Germany. [1] He discussed labor rents in various countries with a dynamic view of changes always in mind. After having observed them in different countries, he gave a short summary of the most marked feature of rent common to the system in all its modifications. He started from particular facts and reached a general conclusion, employing the inductive method to advantage. His criticisms of labor rents from the economic point of view fall under four headings. Firstly, there is a strict connection between the wages of labor

---

[1]   After describing the servile condition of the Russian serfs, Jones maintained that they were in a state of rapid change. Three days of labor for rent in each week had been the rule. The tenants on the royal domains appeared to be, on the whole, in a better condition than the serfs belonging to individuals. The number of royal serfs was estimated in 1782 as ten millions and a half. In Hungary, such peasants occupied about half the cultivated surface of the country in 1777, and all paid labor rents. Till the reign of Maria Theresa, their situation was quite similar to that of the Russian serfs. By her edict, the quantity of labor due to the proprietor of each session (about the size of 35 to 40 English acres) was fixed at 104 days per annum. Besides this the peasant had to give four fowls, twelve eggs and a pound and a half of butter. In Germany the situation was more hopeful for such workers. Some tenants, under the name of "Amdmen," were prosperous. There were others called "Leibeigeners" and "Meyers." The former paid a labor rent in kind and cultivated the land of the landlord for a certain number of days in the year. The latter had commuted their labor rent into a money or corn rent The proprietor could not raise the rent nor could he refuse to renew the lease unless the heir was an idiot, or the rent in arrears.

and the rent—the dependence of wages on rents. Where claims upon the serf's time are multiplied, his own ground must be imperfectly tilled, and thus the produce of his allotment must become less. Secondly, this kind of tenancy has a singular effect in degrading the industrious habits of the laborers. Thirdly, the lax superintendence, or the imperfect assistance, of the landed proprietors makes the inefficiency of agricultural labor still worse. And lastly, since the inefficiency of agricultural labor results in only a small amount of raw produce the non-agricultural classes maintained by it must be small.

In addition to the above-mentioned economic aspects of labor rent, Jones made three further remarks on its influence upon the political and social conditions of nations. The constant coercion and arbitrary authority of landlords over the tenants, the great power and influence of the aristocracy, and the want of a third estate in the political constitution of those countries all combined to produce a dark and melancholy picture of labor rent. He also suggested a tentative plan for their improvement, embracing the substitution of produce or money rent.

Métayer rent, the second kind of peasant rent, is present in a state of society more advanced than that of labor rent. The métayer is a peasant tenant who extracts his own wages and subsistence from the soil. He pays a produce rent to the owner of the land. The landlord, besides supplying him with the land, supplies him also with the stock by which he is assisted in his labor. The payment to the landlord may be considered, therefore, to consist of two distinct portions: one constitutes the profits of his stock, the other his rent. Jones' survey of métayer rent covers the western division of continental Europe as well as the nations of antiquity. ①

In passing a critical judgment on métayer rent as a whole, Jones balanced its advantages and disadvantages from a productive viewpoint. So far as the advantages are concerned, the fact that the métayer is entrusted with the whole care of the cultivation is a circumstance which not only indicates his superior rank in society, but brings with it substantial improvement in his condition. Furthermore, since the landlord's rent depends upon the amount of the produce, he has an obvious interest in preventing the energy

---

① In tracing the métayer rents in Greece, Jones consulted many authorities, including Xenophon and Aristotle. He tried to discover the causes which destroyed the system of slave cultivation and those which brought the métayer rents into effect. As Greece became consolidated, first by the Macedonian, then by the Roman influence, the possessions of individual proprietors naturally extended themselves over a large space, and profitable management by slave agents must have become more and more impracticable. At last a tenant was introduced who, receiving from the landowner his land and stock, became responsible to him for a certain proportion, usually half, of the produce. The causes which introduced the métayer system in Rome were similar to those which ultimately established in Greece. On this topic Jones made a careful study of the agricultural literature written by Cato and Virgil. Before the introduction of the métayer system, Virgil recommended alternate husbandry. As the empire became larger and the size of estates increased, the superintendence of husbandry became ineffcient and the lands were given up to the discretion of an inferior class of slaves. Columella was the only one who recommended that all such estates should be let.

The terms on which the French métayers held their farms differed much from age to age, but the normal rate was half, from which the original name of "Medéetarius" was derived. In Italy the métayers were fewer than in France. The number of acres which a métayer can manage must depend largely on the course of crops and mode of tillage.

or the means of the tenant from being lessened by oppression. ① As to the disadvantages, it is apparent that the divided interest which exists in the produce of cultivation mars almost every attempt at improvement. ②The tenant is unwilling to listen to the suggestions of the landlord, the landlord is reluctant to entrust additional means to the hands of a prejudiced and usually very ignorant tenant. The tenant's dread of innovation is natural; he exists under a system of cultivation familiar to him; the failure of an experiment might leave him to starve. This dread makes it almost impossible to introduce improvements into the practice of the métayer system. While the tenant is frightened at a change of system, the landlord hangs back, with a hardly less mischievous reluctance, from the advances necessary to carry on efficiently any system whatever. When stock is to be advanced by one party and used by another for their common benefit it brings about some waste and carelessness in the receiving party and great jealousy and reluc-

---

① Charles Gide estimates highly the benefits of métayer rents. His argument may be briefly stated as follows:

In the first place the nétayer system establishes a unity of interests between the owner and the métayer. They share alike in good and bad fortune; there is a real association between them, and it is one of the oldest and most admirable forms of profit sharing. Secondly, the métayer is never straitened by the mode of payment, because he pays in kind. He only gives the proprietor what the earth itself gives: nothing, if it yields nothing; much, if it yields generously. Thirdly, the métayer system, by customarily fixing the division of the product in halves, wards off completely the influence of competition on price and quenches all controversy as to the amount of the rent. It also assures a long duration of lease. Finally, intercourse is more intimate and even more familiar between the owner and the métayer. For all these reasons the métayer system may be considered as an element of social peace and as capable of solving in certain cases the agrarian question. (*Dictionary of Political Economy*, Vol. II, p. 738).

② Adam Smith mentioned this point in *The Wealth of Nations* (Book III, chapter 2), "It could never be the interest of this species of cultivation to lay out, in the further improvement of the land, any part of the little stock which they might save from their own share of the produce, because the lord, who laid out nothing, was to get one half of whatever it produced."

tance in the contributing party. ①

Having balanced the merits and demerits of the métayer rent, Jones pointed out its special features as a weapon with which to attack the Ricardian theory of rent, based upon differences in the fertility of soils. The existence of rent in the métayer system is in no degree dependent upon the existence of different qualities of soil or of different returns to the stock and labor employed. In any country the landlords, who, with small quantities of stock, have quantities of land sufficient to enable a body of peasant laborers to maintain themselves, would continue to derive a revenue as landowners through sharing the produce of the industry of those laborers, though all the lands in the country were perfectly equal in quality. He also touched upon the wage question in this connection. In countries employing the métayer system, the wages of the main body of the people depend upon the rent they pay. The division of the produce on which their wage depends is determined by their contracts with their landlords. In like manner the amount of rent in such countries is determined by the amount of wages.

Ryot rents are produce rents paid by a laborer gaining his own wages from the soil to the sovereign as its proprietor. These rents originate in the rights of the sovereign as the sole proprietor of the soil of his dominions.

---

① Arthur Young has discussed the disadvantages of the métayer system: "There is not one word to be said in favor of the Métayer System, and a thousand arguments that might be used against it. In this most miserable of all the modes of letting land, the defrauded landlord receives a contemptible rent; the farmer is in the lowest state of poverty; the land is miserably cultivated; and the nation suffers as severaly as the parties themselves. Wherever this system prevails. it may be taken for granted that a useless and miserable population is found. " (Travels, Vol. II, p. 153) .

The survey of ryot rents made by Jones was limited to Asiatic nations. ①In judging the merits and defects of this kind of tenure he decided that there is nothing mischievous in the direct effect of ryot rents. They are usually moderate if collected peacefully and fairly and become a species of land tax, leaving the tenant a beneficial hereditary state. But their indirect effeets are full of evils. They nurse and foster Asiatic despotism on the one hand, and reduce the citizens to the most helpless and prostrate condition on the other. In countries cultivated by ryots, the wages of the main body of the people are determined by the rent they pay, as is the case under all varieties of peasant rents. In like manner the abount of rent in such countries is determined by the abount of wages. The existence and progress of rents under this system or tenure is also in no degree dependent upon the existence of different qualities of soil, or different refurns to the stock and

---

① In India he found the cultivator was under a Zemindar, a functionary who took charge of collecting revenues in the Hindoo Government. The system was very disastrous, due to the corruption of the officials. In Persia, the tenant was obliged to pay one-fifth of the produce to the Shah. In Turkey, the rate of ryot rent differed according to the religion: one-seventh of the produce where the cultivator was a Turk, one-fifth where he was a Christian. Concerning the rent of the Chinese peasantry, Jones honestly confessed that he did not know enough to judge accurately of the peculiar modifications which this system of imperial ownership had received in that country. As we know, no one can be, according to Confucius' doctrine, the true landlord except the emperor. The Canon of Poetry says: "Under the wide Heaven all is the King's land." Since the government was the landowner, there was no distinction between a land tax and rent. Under the Tsing Tien System the center lot of each Tsing was cultivated in common by the adjoining landholders for the government as a tax. Land was distributed to eight families and rent was paid in terms of labor, not in produce, as Jones defined a ryot rent. In China, land was held by the government and granted in various sizes of tracts to successive generations of farmers in different dynasties. The farmer had a species of life tenure, from the time he started farming, at about thirty years of age, until sixty, when the land reverted to the government. After about twenty-five centuries of tenure of this general type private ownership came into existence. According to the historical facts, the earliest custom of paying rent was the métayer system. The cultivator retained one-half of the harvest and paid the other half to the landlord as rent. Such a prachce has existed from the Chin Dynasty to the present day, since Shong Yang accomplished the destruction of the Tsing Tien System. In this case Jones was right in regarding it as a produce rent.

labor employed on each.

Under the head of cottier rents, the fourth of the peasant rents, we may include all rents contracted to be paid in money by tenants extracting their own subsistence from the soil. The cottier tenant is bound by contract, whatever the quantity or value of produce may be, to pay a fixed sum of money to the proprietor. The reason that this system prevails in Ireland is simply because it is in the neighborhood of England, and the connection between the two countries enables the Irish peasant to obtain cash for a portion of his produce. The disadvantages of cottier rents may be ranged under three heads. The first of these is in connection with the question of population. Where labor or métayer rents prevail, some external causes of repression are found in the interference of the landlords for their own interests. Where ryot rents are established the external causes of repression are found in vices and mismanagement; where cottier rents exist, no such external causes are present and the unchecked disposition of the people leads to a multiplication which ends in wretchedness. The second disadvantage is the want of any influence of custom and prescription in keeping the terms of the contract between the proprietors and their tenantry steady and fixed. The third disadvantage is the absence of such direct and obvious common interest between landlord and tenant as might secure to the cultivator assistance when in distress. The principal advantage which the cottier derives from this form of tenure is the great facility with which, when circumstances are favorable to him, he changes his condition in society altogether.

After a survey of these various forms of land systems, Jones was in an excellent position to declare that no one type of land tenure could be taken as the basis of a theory of rent. With the aid of history and economic data he boldly expressed his opinion that the income from land owed neither its origin nor its continuance to the existence of gradations in the qualities of soil; that with improvements in agriculture the amount of produce which formed the annual rents had steadily increased; that the landlords would find that they became wealthier as the labor of their peasant tenantry produced more from the earth, and that they became poorper as it produced less; that increasing produce converted into increased rents constituted a fresh creation of material riches;[①] and that under all forms of peasant tenures the interests of the landlords are indissolubly connected with those of their tenantry and of the community at large. All these points, supported by a study of various economic institutions of different nations, were used by Jones to attack the Ricardian theory of rent.

Here we must be careful to notice, however, as will be pointed out later, that Jones' concept of rent is different from Ricardo's. The former employs this term in the popular sense, while the latter uses it in the narrow sense of economic rent only.

Ⅱ. *Farmer Rent*

In discussing peasant rents Jones was successful in pointing out the narrowness and lack of general applicability of the Ricardian theory of rent. He then proceeded to discuss "farmer rent" (the English type of farming). The origin of farmers' rent, he held, was due to the rise of the

---

① "Increased rents originating in the accumulation of capital on the land, and in increased production, are not only themselves a clear addition to the resources of a country, but necessarily indicate a yet greater addition in the hands of the producing classes; an addition which is substantially equivalent to the progressive enlargement of the territory itself. " (*Distribution of Wealth*, p. 203) .

capitalist classes, who advanced from their own funds the wage of labor and took charge of the varied industry of a population. Rent, in such a case, necessarily consists merely of surplus profits, that is, of all that can be gained by employing a certain quantity of capital and labor upon the land instead of in any other occupation. ①

Before proceeding to discuss farmers' rent we must say a few words about the distinction between farmers' rent and peasant rent. In the first place, according to Jones, the origin of peasant rent is the appropriation of the soil, while that of farmers' rent is due to the rise of the capitalist class. In the second place, custom and contract play an important role in peasant rent, while competition is the essential factor in farmers' rent. Thirdly, in the development of economic stages the former is still in the barter economy, while the latter is in the money economy. Fourthly, as far as the distributive process is concerned, the former system is a kind of two-fold division of produce, while the latter is a three fold division of produce. Fifthly, the rent has a great influence on wages in the case of peasant rents, but this influence ceases in the case of farmers' rents. Sixthly, in the system of peasant rent the central figure is the landlord; in that of farmers' rent, the capitalist is the most prominent figure. Lastly, from the standpoint of national economy Jones put more emphasis on peasant rents. than upon

---

① *Distribution of Wealth*, p. 177. He borrowed this idea of surplus profit from Adam Smith. "Rent is the produce which is over what is necessary to pay the farmer ordinary profit." *Wealth of Nations*. Book I, p. 145.

The terms "rent" and "surplus" have come to be used interchangeably. If a form of income appears to be a surplus, it is at once treated as a kind of rent; if it presents some of the peculiarities of rent it is forthwith christened surplus. If rent is regarded as characteristically a differential, all incomes that contain differentials from one point of view or another are called surplus. If surplus income is defined as residual, all residual incomes are termed rents. (See Johnson's *Rent in Modern Economic Theory*, p. 19).

farmers' rent, claiming that peasant rents under their various forms are the most numerous and important, not only in deciding the economic relations of landlord and tenants, but also in influencing the political and social condition of the mass of the people.

At the outset Jones presents several problems in connection with farmers' rent. Here the capitalist class plays a prominent role, comparable, as we have already said to that of the landlord in peasant rent. The function of capital therefore is brought to the foreground and it actually occupies two-thirds of the Second Book of Jones' work, in a discussion of the ways of increasing rents. He attacks the question of differential returns, which was regarded by Ricardo as the sole explanation of the cause of rent. He also gives some indication of the real sources of increasing rents and brings out his theory of social harmony in contrast to Ricardo's theory of the class struggle.

Jones mentions three methods or causes of increasing farmers' rent which, he holds, consists merely of surplus profit: first, an increase of produce from the accumulation of larger quantities of capital in its cultivation; second, the more efficient application of capital already employed; third, a diminution of the share of the producing classes and a corresponding increase in the share of the landlord. [1] He insists upon the fact that the obvious cause of the actual rise of rent in England was not that the most costly portion of agricultural produce was obtained at greater cost, but simply that a larger amount of produce was obtained.

As to the first method of increasing farmers' rent, by employing larger quantities of capital in its cultivation, Jones argues with Ricardo on the

---

[1]   These three methods of increasing farmers' rent had been discussed by Adam Smith: *Wealth of Nations*, Book I, chapter 2, p. 247.

question of the relative fertility of soils and the law of diminishing returns. According to Ricardo rent is "that portion of the produce of the earth which is paid to the landlord for the use of the original and indestructible powers of the soil. " It is "always the difference between the produce obtained by the employment of two equal quantities of capital and labor," and "with every step in the progress of population, which shall oblige a country to have recourse to land of a worse quality, to enable it to raise its supply of food, rent, on all the more fertile land, will rise. "[1] This Ricardian law of rent embraces two complementary phases: a resort to inferior soils and an extensive margin, and a law of diminishing returns leading to an intensive margin. Jones first takes up the law of diminishing returns and argues that the increasing amount of capital employed on the land of a developing country necessarily elevates rents on the better soils, and this quite independently of alterations either in the relative fertility of the soils cultivated or in the amount of produce obtained by the application of given quantities of capital to the inferior soils:

"Let A have been formerly cultivated with 100£ , yielding annually 114£ , 10£ being the ordinary profits on stock: and B with 100£ , yielding 115£ : and C with 100£ , yielding 120£ , and so on to Z. As all above 110£ on each would be surplus profits, or rent, the rent of B would be 5£ , and that of C 10£ , etc. In some indefinite time let each of these qualities of soils be cultivated with a capital of 200£ , and their relative fertility remaining as before, let their produce be proportionally increased. A will produce 220£ , B, 230£ , C, 240£ . All above 200£ on each will now be surplus profits or rent. The rent of

---

[1] J. R. McCulloch: *The Works of David Ricardo*. London, John Murray, 1888, pp. 34, 36, 37.

Alfred Marshall says that those free gifts of nature which Ricardo classed as the inherent and indestructible properties of the soil have been largely modified, partly impoverished and partly enriched by the work of many generations of men. (*Principles of Economics*, 8th edition, p. 147) .

B, therefore, will have become 10£ , that of C 20£ that is, the rent of each will have doubled. "①

The general accumulation of capital employed in cultivation, while it augments the produce of all gradations of soils somewhat in proportion to their original fertility, must of itself raise rents without reference to any progressive diminution in the return to the labor and capital employed. Jones concludes that a general increase of the produce of land, following the application of additional capital and labor for its more perfect cultivation, seems a very natural and obvious cause of a rise of rents.

Jones also states that, supposing we grant that the difference between the relative fertility of soils is the sole cause of rents, it would not follow that nothing could raise rent but some cause which altered the relative fertility of the land cultivated, since any cause would raise rents which increased the amount of produce of all, though it left their relative fertility untouched.

"We have attempted to show that increasing produce from all the qualities of soil in a country, produced by the application of more capital and labor, will necessarily raise rents in an extensive country farmed by capitalists, from the unequal returns to that capital and labor on lands of unequal goodness: that rents will thus be raised without its being necessary to suppose any alteration in the relative fertility of the soils cultivated any sort of inferior soils, or any diminution in the produce obtained by agricultural labor on the old soils; and that there is no foundation whatever for the opinion that, in every stage of such a process, every portion of additional produce successively got from the same lands must necessarily be

---

① *The Distribution of Wealth*, p. 182.

obtained by a less advantageous expenditure of labor and capital. " ①

Jones not only refuses to accept the theory that the difference between the relative fertility of soils is the sole cause of rent; he even denies the fertility of soils as a fixed quantity. "We must take into calculation the increased power gained by increased skill in the combination and succession of different crops, and the mode of consuming them, and making them react on the fertility of the farms. " ② A soil which is suitable for one crop may be more or less suited for another, and the differential advantage of different soils, as respects their fertility, may conceivably vary in opposite directions or different degrees in the case of different crops, while their advantage as respects their situation and the cost of conveying their produce to the market may be subject to variations of a similar character if one crop is more bulky or perishable than another and more likely to be injured by delay or rough handling in transit. Once more, the cost of conveyance to the market may differ according to the market in view, and lands favorably situated for one market may be disadvantageously placed for another. ③The increased skill in the combination and succession of different crops which reacts on the fertility of farms is a strong argument used by Jones against the Ricardian theory of rent.

The reaction of the modes of consumption on the fertility of the farms to which Jones directed attention is a real contribution to the theory of con-

---

① *Distribution of Wealth*, pp. 196-197.

Rogers regarded the use of manures as a factor in checking the effect of diminishing returns. "The greatly increased produce of the 18th century was entirely due to the increased use of natural manures. " *Six Centurie of Work and Wages*, p. 476) . F. L. Patton also mentioned the introduction of crop rotations as a delay to the law of diminishing returns. (*Diminishing Returns in Agriculture*) .

② *Distribution of Wealth*, p. 188.

③ L. L. Price: "Some Aspects of the Theory of Rent, " *Economic Journal*, Vol. I.

sumption. If our food habits change from time to time there will be no absolute measure of the richness or fertility of land. One piece of land which is
fertile for the production of crop A is not necessary for crop B. The scarcity
of fertile land exists purely relatively to demand. Fundamental changes in
habits of consumption, by affecting demand, affect also the relative scarcity of fertile land. We cannot call one piece of land more fertile than another until we know something about the skill and enterprise of its cultivators
and the amount of capital and labor at their disposal, and until we know
whether the demand for produce is such as to make cultivation profitable.
The fertility of different soils is liable to be changed by the method of cultivation and through the relative value of different crops. With poor culture
all lands soon become equally poor, while with proper culture the poor land
will become fertile. ①The term fertility has no meaning except with reference to the special circumstances of a particular time and place.

Jones emphasizes a "limit point" in the operation of the law of diminishing returns: the law is true up to a certain point, beyond which additional capital and labor applied to land will yield less returns proportionately. But it is not true to say that no additional labor can at any time be bestowed upon the earth without a return less in proportion than that yielded
to the labor formerly applied

"The stature of man is limited: there is a point beyond which we know that it would be idle
to expect that a human being should increase in height, without decreasing in strength and
energy. If we were to argue that every inch added to a young person's stature in his progress
to maturity must be followed by increasing debility, we should argue very ill but not worse

---

①　Alfred Marshall says that even if there be no change in the arts of production, a mere increase
in the demand for produce may invert the order in which two adjacent pieces of land rank as regards fertility. (Marshall: *Principles of Economics*, 8th edition, Macmillan & Co. p. 157).

than those who, having observed that in the culture of the earth there is a point beyond which fresh labour bestowed must produce feebler results, lay it down as a law of nature, that with every increased portion of capital employed upon the land, then will be a decreased rate of production. " ①

He went further and argued that if the statement that an additional quantity of labor employed on the land results in a proportionately less return is true, then we can observe two consequences: either the industry of a larger proportion of the population must be devoted to agriculture, or the proportion of the gross produce paid to the landlord as rent must have increased. If these two results are not observable, these rents must have increased from some other cause or causes than from the employment of additional labor in agriculture with a proportionately less return. Then he appeals to the statistical history of England to show three important facts. First, there has been a spread of tillage, accompanied by a rise in the general rental of the country. Secondly, there has been a diminution in the proportion of people employed in agriculture. Thirdly, there has been a decrease in the landlord's proportion of the produce. ② From these facts he reached the conclusion that in England rents have risen, the proportion of hands employed in cultivation has become much smaller than formerly, and the proportion of the gross produce taken by the landlord as rent has diminished; that the general rise of rents which has taken place has not proceeded from the employment of an additional quantity of labor with a proportionately less return, but from some cause or causes essentially distinct from that one and

---

① *Distribution of Wealth*, p. 190.

② Jones quoted one statement of Adam Smith to support his own argument. "In the progress of improvement, rent, though it increases in proportion to the extent, diminishes in proportion to the produce of the land. "

attended by opposite results; and that increased rents in England have proceeded from better farming and greater produce. ①

The law of diminishing returns is supposed to assume as one of its important qualifications that the efficiency of capital and labor remain constant. On this point Jones replies that in the progress of those improvements in the art of cultivation by which the most profitable amount of produce is approached, it may be possible that each successive portion of capital and labor concentrated on the land is more economically and efficiently applied than the last. ② Thus the tendency to diminishing returns must be understood with reference to a given stage in agricutural art. Agricultural improvement may counteract this tendency and push the limiting point still further.

Diminishing returns are usually accompanied by increased total returns. There is not an absolute decrease of returns of produce, but merely a diminishing rate of increase. Rent will rise, even while the difference between the relative fertility of the soil is diminishing, provided that the abso-

---

① This view has been accepted even by J. S. Mill. In spite of Mill's early expressions, derived from economists who believed that returns do, as a general rule, diminish, he made a concession after observing the actual facts. He said that the fact that the produce of land increases in a diminishing ratio to the increase in the labors employed is the universal law of agricultural industry; that this principle, however, has been denied, and experience confidently appealed to in proof that the returns from land are not less but greater, in an advanced rather than in an early stage of civilization, when much capital rather than little capital is applied to agriculture; and that unquestionably a much smaller proportion of the population is now occupied in producing food for the whole than in the early times of our history. (*Principles of Political Economy*, Book I, Chapter 12) .

② According to Roger's estimate, land in England produces probably seven times as much as it did five hundred years ago, and the increased production is due in the last resort to the increase of intelligence in the methods of production. In fact, as J. S. Mill has often shown, there is scarcely any advance in general civilization which may not indirectly counteract the law of diminishing returns. (See Nicholson's *Tenants Gain Not Landlord's Loss*, p. 39) .

lute quantity of produce in, each class is increasing. [1]Thus the difference between Ricardo and Jones lies in the fact that the former calculates the ratio while the latter estimates the amounts. [2] One takes the average return for consideration and the other the total returns only. The average return in the physical sense, as a rule, increases up to a certain point, beyond which there is a tendency to diminish. The total returns always increase as the amount of outlay increases.

On the law of diminishing returns, however, modern writers such as Professor Seligman and Fetter try to strike a compromise between Ricardo and Jones. Contrary to Jones they insist that there is a law of diminishing returns, and at the same time they modify Ricardo's doctrine by showing that the law is not so rigid as advocated by him in being applied only to agriculture. Professor Seligman says that the law of diminishing returns is universal and applies to everything that possess value; it explains the rent of land and will equally explain the interest of capital and wages of labor. [3] Professor seligman also cautiously remarks that a "certain point is the point of full utilization. It frequently happens that this point has not been

---

[1]   If 100£ be employed on classes A, B, C, with a produce of 100£, 115£, and 120£ and consequently 200£, with returns of 200£, 228£ and 235£, the relative differences of the produce will have diminished, and the soil will have approximated in fertility; still the difference of the amounts of their products will be increased from 5£ and 10£ to 8£ and 15£ and rents will have risen accordingly. " *Distribution of Wealth*, p. 196.

[2]   Alfred Marshall says: "Ricardo's wording of the law of diminishing returns was inexact. It is, however, probable that the inaccuracy was due not to careless thinking but only to careless writing. In any case he would have been justified in thinking that these conditions were not of great importance in the peculiar circumstances of England at the time at which he wrote, and for the special purposes of the particular practical problems he had in view. Of course he could not anticipate the great series of inventions which were about to open up new sources of supply, and, with the aid of free trade, to revolutionize English agriculture; but the agricultural history of England and other countries might have led him to lay greater stress on the probability of a change. (*Principles of Economics*, p. 163) .

[3]   Seligman: *Principles of Economics*, p. 375.

reached. " ① Professor Fetter makes a further distinction between technical diminishing returns and historical diminishing returns, a distinction which has been confused by Ricardo and ignored by Jones. Professor Fetter says:

"The principle of technical diminishing returns is that at any given moment the uses obtainable from any indirect agent can not be indefinitely increased without increasing difficulty. Historical diminishing returns occur when, in fact, human effort is less bountifully rewarded in a later period than in an earlier one. If to-day a day's labor in agriculture produces less than fifty years ago, historical diminishing returns would have occurred. In fact, labor is more, bountifully rewarded in agriculture than fifty years ago, yet it is true today that there are few fields or appliances which, if used more intensively with the prevailing prices of labor and material, would not show a diminishing return to the additional capital applied. Therefore, in the historical sense, increasing returns have prevailed, yet at every moment it has been necessary to apply resources under the guidance of the principle of diminishing returns. " ②

The dispute between Ricardo and Jones on the law of diminishing returns has, therefore, been peacefully settled. Ricardo was right as to technical diminishing returns, but wrong as to historical diminishing returns. Jones was right in the historical sense but was not fair in ignoring the technical law of diminishing returns. There is no one law of diminishing returns, but in its place there must be at least several groups of statements:

---

① Seligman: *Principles of Economics*, p. 252.

② Fetter: *Economic Principles*, p. 69.

technical, the entrepreneurial, and secular returns. ①

The criticism of the law of diminishing returns offered by Jones was highly useful in stimulating further examination and revision of the form of the statement. Since his time the law has come to be thought of chiefly as a statement of potentialities, holding true at a given time rather than as having to do with the historical progress of industry. It has also gained recognition as the statement of a tendency rather than as a description of necessary or inevitable facts.

Jones further attacks the supposed indication of the decreasing efficiency of agricultural labor along three different lines. In the first place a fall of profits, he says, is no proof of the decreasing efficiency of the agricultural occupation. A fall of profits, he holds, might be due to a rise of wages. Here he considers that real wages are changeable and that their variation has influence upon the rate of profit. This is the extreme opposition to Ricardo who assumes the permanent immutability of real wages and then shifts the whole responsibility for a fall of profit to a decreasing efficiency of agriculture. Ricardo's proposition is perfectly logical because, one of the three productive factors being fixed, there must be a mutual influence between the other two. That profit falls must be due to the rise of rent which, Ricardo assumes, is conditioned by the cultivation of the poor soil which,

---

① This conclusion has been reached by F. L. Patton in his study, *Diminishing Returns in Agriculture*, 1926. He said: "The first of these groups includes all data relating to physical, experimental or technical diminishing returns. The second group contains all data as to diminishing returns of profits arising out of the profit-seeking activities of agrticultural entrepreneurs. It can perhaps best be called entrepreneurial or money returns. The third group of data relates to what will here be called secular diminishing returns. " (p. 13) .

Professor Fetter says, "There are at least three distinct problems:

(1) technical proportion, the best mechanical or physical combination; (2) profitable proportion, the entrepriser's best combination, and (3) the socio-economic problem of the relation of population to resources" (*Economic Principles*, p. 440, footnote) .

again, is due to the decreasing productivity of agriculture. ① Jones, on the contrary, maintains that different rates of real wages prevail in countries with similar climate and soils, and sometimes under the same government; that alterations in the food, clothing, habits and general mode of maintenance of the people take place from generation to generation in the same countries; that a change in the rate of wages is sufficient, while the productive power of industry remains the same, to produce a change in the rate of profits; and that a fall of profits is never an unequivocal proof of a diminution in the efficiency of agriculture. ②

In the second place, Jones declares that an increasing relative value of raw produce is no proof of the decreasing efficiency of agriculture. He argues that the relative value of raw produce might be due to the greater improvement in the skill of manufacture than in that of agriculture:

"In the progress of nations an increase of manufacturing power and skill usually occurs greater than that which can be expected in the agriculture of an increasing people. This is an unquestionable and familiar truth. A rise in the relative value of raw produce may, therefore, be expected in the advance of nations, and this from a cause quite distinct from any positive decrease in the efficiency of agriculture. " (Distribution of Wealth, p. 249).

---

① Ricardo maintains that it is absolutely necessary that money wages should increase, since the price of commodities is continually rising. Money wages will show a tendency to rise in sympathy with the rising price of corn, so that the workman will always be able to procure just the same quantity of bread, no more and no less.

② *Distribution of Wealth*, pp. 247-248.

Ricardo seems, however, to make use of the same expression in saying that "it is not to be understood that the natural price of labour, estimated even in food and necessaries, is absolutely fixed and constant. It varies at different times in the same country, and very materially differs in different countries. " (McCulloch: *The Works of David Ricardo*, p. 52) . But his fundamental law of wages is that the natural price of labor is that price which is necessary to enable the laborers one with another to subsist and to perpetuate their race without either increase or diminution. If a working man has more children than are necessary for replacing their parents then their wages fall below the normal rate until increased mortality shall have again established equilibrium.

Lastly, Jones emphasizes the point that an increasing money value of raw produce, compared with prices in other countries, is no proof of the decreasing efficiency of agriculture. It may, he assumes, proceed from paying higher wages or heavy taxation, or it may proceed from different values of precious metals. [1] He traces the increasing relative value of agricultural products from the increasing efficiency of manufactured goods, and the increasing money value of raw produce from the causes arising from the monetary side of the price equation, not from the goods side.

After the discussion of the law of diminishing returns Jones presents his theory of economic harmony, which appears in his argument against the claim that the economic interest of the landlord is in conflict with the community as maintained by Ricardo. The question of economics interest is, at bottom, a question of whether agricultural improvements are detrimental to the landlords. According to Ricardo's opinion.

"If the interests of the landlord be of sufficient consequence to determine us not to avail ourselves of all the benefits which would follow from importing corn at a cheap price, they should also influence us in rejecting all improvement in agriculture and in the implements of husbandry, for it is certain that if corn is rendered cheap, rents are lowered, and the ability of the landlord to pay taxes is, for a time at least, as much impaired by such im-

---

[1]   In this connection Jones followed the opinion of Malthus, who maintained that the differences in the price of corn, so easily observable in different countries, might be due to a difference in the value of the precious metals in different countries under different circumstances. More than three-fourths of the difference between the price of corn in Bengal and England is probably occasioned by the difference in the value of money in the two countries. (*Principles of Political Economy*, p. 193) .

The same idea was expressed even by Ricardo himself, when he said that when any particular country excels in manufactures, so as to occasion an influx of money towards it, the value of money will be lower and the prices of corn and labor will be relatively higher in that country than in any other. (*Principles of Political Economy and Taxation*, p. 163) .

provements as by the importation of corn. " ①

He also distinguishes the improvements in agriculture as being of two kinds: those which increase the productive powers of the land, and those which enable us, by improving our machinery, to obtain its produce with less labor. They both lead to a fall in the price of raw produce; they both affect rent. ②

Again, in his criticism of Malthus' opinion on rent, Ricardo holds that

" both the improvement in agriculture, and the superior fertility, will give to the land a capability of bearing at some future period a higher rent, becauae with the same price of food there will be a great additional quantity; but still if the increase of population be in the same proportion the additional quantity of goods would not be required, and, therefore, rents would be lowered and not raised. ③

So he concludes that " independently of these improvements, in which the community have an immediate and the landlord a remote interest, the interest of the landlord is always opposed to that of the consumer and manufacturer. " ④ We observe in his statements that he assumes a stationary condition of population and a sudden introduction of an improvement which makes the raw produce cheaper and tbe rent lower. Here Jones argues that

---

① Ricardo: "Essay on the Influence of a Low Price of Corn on the Profis of Stock" in the *Works of David Ricardo*, ed. by McCulloch, p. 390.

② McCulloch: *The Works of David Ricardo*, p. 42.

③ *Ibid*, p. 251.

In his chapter on rent, Ricardo also maintains that " it is undoubtedly true, that the fall in the refative price of raw produce, in consequence of the improvement in agriculture, or rather in consequence of less labor being bestowed on its production, would naturally Iead to increased accumulation; for the profit of stock would be greatly augmented. This accumulation would lead to an increased demand for labor, to higher wages, to an increased cultivation. It is only, however, after the increase in the population, that rent would be as high as before; that is to say, after No. 3 was taken into cultivation. A considerable period would have elapsed, attended with a positive diminution of rent. " (*Ibid*, p. 42) .

④ McCulloch: *The Works of David Ricardo*, p. 202.

population will not be stationary, and from Malthus he borrows the idea that food creates its own demand. [1] Jones says: "In the process by which increased supplies of food are produced for an increasing population, we observe no such wide dislocations between supply and demand. "[2] He also states that as the mass of people slowly increase, we see the gradual pressure of demand stimulating the agriculturists to improvements, which, by an imperceptible progression of the supply, keep the people fed; that while these processes are going on, every increase of produce occasioned by the general application to the soils of more capital, acting upon them with unequal effect according to the differences in their original fertility, raises rents; and that the interests of the landlords are at no moment opposed to improvements, which, while they increase the mass of raw produce, are as favorable to the augmentation of the revenues of the owners of the soil as they are essential to the well-being of the people. He further mentions that it is necessary to remember the slow manner in which agricultural improvements are discovered, completed, put to practical use, and spread. This view has been supported by Rogers, who said that it is the characteristic of agriculture that its improvements are so gradual as to be almost imperceptible. [3] Agricultural knowledge is not gained overnight.

Jones also points out the difference between the temporary and the permanent prosperity of the landlord in his theory of economic harmony. His arguments run as follows:

---

[1]　Rent, Malthus says. is paid because (1) the land produces more than enough to maintain its cultivation; (2) the necessaries of life bave a peculiar quality of being able to create their own demand, to raise up a number of demanders in proportion to the quantity of necessaries produced; and (3) the most fertile land is comparatively scarce. (Malthus: *Principles of Political Economy*, 1820, p. 139) .

[2]　*Distribution of Wealth*, p. 200.

[3]　Rogers: *Six Centuries of Work and Wages*, p. 469.

"It is true that there are cases in which the landlords may derive a limited advantage from circumstances which are diminishing the means of the body of the people, but their permanent prosperity must emanate from more wholesome and more abundant sources. " "When the revenues of any class increase, that increase may in every case proceed from two causes: first from an invasion of the revenues of some other classes, the aggregate revenues of the state remaining what it was, or secondly from increased production, leaving the revenues of all the other class untouched, presenting a clear addition to the aggregate revenue of the nation. " "A little consideration will show us that it is only in the last that is the most advantageous manner, that the revenue of any class can increase progressively and securely in the progress of nations. " "The fact is, that the prosperity which each class can grasp by the depression of other is limited and insecure, The advantages which each may draw from sources of increasing wealth common to all, or at least injurious to none, are safe, and capable of being pushed to an extent of which the limits lie beyond our experience, or means of calculation. " (Distribution of Wealth, p. 270) .

Then Jones concludes that a diminution in the share of the producing classes in the produce is certainly a possible, but as certainly only a limited and very rare, source of advance in the revenue of the landlords; that a gradual increase of their means, which keeps pace with the riches of other branches of the community, flows from healthier and more copious fountains; that the circumstances which are most essential to the continuous prosperity of the landlords are also most conducive to the increasing wealth and strength of the nation; that it is an error to suppose that there is anything peculiar to the landlords in the fact that they have occasionally a limited interest opposed to that of the other bodies which compose the state. ①

The second source of the increase of farmers' rent, Jones maintains, is the increasing efficiency of the capital employed. The first source of the increase of farmers' rent was a quantitative accumulation, but this second one is a qualitative improvement in the utilization of capital. The efficiency of the capital employed in cultivation may show itself in two ways: first, less capital may be necessary to produce a given quantity of produce from a spot of ground; second, the same capital may produce from the same spot of ground a larger produce than it yielded before. Whichever the result, however, the increasing efficiency of the capital employed shows itself, rent will rise, and unless the progress of improvement outstrips the progress of population, and the growth of produce exceeds the growth of demand, this rise of rent will be permanent. The rise of rent from the increased efficiency of capital employed, Jones assumes, will ordinarily coincide with an extension of agricultural wealth, the population, the strength and the resources of the country. ② He also assumes that such a rise of rents might take place, and go on increasing with the increase of population indefinite-

---

① Here Jones had closely followed Malthus who undertook, in three sections of his book, (*Principles of Political Economy*,) to establish the strict and necessary connection of the interest of the landlord and of the state, whether the country raised its own food supply or imported a major part. Malthus was convinced that advancing rents were a symptom of national progress.

② Jones, however, makes the remark that increased rents from the increased efficiency of capital, though an addition to national wealth and resources, do not indicate so large an addition to those resources as increased rents proceeding from the accumulation of capital in cultivation. "When 100£ produce (prices being the same) corn worth 120£ instead of corn worth 110£ , the wealth of the nation is increased by 10£ 's worth of corn and no more. When 90£ will produce the same quantity of corn which 100£ did produce, the nation is enriched to the same amount in another shape; for 10£ may be withdrawn from agriculture without its produce being diminished and the nation will be enriched by being put in possession of any other commodities which the capital of 10£ may be employed to produce. The increase of national wealth will in either case be confined to the amount of 10£ , the same sum by which rents rise. " (*Distribution of Wealth*, p. 224) . Here we can observe the turn of mind of Jones, who always emphasizes the amount of increase instead of the rate of increase.

ly, though no inferior gradations of soil were in existence. Still further, he considers the tillage of poor soil as the consequence of the increased efficiency of capital which is the source of the increase of rent.

"The same increased productiveness of agricul tural capital which occasions a rise of rents on old lands usually makes it possible to extend tillage to lands of inferior natural fertility with as ample return as that obtained from the old soils before the improvement took place. "①

On this point Jones clashes with Ricardo. The latter regards the cultivation of poor soil as the cause of the rise of rents, while the former insists that whenever a rise of rents takes place from the increased demand for agricultural produce, the spread of tillage to inferior soils presents a practical limit to that rise. ② Jones' arguments may be briefly stated as follows: it is clear that if, as population increased, all fresh supplies were necessarily extracted from the old soils alone, there would be no assignable limit to the increase of the relative value of raw produce, of the surplus profits made on the land, or of rents. But while additional quantities of produce can be obtained from inferior gradations of soils, the price of raw produce will never exceed the cost of producing it from the lowest gradation which it is

---

① *Distribution of Wealth*, p. 225.

② *Distribution of Wealth*, p. 228.

In *Social Economics* Professor Cassel expressed the same idea: "The one-sided stress on the differential element is apt to give the idea that the existence of inferior land is somehow essential to the ground rent of better. As a matter of fact this ground rent by no means depends for its existence upon the presenee of the inferior land; on the contrary, it is merely reduced on that amount. " (p. 227.)

In the discussion of the third source of increasing farmers' rent, Jones also declares that the decrease of the share of the producing classes and corresponding rise of rent have been wholly unconnected with the cultivation, or even the existence, of poor soils. "If a country had no soils to resort to besides those already cultivated, the demand might keep constantly ahead of the slowly increasing supply, and the possible increase in the relative value of ˉaw produce, and the consequent rise of rents, would be indefinite. But when inferior gradations of soil exist, and can be resorted to, the rise in the exchangeable value of raw produce is limited. " (*Distribution of Wealth*, p. 231) .

found expedient to cultivate, and if, from the increasing efficiency of agricultural capital, the cost of getting produce from that gradation is not greater than it was on the old soils before the improvement, the price of raw produce will not rise at all. The inferior soils, though their cultivation is not essential to a rise of rent, present alwayls a boundary to that rise. Their existence is a protection to the interests of the consumers, without interfering with those of the landed proprietors. They prevent corn being sold at a monopoly price. In a word, the presence of poor lands checks the rise of rent. [1]

In his discussion of the efficiency of capital, Jones also approached the modern view of the law of proportionality in dealing with all productive factors. As agricultural knowledge is improved, machinery will be used and human labor will be reduced. The progress will be made through various experiments which will test the efficiency of the two factors Jones believed that in countries where capital abounds the owners of it are always impelled by self-interest to use the various factors which they employ as much as possible in the shape of auxiliary capital, and as little as they can help in the shape of wages of labor. [2]

The third source of the increase of farmers' rent, Jones states, lies in a decrease in the share of the producing class, while the produce remains

---

[1] Alfred Marshall also mentions the fact that the existence of inferior agents does not raise, but lowers, the rents of superior agents. "In this connection it may be noted that the opinion that the existence of inferior land, or other agents of production tends to raise the rents of the better agents is not merely untrue. It is the reverse of the truth. For, if the bad land were to be flooded and rendered incapable of producing anything at all, the cultivation of other land would need to be more intensive; and therefore, the price of the product would be higher, and rents generally would be higher than if the land had been a poor contributor to the total stock of produce." (*Principles of Economics*, p. 424).

[2] *Distribution of Wealth*, p. 227. The "various conditions" mentioned by him express exactly the idea of modern agricultural experiments and this law of proportionality can be applied to any kind of industry.

the same. In this case, he assumes that the produce is stationary and the farmers' ordinary profit remains the same, but his share in the produce of the soil shrinks as the price of the raw produce rises, proceeding always from an increasing demand without a corresponding increase of the supply.

"A rise in the relative value of raw produce, from whatever cause the rise proceeds, will always be followed by a decrease of the share of the producing classes in the products of the soil, relative to the labor and capital they employ, and by a corresponding rise in the produce rents to the landlords. "①

The rise of rents in this case forms no addition to the resources of a country. Jones himself perceives that the increased rents of old soils are a mere transfer of a portion of the wealth already existing from the producing classes to the landlords. Yet he still refuses to accept the dark picture drawn by Ricardo that as rents rise, profits will necessarily fall and wages will remain stationary. He says:

"Such a diminution in the power of agriculture, though a possible event, takes place in the progress of the wealthy people very rarely. I doubt if it ever takes place at all; and, when it does take place, we must not hastily conclude that, because the quantity of corn remaining in the hands of the producing agricultural classes is diminished, there must therefore be a fall either in profits or wages, or that such producing classes would have the means of consuming either less corn, or less of any other commodity, than they did before the reduction of their share in the produce of the soil. "②

Human industry, he holds, is not wholly employed in turning out raw produce and its increasing in other departments may balance the decreasing powers of agriculture. The effects of the failure in productive power of one branch of the population will be balanced by the increased productive pow-

---

① *Distribution of Wealth*, p. 231.

② *Distribution of Wealth*, p. 233.

er of another branch. Those who produce less will find their commodities rising in exchangeable value; those who produce more will find them falling. These variations in relative value will distribute equally all the advantages and disadvantages of the variations which take place in the producing power of different branches of industry. The decreasing efficiency of agricultural capital must, however, be disadvantageous, though it is not necessarily followed by any actual impoverishment. [1] His points of view on economic problems are always cheerful and optimistic: in the case of the increasing efficiency of agriculture he maintains that more non-agricultural classes can be supported, and in the case of decreasing effeiency he argues that it can be balanced by the increasing efficiency of manufacturing labor.

He concludes that the erroneous views in which these positions originated proceeded no doubt from imperfect observation and hasty reasoning. He blames the Ricardian School for not having directed enough observation to foreign lands.

"We are all as Englishman occasionally, more liable than could be wished to some of these mistakes. We are much too prone to consider the state of society in which we exist as a type of all others and this narrow and mistaken assumption is necessarily the parent of much ignorance and many errors. England is, in fact, at the extreme and verge of the economic career of nations. " [2]

He considers his own theory a new one, but he is very cautious in

---

[1] "A decrease in the share of one of the producing classes, that is, a fall in the rate either of wages or of profits, is never necessarily the result of the diminished productive power of human industry in any of its branches. " (*Distribution of Wealth*, p. 241) .

But according to Ricardo's opinion: "profits of stock fall only because land equally well adapted to produce food cannot be procured; and the degree of the fall of profits, and the rise of rents, depends wholly on the increased expense of production. " — (McCulloch: *The Works of David Ricardo*, p. 375) .

[2] *Distribution of Wealth*, p. 286.

avoiding the claim of being omniscient, and always keeps in mind the relativity of economic doctrine. ①

So far we have studied the arguments of Jones against Ricardo and we are now in a position to present the differences between the two men on the theory of rent. ② The primary cause of the differences in opinion between Ricardo and Jones lies in the distinction between differential rent and scarcity rent. Their conceptions of rent are not the same. According to Ricardo it is convenient to estimate the rent of a particular agent by comparing its yield to that of an inferior agent, when similarly worked with appropriate appliances. According to Jones it is best to go straight to the fundamental relations of demand to the scarcity or abundance of the means for the production of those commodities for making which the agent is serviceable③. In his theory of peasant rent Jones attributes to the origin of rent the appropriation of soil which is in turn, due to the overwhelming necessity of the inhabitants. The whole land of a country is required for cultivation. The cause of rent is the growth of demand and not the cultivation of "land No. 2," or poorer land, because the cultivation only take place when the prise has risen. If in any country the last type of land used were scarce relatively

---

① "The rents paid by the smallest, but to us the most interesting class of tenantry, agricultural capitalists or farmers, I have treated with Mr. Malthus and others simply as surplus profit. This view, however, taken here of the different modes by which these surplus profits. may increase and accumulate on the soil is, I believe new. Certainly it is cheering and strips away at once all that was harsh and repulsive in the false aspect lately so laboriously given to the causes and sources of increase in this class of rents. " (*Distribution of Wealth*, p. 286) .

"In the meantime, as I am conscious that the wide outline I have drawn, and such details as I have introduced, are faithful and impartial, I cannot, and do not doubt that the productive supply of detailed information will conform to the principles I have pointed out, while it may probably modify and correct to some extent their local application" (*Distribution of Wealth*, p. 306) .

② See Appendix B.

③ Marshall: *Principles of Economics*, 8th edition, p. 423.

to the demand, it would have to bear a rent. The ground rent of land of a certain quality is by its nature a scarcity price. It is the payment secured for the use of marginal land. ① This copcept of marginal or scarcity rent denies the existence in actual cultivation of no-rent land. It is shown that the various uses to which the same piece of land may be put ordinarily permit marginal land to command a rent. Marginal produce is derived from rent-paying land, and rent to that extent is held to enter into the cost of marginal produce. Such is the theory of rent quite independent of the law of diminishing returns and the marginal fertility of land. ② The fertility of the soil is not one bit more important to the farmer than the proper amount of sunshine and rainfall. Yet the farmer pays a price for the use of soil whereas he receives free the use of sun and rain. This contrast leads the way to an explanation of the basic relation which supply of land bears to the price paid for the use of it. ③

Now we can say that commonly the marginal land, for any particular use, itself affords a rent because, though morginal for the given use, it is above the mangins for some other use to which it might be applied. Rent is thus composed usually of a differential and of a marginal element. The dif-

---

① The dictum that rent does not enter into normal cost is entirely true only in connection with the assumption of the employment of land for a single productive use and the consequent availability of a body of free or no-rent soil. Under modern industrial conditions land is capable of a series of uses. The poorest or marginal land utilized for any particular purpose is above the margin of utilization of rent-paying land with respect to the next lower purpose. To be retained in the first use, it must yield a marginal rent equivalent to that which it would pay if devoted to the second use.

② The description of rent as a differential return is of theoretical importance if rent is not a cost, if it does not enter into price. Until it is independently proved that rent is not a cost the differential analysis which is based upon a comparison of the productivity of unlike units is incapable of distinguishing rent from wages and interest.

③ In the case of farmers' rent Jones considers rent as a surplus profit. All that is needed is an intense demand for a supply that is never equal to that demand, so that the price is above the cost of production.

ferential element is an expense of production only to enterprisers using superior land for a given purpose, while the marginal element must be paid by all enterprisers engaged in a given branch of production and figures as an element in the normal expense of production. Thus Ricardo's concept of rent should be broadened rather than shaken by Jones' attack. Rent is a cost for those theorists concerned primarily with the competing uses of land; it is not a cost for those who regard it as a distributive share arising from all the employments of land, treated as though they were one. With Ricardo the latter view appears predominantly.

Ricardo seeks in the theory of rent one general principle which will solve all land problems. But such a theory is an impossibility. In addition to the differential analysis we need some other principles: first, the principle of scarcity reflects a factor influencing prices; second, the substitution principle governs the shifting of land from one use to another; and third, the principle of proportionality means the proportionality of the economically available supply of land among its uses in such a way that all demands will be adequately met.

Since the time of Jones' criticism of the Ricardian School, all the assumptions of the theory of rent have been assailed. The assumption that the powers of the soil are original or non-produced by men has been attacked. The assumption that the powers of the soil are indestructible has been denied and the assumption that rent is a species of income wholly different from other incomes has been modified. ①It has been realized that agriculture is by no means the only domain in which capital and labor yield unequal returns. Degrees of productivity and differences in returns are equally evident in the case of capital. Similarly, the production of one worker as compared with another is frequently unequal. Differences in induetrial revenues are quite analogous to the differences in agricultural incomes. Still more, the supply of land has come to be viewed from two standpoints: physical supply and economic supply. One is constant and the other always changing. Ricardo's historical theory of rent-the order of cultivation from good to bad soil-has been challenged by American agricultural experiments. His static theory of the economic forces tending to determine rents at the present time has been modified and extended to all other factors of production. And his dynamic theory of the causes continually tending to increase rent as wealth and population increase has been proved to be untrue by the economic facts of history.

---

① The analogy between returns from land and capital has already been expressed by J. Craig, in 1831. "So much do these sources of revenue resemble each other, that even in ordinary language the return for fixed capital, when the necessary circulating capital is supplied by a different person, is always denominated its rents. " (*Remarks on Some Fundamental Doctrines in Political Economy*, p. 138) .

Again, S. Bailey in 1825 established the analogy between land rent and labor rent. "The extraordinary profit out of which rent arises is analogous to the extraordinary remuneration which an artisan of more than common dexterity obtains beyond the wages given to the workman of ordinary skill. In one case the monopoly is bounded by the existence of inferior soils, in the other by the existence of inferior degrees of dexterity. " (*A Critical Dissertation on Value*, p. 185) .

J. S. Mill has broadened the meaning of rent. "All advantages which one competitor has over another, whether natural or acquired, whether personal or the result of social arrangement, assimulate the possessor of the advantage to a receiver of rent. " (*Principles*, Book III, chapter 5.)

Later J. B. Clark definitely declares, "The principle that has been made to govern the income derived from land actually governs those derived from capital and from labor. " ("Distribution as Determined by a Law of Rent," *Quarterly Journal of Economics*, 1890, p. 289) .

All these writers were trying to extend the term "rent" to every differential gain. We have a number of differential revenues which are exactly analogous to the rent of land.

Therefore, the revolt against Ricardo's theory of rent, initiated by Jones, has been successful. Jones' study of economic institutions has been proved useful in pointing out the narrowness and inapplicability of the Ricardian system of political economy,[1] and Jones' arguments against the law of diminishing returns, the origin of rent from the unequal fertility of soil, and the economic conflict between the landlord and the other classes seem to have been justified and supported by later writers.

---

[1]   "Mr. Ricrardo, however, overlooking the limited extent of the field to which these principles were really applicable, undertook from them alone to deduce the laws which regulate the nature and amount of the revenue derived from land at all places and under all circumstances; and, not content with this, proceeded from the same narrow and limited data to construct a general system of the distribution of wealth, and to explain the causes of variations which take place in the rate of profits or amount of wages over the surface of the globe. " (*Distribution of Wealth*, *Preface*, p. 8) .

CHAPTER V
THE THEORY OF WAGES

I. *The Classification of Laborers and*
the Doctrine of the Wage-Fund

ACCORDING to Jones' system of political economy, the theory of wages should follow the theory of rent. He believed that the next, and a more important, division of the annual produce, is that which is consumed as wages of labor, but it is taken in the second, instead of in the first place, because a clear perception of the causes which affect the amount of the remuneration received by the majority of the laborers in the world can only be attained after a survey of the forms and conditions of the various rents they pay. [1] In discussing the theory of wages, he employs the same method of approach as he used in the theory of rent, appealing to the experience of the past, and examining the present. His discussion of the theory of rent centers on peasant rent, which was entirely ignored by Ricardo; in like manner, in dealing with the theory of wages, his attention is chiefly paid to groups of laborers which the Ricardian School has completely left out of

---

[1] *Distribution of Wealth*, Preface, XXVI.

consideration. His inquiry into this subject consists of two main questions: what are the funds which support the laboring population of the globe, and what are the laws by which the numbers of those who are to share those funds are determined? He studied these topics from the standpoints both of production and of distribution.

The early nineteenth century economists talked of wages as if the term included all remuneration of labor; yet they thought of no labor except that type which earns "wages" in the common, narrow acceptation of the word. They thought that all laborers were hired by capitalists. It happened that in England, at the time when the Classical economists were developing their system, a larger proportion of manual workers were in this situation than had been the case, hence, the easy assumption of such a condition by these writers, and hence their easy acceptance of the wage-fund doctrine. In order to attack the current theory of wages, Jones first introduces a three-fold classification of laborers. First, "unhired laborers," are those who cultivate the ground they occupy as peasant cultivators and live on self-produced wages. Secondly, "paid dependents" are those who are paid out of the revenues or income of their employers. Thirdly, "hired laborers" are those who are paid out of the capital of their employers. [1]This kind of three-fold division of laborers is founded entirely on the difference in the nature and the formation of the funds which supply their wages. The first group is self-supporting, and there is an intimate relation between wages and rent. The difference between the second and the third

---

[1]   "The third class of hired laborer, paid from capital, has so exclusively met the eyes and occupied the thoughts of English writers on wages, that it has led them into some serious and very unfortunate mistakes as to the nature, extent, and formation of the funds out of which the laboring population of the globe is fed, and as usual, they have misied foreign matters. " (*Literary Remains*, p. 14) .

groups lies in the fact that the second group is supported, not from a fund which has been accumulated and saved with a view to profit, but by expenditure of income, while the third group is employed by the capitalists, out of a view to profit. The profit motive marks the difference between the two.

Jones possesses a broad-minded view of the great variations in the machinery of production and distribution among different communities and in different times. Instead of one kind of wage-fund he offers three. The first portion is a quantity of wealth produced by the laborer himself as the occupier of the soil. This branch of the labor fund supports a far greater proportion of the laboring classes of the earth than either of the other two. In the infancy of society men are wholly dependent on what they can themselves produce from the earth, first by collecting its spontaneous produce, and then by what they can obtain by cultivation. As society advances in civilization, the process of property in the soil begins. It is vested in those who so represent the community. The state may be the supreme owner of the soil, and the occupiers cultivate under conditions imposed by the state. Here we have hereditary occupiers. Gradually a body of landowners, intermediate between the occupiers and the state, may impose the conditions under which the occupiers cultivate; these cultivators will be called tenants. Hereditary occupiers and the tenants cover the vast majority of the cultivators of our earth. The conditions imposed upon them determine the rate of wages. Of the produce of the soil, a part is left in the hands of the occupier, it constitutes his wages; a part goes to the owner of the soil, it constitutes his rent. If the produce remains stationary, you cannot increase the one without diminishing the other of these quantities. There is, however, a certain limit beyond which all demands of the landlord must not go. Enough must be left to the laborers to maintain themselves and rear such families as will secure another generation of laboring occupiers. If the peasants have need of ground, the landlords have need of tenants. Thus is established the minimum wage of occupying cultivators. From observation and experience Jones concludes that the fund for the maintenance of this group of laboreres-probably the most numerous in the world-forms no part of the saved and accumulated capital of nations, but is a revenue produced by themselves from the soil, and that the produce of their land being taken as a given quantity, it is the rent they pay which determines what shall be left to them as wages. [1]

The second portion of the wage-fund is derived from the revenues of superior classes expended on the maintenance of laborers. Before capitalists appear as the advancers of wages, there is a long interval during which the owners of revenue must apply it themselves, in support of the workman who produces the commodities they desire. The early dependence of the artisans directly on the revenues of consumers is a matter of necessity. They cannot be supported by advances from accumulated stock when neither capital nor capitalist exist for the purpose. It is in Asia, Jones assumes, that we observe, this peculiar fund for the maintenance of non-agricultural laborers in full and continued activity and predominance. Bear in mind the two facts, he says, that a body of such workmen can exist only in the employment of the distributors of revenue, and that the great distributor in Asia is the State, In Asia, the surplus produce of the soil has been distributed mainly by the king's officers to the non-agricultural population, and that non-agricultural population has swarmed about the court of an

---

[1]   *Literary Remains* pp. 433-434.

Eastern Monarch. It has happened in times past that these Oriental States, often supplying the expenses of their civil and military establishments, have found themselves in possession of a surplus which they could apply to works of magnificence, and in the construction of these their command over the hands and arms of almost the entire non-agricultural population has produced stupendous monuments, such as the Great Wall of China.

There are one or two propositions which it is well to bear in mind, Jones states, while tracing the functions of this particular part of the wage-fund. The surplus produce of agriculture consists of all the produce not consumed or used by the cultivators during the task of cultivation. It always limits the non-agricultural population of the whole earth. It also determines, by the mode of its distribution, the occupations of the non-agriculturists, and the nature of the commodities produced by such of them as produce wealth. It is obvious that this surplus may come into the hands of, and be expended by very different men, or classes of men, and these differences must affect powerfully both the occupations of the non-agriculturists and the nature of the commodities they produce. This surplus produce may be distributed by the state, by a body of landholders distinct from the cultivators, by the cultivators themselves, or by all three in different proportions.

The third portion of the wage-fund is the wealth accumulated and saved from revenue and advanced to the laborers with a view to the profits of its owners. It prevails more widely and exclusively in England than anywhere else. Jones asserts that there are two prominent circumstances affecting their positions and fortunes which broadly distinguish this class of laborers from both unhired laborers and hired dependents. ①In the first place, the whole fund from which they are paid is a fund which has to be saved, which goes through a process of accumulation with a view to profit, and, as their numbers increase, it is necessary for their continuous prosperity that the community, of which they form a part, should save and accumulate capital at least as fast as they are multiplying their numbers. This is not the case, either with unhired laborers or hired dependents. The wages of the unhired workman never exist in any other form than that of a stock destined for immediate consumption; his welfare is quite independent of the savings of any part of the community. The funds, likewise, on which the hired dependent lives go through no process of saving; his subsistence depends not on the economy and accumulation of the class which employs him, but on expenditure of the funds for the purpose of immediate enjoyment. The second circumstance is that the continuous employment of the hired laborer may be dependent upon the existence of a demand for the products of his labor rather than the demands of his immediate employer, that is, there must be a market for the commodities he produces. His condition and livelihood are affected by fluctuations in the taste and consumption of the most ditant parts of the world. The wages of such laborers depend on the relative growth of capital and population. Jones gives little space to the discussion of this class of laborers. He maintains that the organization of industry by which laborers are hired by capitalists represents an advance in the method of production. The laborers work more continuously and efficiently.

The differences which he points out between modern advanced socie-

---

① *Literary Remains*, p. 173.

ties and old communities having a fundamentally different organization of industry, deserved much more attention than they received. The English economists of that time had a singularly insular horizon. They regarded only the phenomena that were before their eyes in their own country, and generalized from them with a strange disregard of the absence elsewhere of the conditions on which their generalization rested. Wages were described to mean any reward for immediate exertions, regardless of the mode in which the reward comes. In the detailed discussion of wages, the case of the hired laborer and of what the employer would pay him occupied the chief place. The large array of persons who received a return for labor in a different manner were left without any distinctive designation. Jones' protests against the undiscriminating rashness with which they applied their doctrines should be considered as an important contribution to the study of the problem.

Jones also mentions the advantages of the capitalist syetem to the laborer, because it brings competition for his services.

"As accumulation goes on, however, and the mass of capital becomes greater relative to the number of the laborers, there must be a struggle and competition in the labor market to invest some of the fresh capital in wages-its owners cannot escape from this necessity. No fresh machinery can be provided or managed except with the assistance of labor. The struggle, during the relative advance of auxiliary capital, is constantly supporting and bring up the rate of wages, and abstracted from all other causes, this progress secures the interest of the laborers, and tends to carry their wages to the highest point which the capitalist can pay, consistently with his making a reasonable profit on his capital."[1]

But he is very careful to add a qualifying statement: "It is to be re-

---

[1] *Literary Remains*, p. 460.

membered, however, that this is only true where the mass of capital is increasing faster than the population. If the capital increases only as fast as the population, or slower than the population, other results follow. " ①

II. *The Theory of Population*

This leads us to study his theory of population. Jones states that the subject of population is connected with political economy mainly because the understanding of it is necessary to comprehend the causes of fluctuations in the rate of wages and profits. ② He divided the subject of population into three parts, namely, the causes which affect the progress of population generally, the causes which affect the progress of the laboring class in particular, and the causes which determine the ultimate incidence of taxes laid on such commodities as are consumed by the laboring classes. ③The last of these topics, however, has no direct bearing upon the subject of population. We will discuss it later in the Chapter on taxation.

He definitely declares that vice, misery, and moral restraint (suggested by Malthus) do not comprise all the checks to population, and that on the whole subject of population we should gain in clearness of concep-

---

① *Literary Remains*, p. 460.

② *Lecture on Population*, p. 153. (Reprinted in *Literary Remains*) . Also in the *Preface* of his *Distribution of Wealth*, he says that the facts on the subject of population which Malthus brought to light must always hold a prominent place in "every inquiry into the causes which determine the social progress and conditions of nations, and the most prominent place in such branches of those inquiries as have for their especial object the explanation of the laws which governs the rate of wages. " (*Preface* p. 9) .

③ He treats of the general subject of population as subordinate to the last two heads of inquiry. His third inquiry will be discussed in connection with his theory of taxation.

tion and avoid exaggeration if we were to get rid altogether of this three-fold division of the checks, and should separate them into two classes, consisting, first, of the causes which increase the number of deaths, and second, of the causes which diminish the number of births. [1]In other words, these checks must comprise every circumstance which makes the numbers of birth fewer, or the number of deaths greater, than they would otherwise be. He first tries to explain some habits that increase mortality which are not vicious, nor referable to misery:

"If, indeed, we include under the head of vice every voluntary habit, however, far from moral taint, which increases mortality, and if, under the head of misery, we include all causes of increased mortality which arise from the absence of more sufficient means, though free from conscious suffering, we may certainly extend our notions of the effects of sin and misery to an indefinite extent. The lawyers, the students, who talk or read them selves to death, are the victims of their vices. The man who dies because he cannot afford the expense of a voyage to Italy or Madeira, is a victim of misery. We may thus introduce into action sin and misery, on a new scale, and convey the most unfounded alarms as to the influence of these evil things in controlling the progress of the numbers of mankind. "[2]

Then he denounces Malthus' narrow division of moral restraint as defective in excluding partial restraint and confounding the lapses of infirmity

---

① *Lecture on Population*, p. 162.
② *Literary Remains*, p. 95.

with the deliberate and regular course of vice. ①

He offers the term "voluntary restraint" in place of moral restraint. The dominion of voluntary restraint, he says, rests upon two points in the rational and moral constitution of man, on his foresight and on the habit of indulging secondary wants. In order to examine the exact mode of increase in the influence of foresight in retarding the age of marriage, he found it convenient to divide the wants and requirements of mankind into two classes. All the means that any rank of the community require to satisfy their wants and tastes, the satisfaction of which they believe essential to their respectability or comfort, may be called their "means of maintenance." The means which they require to support a bare healthy existence, may be called their "means of subsistence." The means of maintenance, therefore, will always include the means of subsistence, but the means of subsistence may be very far from including the means of maintenance. The means of subsistence of families are limited and stationary in amount, or, very nearly so, while the means of maintenance may vary, and become enlarged indefinitely with the different tastes and habits and means of different ranks in the same nation. In other places, he employs the terms "primary wants" and "secondary wants" instead of means of subsistence and maintenance.

---

① "In order to make the erroneous views arising out of this faulty division of checks more apparent, let us observe the career of a professional man refraining from marriage till the age of thirty-five, and keeping constantly in prospect the establishment of a home and a station for himself and his children; it is not too much to assume that, to attain the end he has in view, his career, during the time, has been honorable and useful; that he has been careful of his own selfrespect, jealous of his honor, zealous in his exertions, and that sociery is both served and adorned by a class of such members. Yet let the frailty of nature overcome him once during his career, and at once, according to Mr. Malthus, the whole check on rapid multiplication, established by the existence of such a class of men, becomes converted into a mass of unmixed vice." (*Literary Remains*, p. 154) .

"The wants of mankind are divided into primary and secondary. Primary wants are a given quantity and include whatever is necessary to subsistence and health. Secondary wants are an unlimited quantity, embracing whatever contribute to comfort and enjoyment." [1]

Concerning the relative influence of these two kinds of wants in checking population, Jones says that the foresight which warns men of the danger of their not being able to satisfy their primary wants has a limited influence, because the wants themselves are limited, and the influence of precedence ceases when the means of satisfying them are found. But it is different with secondary wants; they are indefinite. The multiplication of secondary wants has no limits that we can discern, and their influence in creating habits of prudence increases almost step by step with increase of their numbers. [2]Secondary wants increase as men rise in the scale of society. Throughout the whole mass of human society, he maintains, it is the multiplication of the means of comfort and of enjoyment which, during the career of nations, is the great and efficient cause which prompts men voluntarily to refrain from the greatest possible exercise of their power to increase their numbers and in proportion as wealth increases and spreads throughout the nation, the motive for, and habit of, such voluntary restraint acquire a stronger influence over the progress of the population. [3]The importance of secondary wants as a check to the growth of popu-

---

[1] *Literary Remains*, p. 467.

Jevons, on the subject of human wants, mentioned T. E. Banfield as the most important writer in the discussion of primary and secondary wants. But as a matter of fact, Banfield's *The Organization of Industry* was published in 1844, several years later than the appearance of Jones' book on rent, which was published in 1831. Jones also discussed the question in his introductory lecture delivered in King's College in 1833.

[2] *Literary Remains*, p. 102.

[3] *Literary Remains*, p. 165.

lation cannot be over-estimated; It is the multiplication of the means of commanding comforts and luxuries which forms the real check to the growth of population, and not the wants of mere food and necessaries.

In this connection he discusses the relative strength of sexual and all other impulses. He regards the former as stationary and the latter as progressive.

"No doubt the sexual impulse creates a constant tendency in the human race to increase till they approach the limit at which the earth could support its population…But before we contemplate mankind starting on such a career, we must recouect that a tendency imparted by one part of human nature may be by no means the tendency imparted by the whole of human nature, with all its impulses, but may be modified, balanced, or overbalanced, by the aggregate impulses which act in an opposite direction. And here we must remark, that the sexual impulse continues, at most, stationary. I say at most, for there are not wanting facts and arguments to show that it diminishes as the minds and imaginations of men are directed to other objects…But the impulses which lead to its control are not stationary—they go on increasing in number and joint power as the objects of men's desires increase, as the mass of what may be called their secondary wants increases. "[1]

He strongly emphasizes the facts that as secondary wants multiply among the different classes of society, motives of prudence in regard to marriage multiply with them; that weights are increased in one scale while those in the other continue stationary; and that each additional want creates an additional motive for for bearance while the impulse towards marriage remains the same.

Jones' doctrine of secondary wants is based on his theory of consumption, in which he regards imitation as an important factor in the progress of consumption. The fashion of dress and furniture of the nobility and gentry of

---

[1]   *Literary Remains*, pp. 469-470.

one age are found to have passed, and to prevail among the peasantry of a succeeding generation. ①He points out the cumulative effects of imitative power in consumption, thus anticipating Veblen's theory of the leisure class. He also appeals to history to show that in his time people are not worse fed than their forefathers, nor in England are more laborers employed in producing food than formerly.

After discussing the defects of Malthus' division of checks on population, Jones takes up the theory of arithmetic and geometric ratios which, he declares, is incorrect. "Let a country, of which the members have been stationary or increasing slowly, double its members; in twenty years the proportion of fertile females in the young population will be less than it was when the movement began. There will be a larger proportion of female children, under the age of childbearing, and the population will not posses exactly the same powers of doubling, in the given period, that the old one possessed. ②He also refuses to accept the arithmetic ratio, saying that though this may be true in particular cases, and generally at some future time, it is not true in all cases, and at all times. However, Jones' arguments against Malthus are not strong, but often evasive. He did not point out that Malthus seems to have overboked the point that to increase in a geometrical ratio is not necessarily the same thing as doubling every twenty-five years. Nor did he attack Malthus on the arithmetic ratio with the significant fact that since in North American Colonies the population increased for a long period in a geometrical ratio, then this population must have been fed, and consequently the annual produce of food must also have in-

---

① *Literary Remains*, p. 236.
② *Literary Remains*, p. 150.

266

creased in a geometrical ratio. [1]

On the relation between the increase of wages and the growth of population, the economists of his time have sometimes contended, and sometimes taken for granted, that after certain intervals the prices of articles consumed by the laborers would determine the wages of labor by reacting on the supply of labor and thus affecting the relations of demand and supply of labor in the market, which, in turn, at any given time; regulate the price of labor. According to these classical economists a rise in real wages, whether occasioned by a rise of the money amount of the laborer's wages, or a fall in the prices of the articles he consumes, will always give an impulse to population, and will stimulates its vast powers of rapid increase till the numbers of laborers will be greater relative to the demand, so as to bring down the real wages to the amount of commodities which he consumed before the rise took place. Jones considers such a supposition erroneous. Against this "iron law of wages" in relation to population he argues on the basis of social and other considerations.

"When speaking of the progress of population, its movements are frequently reasoned upon as if they depended wholly on the changes in the rate of wages. This is not correct; for various causes, moral and physical, besides the changes in the rate of wages, may contribute powerfully to influence the tendency of population to increase or decrease more slowly or more rapidly at different periods of its existence." [2]

Then he sets forth his general principles that every increase of real wages may either accelerate or retard the progress of population, and that every decrease may also either accelerate or retard that progress. To this general principle he is cautions to make one exception, in the event that

---

[1]   Edwin Cannan: *History of the Theories of Distribution and production*, p. 140.

[2]   *Literary Remains*, p. 167.

the population is already at the minimum of subsistence, and a decrease takes place in the rate of wages. Such a decrease, at such a time, necessarily retards and cannot possibly accelerate the progress of population. This single case excepted, a rise of wages may lead to an increase in the population, as it obviously supplies the means of maintaining larger numbers, or it may lead to the gratification of secondary wants, and so obstruct its increase. A fall of wages may check the increase of population, but such an effect may be obviated by relinquishment of secondary gratifications, which would preserve the means of subsistence undiminished in quantity.

Thus we see that in every case in which the people are not living on the minimum of subsistance, the same variations in the rate of wages may, according to circumstances, act on the rate of increase or decrease of population in two different and opposite directions. There are four possibilities.

A. A Rise in Wages.

1. It may either multiply artificial wants and refined consumption, leaving the rate of increase of population stationary; or

2. It may be extended in primary necessaries and accelerate the rate of increase of population.

B. A Fall in Wages.

1. It may either diminish the consumption of articles induced by artificial wants, leaving the rate of increase of population stationary or accelerated; or

2. It may diminish the consumption of primary necessaries and retard the rate of increase of population.

In attempting to point out the circumstances which help to determine whether changes in the rate of wages shall affect the numbers or the habits of the people, Jones first examines those which determine the results of a rise in the wages of labor. Arranged in order of importance, the "form" in which wages reach the hands of the laborer shoud be mentioned first. When wages are paid in kind, the effect of a rise in wages is to accelerate, and of a fall of wages to retard, the increase of population. But this is not so when wages are paid in money, A rise of wages paid in produce is not so likely to create more secondary wants as to administer to the primary wants of additional numbers. If one laboring family receives an additional income in the shape of raw produce, and another in the shape of money, it seems obvious that the receiver of the money income is more likely to add to his list of comforts than the receiver of raw produce. It is a most natural and easy course for this last-named individual to increase his consumption of primary necessaries. He has received a direct addition to his means of subsistence. The receiver of money has in his hands what may as easily be used to enlarge his maintenance. In all cases, the receiver of wages in money will have greater facilities for buying comforts and luxuries than the receiver of wages in produce. Jones concludes that Malthus was wrong in urging that, because a deficiency of the means of subsistence is a check to population, therefore a superfluity of them must necessarily be a spur to it.

The second modifying circumstance is the length of time during which the change of wages is brought about. A sudden rise of wages will be apt to cause a forward movement of population. A gradual rise of wages will beget a desire for secondary wants. The time consumed in effecting any given change in the rate of wages is very important, because in whatever shape wages are received, if a change of habits is to follow any rise, the progress of the rise must be gradual, and sufficient time must elapse to enable the population both to acquire new tastes and wants, and the habit of considering a command of the means of gratifying them essential to comfort and respectability. A sudden increase of means will ordinarily be used only to gratify more fully tastes and wants already familiar.

The third factor affecting the influence of a rise in wages on numbers of the population will be the abundance or the scarcity of commodities suited to the gratification of secondary wants. To create habits of consumption among a population in possession of increasing wages, several requirements will be necessary. The people must acquire a knowledge suited to their tastes. Cheapness is the main instrument of familiarity with humble comforts. Commodities must be presented to the people at such a reasonable price as to be within the reach of the successive additions to their means. In a country which has no domestic manufacturers, the first step, certainly, towards familiarizing the people with them is to admit the best and cheapest that can be procured from abroad. The next step is to remove all obstacles which obstruct the production of home commodities suited to the new and growing wants of the people.

In the fourth place, the existence or non-existence of many classes approximating, but not confounded with, each other, and of all intermediate classes between the highest and lowest ranks of society, will have great influence in determining the effects of a rise in wages on the size of the population. The presence of numerous gradations in the rank and wealth of the population will develop imitative power in consumption very easily. All classes in the society will form a long chain, conveying by a sure and gradual communication some of the feelings and habits of the highest successively downwards to the very lowest ranks. The influence of this fact on the habits of the laboring classes during an advance of wages becomes necessarily greater as the increased means can be applied to the acquisition of comforts and luxuries.

Fifthly, the degree of civil liberty enjoyed by the people and the hope of elevation into the upper walks of society will be a powerful motive to the deferring of marriage and hence of an increase in population. If there are laws which impede changes in the occupations of families and if there are differences of ranks perpetuated and enforced by habits, imitative power and foresight of a people will not be encouraged.

The sixth circumstance will be the influence of parents in determining the age of marriage of their children. In addition, the facilities for investment of the savings of the laboring class will have great influence upon the growth of their numbers during the advance of wages. And the best factor is the extent and nature of the education of the laboring classes. This question of education enters largerly into all views of the causes which promote foresight and self-respect among the people.

On the other hand, the effects on the size of the population of falls in the wages of labor will be conditioned, according to Jones, by the same circustances as those that influence the results of a rise. Thus, if the fall of wages is sudden, it will be injurious to the health of the people; if gradual, it will be less harmful. As to the other circumstances, a reference to what we have said of their operation during the process of a rise will sufficiently indicate their tendencies and influences during a fall.

In summary, it may be said that Jones discussed in his theory of wages two problems, the doctrine of the wages fund and the principle of population. He did not offer a general theory of wages. In his first group of laborers, the hereditary occupiers and tenants, he considered wages as a "flow" rather than a "fund. " They are composed of food and necessaries, and their amount is fixed by rent contracts with the landowners. The wages of the second group of laborers, the hired dependents, are also derived from current income, not from capital. These wages may be paid either in terms of raw produce or in terms of money. Only the wages of the third class of laborers comefrom capital. Here he offered a demand-supply theory of wages. [1]Against the rigidity and predetermination of the wage-fund Jones argues that wages are various and different. He thus questions rather the scope of the classical doctrine than its validity where the assumed conditions are to be found. [2]

Economists of his time often discussed the problem of population in connection with the law of diminishing returns. But Jones was interested in the relationship between the fluctuations of wages and the size of the population. He set forth his doctrine of secondary wants as a real check to the growth of numbers. He examined the relative strength of human impulses during the progress of civilization, and emphasized the instinct of imitation as an important factor in the progress of consumption.

---

[1] He says the price of labor, like the price of every other commodity, depends at any time and moment on the supply of labor in the market compared with the demand for it. (*Literary Remains*, p. 146) .

[2] E. W. Taussig: *Wages and Capital*, p. 210.

CHAPTER VI
THEORY OF PROFIT

I. *The Source of Capital*

WE have mentioned that Jones' theories of rent and of wages, though appearing in his *Distribution of Wealth*, were discussed from the viewpoint of production. Similarly, his theoly of profit is largely a theory of production rather than an analysis of factors determining the amount of profits.

In Jones' theory of profit we notice three differentiating and important characteristics. In the first place, the economists of his time all looked upon circulating capital as the most important part of capital, and upon the funds for the maintenance of labor as almost the only component of that circulating capital. Fixed capital was sometimes so completely forgotten that capital could be used to indicate the funds for the maintenance of labor only, machinery being put in a separate category. Ricardo, in the preface to his book, makes machinery a requisite of production, in addition to capital. [1]It was Jones who emphasized the importance of auxiliary capital in the production of wealth.

In the second place, Jones maintained that capital is not accumulated solely from the profits of stock, and that it is not necessarily true that the accumulation from profits will be great where the rate of profits is high, and small where the rate of profits is low. His criticism of the contemporary theory of the accumulation of capital has been noted and appreciated by later writers. [2]

Consequently, in his theory of profit, he discusses three problems, namely, the source of capital, the accumulation of capital, and the function of capital. Capital consists, as he conceives it, of all such commodities as are employed in producing wealth, or are advanced towards the maintenance of those who produce wealth, Capital is something saved from revenue, and employed for the purpose of producing wealth, or with a view to profit. Jones put more emphasis upon the production than upon the distribution of wealth.

Capital, being something saved from revenue for the purpose of assisting production, the sources of capital consist of all the revenues of the population of every country from which it is possible that any portion can be saved Hence, it follows that whatever is a source of revenue may be a source of capital. The particular classes of revenue which contribute most a-

---

[1] "The produce of the earth-all that is derived from its surface by the united application of labor, machinery, and capital, is divided among three classes of the community; namely, the proprietor of the land, the owner of the stock or capital necessary for its cultivation, and the laborers by whose industry it is cultivated. " Ricardo: *Principles of Political Economy and Taxation.* p. 1. (Gonner's Edition)

[2] On the subject of accumulation, Prof. Nicholson says, "Special attention may be called to the criticism by Jones of previous writers. " (*Dictionary of Political Economy*, Vol. 1, p. 7.) .

bundantly to the progress of national capital change at different stages of their progress, and are found entirely different in nations occupyiny different positions in this progress. Since different revenues contribute in unequal proportions to the accumulation of capital of different nations at different stages of their economic progress, profits are never the sole source of accumulation, and what is more, they are the main source of such accumulation only in a few rare instances. [1]The earliest contributions to capital must be from wages. Man originally possesses nothing but his labor; whatever revenue he procures must be the reward of his personal exertions. The reward of personal exertion is wage, and wages are, necessarily, the earliest source of accumulation. They are a considerable source of accumulation in the less advanced nations. Even in England, the first savings deposited in the Saving Bank of England are a proof of this fruithful source of capital. Wages are clearly, therefore, a source of accumulaiton which is not to be neglected when we are calculating the capacities of any nation to increase its capital. [2]

The next source of capital, almost contemporaneous in appearance with wages, is the rent of land, When land has been appropriated and cultivated, Jones holds, such land yields to the labor employed on it more than is necessary to continue the kind of cultivation already bestowed upon it. Whatever it produces beyond this is surplus produce. This surplus pro-

---

[1]   He said that the error of regarding capital as accumulated solely from the profits of stock results from views confined to the state of things in England, where it is chiefly so accumulated, instead of extending to the rest of the world, where it is not so accumulated to any considerable degree. (*Literary Remains*, p. 226) .

[2]   Prof. Bowley has estimated that immediately before the War and for a long time previously some $62\frac{1}{2}$ per cent of the income of the United Kingdom was derived from work and some $37\frac{1}{2}$ per cent from property. (Quoted from pigou's *A Study in Public Finance*, p. 145) .

duce is the source of primitve rents. Over a considerable part of the globe these primitive rents are one great sources of the capital actually employed in agriculture. Even in an advanced state of economic organization, like England, the rent of land remains a most important source of national accumulation. Jones maintains that it is important to remember that there is a long stage in the progress of the productive powers of nations, that stage, indeed, at some point of which most of the nations of the earth are to be found, during which the accumulations from profits necessarily bear a small proportion to the accumulations from wages and rents, simply because that proportion of the revenues of the people which is derived from the profit of stock is exceedingly small when compared with the revenues derived from wages or from rent. [1]

When a considerable advance in the powers of national industry has actually taken place, profits rise into comparative importance as a source of accumulation. On profits, as a source of accumulation, Jones makes the bold statement that the power of a nation to accumulate capital from profits does not vary with the rate of profits; that is, it is great where the rate of profit is low, and small where the rate of profit is high.

"If we look back on the past history of England, we shall find that during the period in which her wealth and capital have been increasing the most rapidly, the rate of profits has been gradually declining; and if any other nations are to proceed from their present position to hers, it is, therefore, not merely possible, but judging from here example, probable, that their increasing quantities of national capital will be accumulated with a de-

---

[1] Jones' opinion has been adopted by Marshall in his *Principles of Economics*, p. 229.

clining rate of profit. "①

He makes a distinction between the rate of profits and the mass of profits,② and denies that the national power of accumulation from profits is dependent upon the rate of profits. Let us assume, he says, any two nations to have equal populations; the power of each nation to accumulate capital from profits would depend on the relative masses of the profits produced by them, which again would depend not alone on the rate of profit in each, but on the rate of profit taken in combination with the relative quantities of capital employed. Here Jones has only the mass of capital in mind; he even declines to accept the rate of profit as a factor in encouraging accumulation. To him, the conception of aggregates is more important than that of averages. So he emphatically decries the notion that a declining rate of profits is necessarlly an indication of a diminishing power to accumulate from profits.

In speaking of the sources of accumulation, Jones has hitherto dwelt exclusively on the three great primary divisions of revenues. But an estimate of the accumulations of the owners of these, he says, will not comprehend all the incomes from which additions are actually made to the capital of nations. In order to calculate the power of nations to accumulate capital from their various sources, we must trace those revenues into the hands of the persons who have ultimately the power of saving or of consuming

----

① *Literary Remains*, p. 370.

The historical fall in the rate of interest is seen to be the natural result of increase of capital in proportion to population, unaccompanied by the discovery of new and profitable means of utilizing capital sufficient to counterbalance the other force.

② He states that the rate of profits is the proportion which the revenue to the owners of stock bears to the amount of capital they employ; while the mass of profits is the proportion which the revenue derived from the capital employed bears to the population and to revenues of every other description. (*Literary Remains*, p. 52) .

them. There is no kind of revenue, from the beggar's alms to the sovereign civil list, which may not contribute something to the accumulating capital of the country. [1]

II. *The Accumulation of Capital*

As to the capacity to save, it is evidently limited by the extent of the surplus revenues of every branch of the population. If these revenues are on the whole abundant, the national capacity to accumulate capital is great; if, on the other hand, they are scanty, the power of the nation to accumulate capital is proportionately small. But the power being given, the will to save may be different among different people. Jones set forth five circumstances which determine the inclination to accumulate.

The first circumstance will be the difference of temperament and disposition in the character of the people. To abstain from present consumption with a view to future advantage obviously requires some degree of prudence, of foresight, and some power of self-denial, and with these moral qualities, it may be said, different nations are, from physical constitution, very differently endowed. But Jones argues that men are much more the creatures of circumstance in which they are placed, than, at first sight, they seem to be; and if, in all other respects, the communities of the various nations were placed in the same position, it is doubtful whether their accumulations would indicate any powerful influence of a difference in moral or physical constitution. At all events, such differences, if they ex-

---

[1] *Literary Remains*, p. 38.

ist, can not be accurately appreciated until the different populations can be observed under precisely the same circumstances. ①

The second circumstance which determines the inclination to accumulate will be the differences in the propertions in which the national revenues are divided among the different classes of the population. We shall find that powers and facilities to accumulate varying quantities of capital to be employed in increasing the fertility of industry often depends very much on institutions springing up in the infancy of societies, which will affect the distribution of their wealth, and upon all the relations and means of the productive classes. Here Jones states three propositions. Where the revenue of each individual is extremely scanty, there is obviously less power of accumulating than where revenues of the same amount are distributed among a smaller number of persons. Again, if there is to be any saving at all, the revenues of individuals must, on the average, be rather more than sufficient to maintain them in their position in society, and if there is to be any considetable saving, the revenues of individuals must considerably exceed that point. Lastly, equal amounts of revenues are distributed in different countries, not only in different proportions, but among classes of society, different descriptions of consumers, and this makes a very considerable difference in the tendency to accumulate capital.

The third circumstance which determines the power to accumulate deals with the different degrees of security in the enjoyment of accumulations. Any kind of violence, whether proceeding from bad government or a badly organized condition of society, is an impediment to the accumulation of capital. This kind of insecurity exists long in the career of many nations,

---

① *Literary Remains*, p. 375.

and is the cause of stationary productive powers over a considerable proportion of the earth's surface. It is impossible to read the history of feudal times in Europe without seeing how completely the lawless violence of the feudal barons must have made the security of the cultivators precarious. In Asia, the insecurity of property, which results from special types of political institutions, is a more lasting and extensive source of mischief. However, open violence is not the only source of insecurity for the enjoyment of accumulation: a bad system of taxation may produce the same effects.

Fourthly, different facilities for the investment of savings may affect the accumulation of capital. Supposing the safety of every man's accumulations secure from open violence of fiscal wrong, we shall even then find different countries differing much in the facilities they offer for the investment of such savings, for example, the creation of savings banks provides facilities for stimulating accumulation. Other things being equal, mere differences in the facility of investing savings promptly, safely, and profitably, would create very appreciable differences in the amount accumulated in a given time. The last circumstances which determine the capacity to save will be the influence of facilities for improving the social position of the accumulator. When there is perfect security for the enjoyment of accumulations, when there are good facilities for investing them, and when obvious means present themselves for making such accumulations the means of advancing the social position of the saving parties, then all the circumstances are combined which impart the will and desire to save through all rank of population. But in the progress of nations, obstacles to any change in the position of large masses of the people are practical and very efficient impediments of the spread of the spirit of accumulation. The economic machinery and political institutions of the majority of nations are opposed to facility in changing social status. Jones mentions three kinds of obstacles in Europe, namely: the distinctions of blood and race, the paucity of non-agricultural occupations, and vicious legislation and regulations as to the privilege of carrying on these occupations.

After a discussion of the circumstances conditioning the accumulation of capital, Jones considers the increase of capital as a consequence of social improvement in the earlier stages of the economic progress of nations. Since social improvement is a great factor for the encouragement of accumulation, it should be emphasized more than the sudden importation of capital from abroad. in this case he seems not in favor of foreign loans which might be used to improve the internal social conditions.

"It is to be remarked that an increase of capital is, in the first instance, the effect and not the cause of social improvement; afterwards they move in a circle, mutually producing and produced. And hence it is that capital imported from abroad into a country can never augment the efficiency of labor so extensively or so permanently as capital generated and accumulated upon the soil itself. "①

III. *The Function of Capital*

When discussing the function of capital Jones first makes a distinction between two kinds of capital. The first is supporting capital, used for the maintenance of laborers, and the second is auxiliary capital, emyloyed in increasing the efficiency of their labor. He discusses different effects of capital employed in these two different ways rather fully in connection with his

---

① *Literary Remains*, pp. 12, 30.

theory of rent. The first difference between the application of capital to industry in the support of additional laborers and that in the shape of implements or anything which is the result of past labor as auxiliary to the efforts of the laborers actually employed is that in the first case the quantity of human power, compared with the capital employed, remains unaltered, while in the second case, it is invariably increased. If a capital is used in employing three men on the soil, and then that capital is doubled, and six are employed, the power employed in production is doubled, but it is not more than doubled; we have no reason for assuming that the labor of the three men last employed will be more efficient than that of the three men first employed. But if, instead of using the new capital in employing three fresh laborers, means are found of applying it in some of the shapes of auxiliary capital to increase the power of the three laborers already employed, we may then safely take it for granted that the efficiency of the human labor employed has been increased, and that the three men assisted by this auxiliary capital will have powers which six men employing all their power directly to the soil would not possess. [1]It is admitted that in agriculture, the effect of auxiliary capital in strengthening human power is less obvious, perhaps, than in manufacturers.

The second difference between the effects of the employment of auxiliary capital, and of capital applied directly to the support of additional labor, is that when a given quantity of additional capital is applied in the shape of the result of past labor, to assist the laborers actually employed, a less annual return will suffice to make the employment of such capital profitable, and, therefore, permanently practicable, than if the same

---

[1] *Distribution of Wealth*, p. 207.

quantity of fresh capital were expended in the support of additional labor-ers. In other words, the difference between auxiliary and the supporting capital lies in the duration of reproduction. [1]Jones affirms that the direct benefit of supporting capital is to help a work to be continuous; that it is limited by the amount of population and the rate of wages, and that it pre-vails only in certain undeveloped nations. He emphasized the accumulation of auxiliary capital, which is very important in tracing the progressive wealth of nations. The progress of auxiliary capital both increases the com-mand of man over the powers of the soil relatively to the amount of labor di-rectly or indirectly employed upon it, and diminishes the annual return necessary to make the progressive employment of given quantities of fresh capital profitable.

In his discussion of the productive power of nations, Jones set forth three factors affecting the efficiency of labor, namely, the continuity with which it is applied; the skill by which it is directed; and the power by which it is aided. All these causes are conditioned by the employment of capital. It is self-evident that labor, steadily continued, must be more productive than that which is desultory. Besides the time obviously lost by

---

[1]   Jones gives the calculation as follows:

"Let us suppose 100£ , employed upon the soil in the maintenance of three men, producing their own wages, and 10 per cent profit on them, or 110£ . Let the capital employed upon this soil be doub-led and first let the fresh capital support three additional laborers. In that case, the increased produce must consist of the full amount of their wages and of the ordinary rate of profit on them. It must consist therefore of the whole 100£ , and the profit on it; or of 110£ . Next, let the same additional capital of 100£ be applied in the shape of implements, manures, or any results of past labor, while the number of actual laborers remains the same. And let this auxiliary capital last on the average five years: The an-nual return to repay the capitalist must now consist of 10£ , his profit, and of 20£ , the annual wear and tear of his capital: or 30£ will be the annual return necessary to make the continuous employment of the second 100£ profitable, instead of 100£ , the amount necessary whem direct labor was em-ployed by it. " (*Distribution of Wealth*, p. 211) .

an intermission of labor, time is always indirectly lost in discontinuing one species of exertion and changing to another. It is capital, or the past results of human labor, that fulfills the conditions on which its continuity is alone possible. ①Secondly, the efficiency of human labor is affected by the degree of knowledge and skill by which it is directed to effect the purpose of the producer. An ignorant savage might hammer a whole day on a piece of cold iron, and not produce a useful object since he lacked a knowledge of the effects of heat on the malleability of the metal. If the continuity of labor is practically the result of the employment of capital in production, the skill with which it is exerted is likewise so. The mind and thought employed in directing human industry is either the mind and thought of the capitalist or that of a skilled laborer paid by him for the purpose. As continuity and skill in the exertion of labor are dependent on the progress of the accumulation of the past results of labor, the third element of efficiency—the power with which it is exerted—is yet more obviously dependent than the other two, since the national mass of auxiliary capital may increase indefinitely, and at every step of such increase there is an increase of mechanical power.

Two great influences of auxiliary capital upon the productive power of nations are mentioned by Jones. The first is the great increase in the relative numbers of the non-agricultural classes. This means that more capital instead of more laborers will be employed in the cultivation of the soil when the factors in production are apportioned. The increase of auxiliary capital is, of course, not the only circumstance which affects the proportionate

---

① *Literary Remains*, p. 12, 30.

number of the two great classes of cultivators and non-cultivators. ①Any cause which increases the efficiency of the actual cultivators may do so, but an increase of auxiliary capital is the only cause which, in the ordinary progress of civilized nations, we are sure must exercise a progressive influence in this respect.

The second influence of auxiliary capital is that its increase adds to the revenues of the intermediate classes. The wealth, the influence and the numbers of capitalists in the community will be proportionately increased as auxiliary capital accumulates. Jones remarks that we can watch the growth of capitalists, and observe them at first scarcely distinguishable as a peculiar body, then separating themselves slowly from tht mass of laborers or landowners with whom they were bebre confounded, assuming a gradually increasing share in the direction of national industry; and influencing at last, in the most decisive manner, not only the productive powers, but the social and political elements of nations. In tracing the economic progress, or in analyzing the respective powers of different nations, he finds the distinctive division of wealth called capital playing a most important part in modifying the ties which connect the different classes of the community, and in determining their respective powers. ②The relative increase in the numbers of the non-agricultural classes, and the relative increase of the revenues and numbers of the intermediate classes are both changes of

---

①   Jones regards the agricultural surplus as the most important thing; its amount limits the numbet of the non-agricultural population of the earth, and its distribution determines the occupation of that portion of the population. This might be true before the development of capitalistic society. In an age preceding the distinctly modern epoch standards of consumption were, for the most part, definite. The surplus of food produced was a rough indication of the probable magnitude of the non-agricultural population. But in modern society, on the contrary, wants are so complex and subject to such great variations that it would be hazardous to predict the result of any but the most striking changes in income.

②   *Literary Remains*, p. 556.

considerable importance in the progress of society.

The use of auxiliary capital will also mark the degree of civilization of different nations. Nations advanced in wealth expend much more of their capital in aiding labor than in paying wages.

"In England, the amount of capital paid to laborers bears a proportion to the amount of auxiliary capital of one to five; while in Russia, capital is almost equally divided between wages and aids to labour. "[1]

In summary, Jones' theory of profit covers a discussion of the source of capital, the accumulation of capital and the function of capital. All these topics he closely relates to the theory of production of wealth. He did not explicitly give the origin and cause of profits. Nor did he offer any distributive theory of profit in a definite form. Contention that capital increases efficiency in the production of wealth seems to imply that the share paid to the capitalist is due to the productive power of capital-aproductivity theory of interest. In tracing the source of capital he just touched the idea of an aggregate profit which depends upon the amount of capital as well as upon the rate of interest. This implies that his distributive theory of profit is not a theory of profit in percentages, but rather a theory which determines the proportions in which the mass profits are divided among the various capitalists.

---

[1] *Literary Remains*, p. 229.

CHAPTER VII
JONES' OTHER THEORETICAL
CONTRIBUTIONS

I. *The Balance of Bargain System*

IN order to comprehend the whole system of Jones' political economy it is necessary, in addition to his theory of rent, wages, and profits, to discuss his historical work on the balance of bargain and his theory of taxation, which includes the question of commutation of tithes. These theories do not deserve the prominence of his other ideas, previously treated, but their significance should not be belittled and no exposition of his work can be complete without something being said on them.

Jones' institutional economics led him to discuss the primitive political economy of England. He was the first to coin the phrase "the system of the balance of bargains."[1] He was also the first to direct his attention to this phase of the whole mercantile system. Although his article first appeared in the Edinburgh Review in April, 1847, the idea had already been discussed in his lectures at Kings' College in 1833. "To draw, then, to this noble

---

[1]   In a modest manner he said that this system might be called, if we wish to give it a name, the balance of bargains system (*Literary Remains*, p. 547) .

realm at least its fair share of the world's stock of gold and silver, two systems prevailed at different periods of our story; but although these systems had this common object, they differed much in their means, their working and effects, and ought never to be confounded, although they are confounded very generally, under the name of the mercantile system, which only made its appearance late, and did not last for a century. Its various parts (of the older system) may be accurately traced in our statute book and ancient documents, but as a systematic whole, it has, I think, escaped the notice of our historians. "[1]

Adam Smith had discussed the aim of the mercantile system in his *Wealth of Nations* (Book 4) but he did not deal much with the means by which the mercantilists were to realize their aim. Jones was the first to bring to light the regulations and various measures of the mercantile system. In criticizing that school, writers frequently emphasized the confusion of precious metals with national wealth as the source of their error. But Jones attacked this problem from another angle, with more insight and more deliberation. He regarded the absence of military conquest and economic imperialism as the logical results of the earlier English legislation, which adopted restrictive means of obtaining precious metals. It was a peaceful method; it had its own justification. "Admitting the non-productiveness of our own mines, and putting conquest and spoliation out of the question, the conclusion seemed very reasonable. "[2]

The provisions of the balance of bargain system divided themselves into two groups: the constructive plan contained those by which it was sought to bring bullion into the country; the preventive plan, those by which it

---

[1] *Literary Remains*, p. 54.
[2] *Literary Remains*, p. 295.

was sought to prevent it from going out of the country. The first plan must precede the second one: the problem is, first to get the bullion, and then to keep it in the country.

Two organizations were used for the constructive purposes—the Staple towns, and the corporation of the Mayor and constables of the Staple. The former was universal on the continent, the latter peculiar to England. The Staple town was named, it is supposed, from the German word *Stapelen*, to heap up, because, as they were perpetual fairs, commodities were to be found heaped up all the year round. The system of the staple consisted in part of the principle of establishing fairs and markets. It was necessary for mutual protection and for regulation of trade and prices that merchants should form a company, and it was also profitable to the king, as both increasing the customs revenue and facilitating its collection. [1]The measures

---

[1]   Before the reign of Edward I the export trade of England was principally carried on by foreigners, of whom the most important were the Hanse merchants. It was in 1313 that this plan of both home and foreign staples was first adopted by England. The staple commoditles of England were wool, hides, leather, lead and tin. wool, especially, was the subject of particular care; it was the sovereign treasure of England, with which she was said to keep the whole world warm. The Mayor and the constables were authorized to select some towns and to punish by fine all dealers carrying wool or wool fells to any other place, and were authorized to change, for a time, the Staple towns at their discretion. The reign of Edward III exhibits more strikingly than any other the influence and results of this plan on the finance and prosperity of tbe country. He established staple courts, staple law, and staple privileges in various towns of England and Ireland. His extraordinary resources in the war with France seem to have been almost entirely derived from duties on the export of wool. The weight of wool for export was to be certified by the Mayor, and at the port it was to be again weighed, and an indenture of the weight made between the Mayor and the custom officers.

Export trade was restricted to aliens under the pain of death. (In this year the Ordinance of the Staple was issued). In 1353 there were ten Staple towns in England. The appointment of home staples only was thought to be advantageous to England because it would break the monopoly of Flanders, and the consequent competition would raise the price of wool, while the foreign merchants would bring in gold and silver of other lands and this the increased revenue from tbe customs, which was heavior for aliens than for Englishmen, would bring in large supplies. But the high duties, as well as the extensive smuggling, prevented the success of the home staples, so in 1363 the Staple was established at Calais where until 1558 it continued to be the most constant and even the sole English staple.

for carrying out the preventive plan, according to Jones, were four in number, namely, the establishment of mints, the searchers and the customers of the outposts, the King's exchanges, and the statutes of employment. Concerning the logical order of these preventive methods, the King's exchangers, and the searchers and the customers should be mentioned first. The King's exchanger was a commercial supervisor in the modern sense, with almost unlimited power over the money transactions of the country. His chief duty was to determine the value of all foreign coins in English money, and the foreign merchant who landed with foreign money in his possession was bound to go to the officer for exchange. In addition to this, the exchanger was authorized to handle the negotiations of foreign bills of exchange. The customers were fiscal agents whose duty it was to collect revenue.

The mint was established for two purposes. In the first place, when the foreign coin had reached England, it might be reexported. In the second place, it might be estimated at some value different from that which the King declared its true value when measured against English coin. The former question was a kind of economic illusion, while the latter involved a legal theory of money. In those days it was believed to be one of the most precious prerogatives of Kings to fix the value of the coinage. No one had the power to interfere with this prerogative, and, according to this principle, no foreign coin should be used in England for any other purpose than that of being exchanged for English coin at the King's mint, or by the King's exchangers. The sovereign always set his own value on his own coin, and no foreigner interfered with his decision. After the par of exchange had been determined, the foreign money was estimated and recoined, and, the King's high prerogative fully vindicated, a next step was necessary to prevent the exportation of money. It was decided that before foreign merchants left the country they must give satisfactory proof that they had employed all the money they had received for their imported cargoes in the purchase of English commodities, so that no money remained in their hands to be carried away. The various acts passed to enforce the rule are called the Statutes of Employment. The most effective machinery for the inspection of all such dealings was the "host" . [1]

A still more peculiar economic phenomenon was the regulation of the sale of pilgrims' bills. For if the selling of pilgrims' bills were in the hands of foreigners they may contrive to smuggle money abroad, and hence it was decreed that whenever such a bill was negotiated, the foreigner should give bond to the exchequer that he would within a given time export to the continent a cargo of English commodities fully equal in value to the money he had received for the bill.

But these regulative measures could hardly be carried out consistently. As soon as the situation changed, the regulations could no longer be maintained. The first blow struck at the system lay in the growth and changed circumstances of England. These circumstances, according to whether they were economic forces or political changes, may be arranged under four heads: the establishment of merchant adventurers which should be reckoned with the foremost among the forces which threw the system of

---

[1]   The Statute of Employment provided that all merchant strangers coming to traffic in any port in England should be under the supervision of certain persons called "hosts," to be assigned to them by the officers of the town. The qualifications of hosts were that they must be creditable persons, expert in trade, and trading in the commodities of their guests. The host was to be privy to all the bargains made by the stranger. He was to keep an accurate book of every bargain made by the foreigner. If any foreign merchant neglected to reprt himself as needing a host, or, having one, failed in obedience to him, he was to be put in prison. These measures not only prevented the exportation of money but also encouraged domestic industry and opened a ready market.

the balance of bargain out of gear; the use of the foreign bill of exchange; the degradation of the currency, and the capture of Calais by the French. After the balance of bargain system was crippled, the balance of trade system was introduced to take its place.

The essential characteristic of the balance of trade system was the constant accession of fresh masses of bullion through foreign trade. It entirely abandoned and repudiated all the expedients and machinery by which the earliest framers of the balance of bargain system had attempted the same object. Jones gave no less credit to Thomas Mun, who was the first to attack the balance of bargain system, than to Adam Smith's work in minimizing the doctrine of mercantilism. He remarked that it took several centuries to expel the fallacy of the balance of bargain system, just as it took hundreds of years to repudiate the mercantile policy. His method was always to discover the origin of a system and then trace its downfall. His historical treatment of economic institutions from primitive to modern times reveals the continuity of economic thought and the dynamics of economic conditions.

II. *Theory of Taxation and Tithes*

Taxes, are, according to Jones, the shares of the government in the revenue of a country, the sources of revenue being rent, wages, and profits. [1]He is in opposition to any single system of of taxation and claims that

---

[1] "Tracing society then once more through its many forms and many stages, we shall endeavor to point out what in each is the nature of revenue drawn by the State from the incomes of the laborers, the landowners, or the Capitalists." (*Distribution of Wealth*, *Preface*, p. 28).

no portion of wealth annually produced and distributed is marked by the peculiarity of yielding no revenue to the state. "We shall attempt to observe the limits of the financial fruitfulness of each class; and to determine the points at which an attemut to press further upon a single division ends in a real burthen upon one or both of the others."[1]

He points out two errors in the system of single land tax. [2]In the first place, rent consists of surplus profits only in a country of capitalists whose capital is endowed with nobility, such as England. This is not so in a country of capitalists whose capital is immovable, like Ireland. Nor is it so in a country where no classes of capitalists are found, as India. In fact, to the actual state of things over a greater portion of the globe, the definition of rent as surplus profits is inapplicable. And even in a country where rents are really surplus profits, it is highly inexpedient to absorb rents by taxation. For a portion of rent is commonly expended by landlords in bettering their land with drains, ditches, etc., and so adding to its value. In the second place, the surplus profits which are said to constitute rents all over the world are not owning, solely or principally, to the superior quality of the soil. Doubtless the different qualities of different soils is one of the circumstances determining the different amounts of their produce. But it is a circumstance of inconsiderable potentiality when compared with the increase of industry, of skill, and of auxiliary capital.

As regards the tax on profits, Jones declares that profits are taxable till capitalists move their capital out of the country rather than pay a tax upon it. [3]A tax upon profit will diminish capital and in turn a diminution of

---

① *Distribution of Wealth*, *Preface*, p. 28.

② *Literary Remains*, p. 273.

③ *Literary Remains*, p. 276.

capital will cause a smaller demand for labor, and, consequently a fall in wages. At what points this result will occur, he admits, is a problem that does not admit of an exact solution.

Of more importance is the subject of a tax on wages. In his theory of population he set forth three problems, the last of which concerns the ultimate incidence of a tax laid on commodities consumed by the laboring class. He maintains that it is impossible to tell beforehand that ultimate incidence of a tax on wages, for this depends upon the effects of the tax upon the growth of population. [1]As taxes on wages are almost identical with a fall in the rate of wages and the abolition of taxes with a rise, their effect is determined by the same laws which regulate the influence of a change in the rate of wages upon the size of the population. It has been mentioned in discussing the theory of population that except on one peculiar occasion any change in the rate of wages may either accelerate or retard the growth of population. Now, suppose a reduction to take place in the rate of wages, in the shape of a tax, under circumstances in which the growth of population would be retarded: the diminution of numbers would certainly raise the rate of wages. In this case, the tax has shifted its incidence from the laborers to their employers, from wage to profits. Again, suppose the same to be laid on wages, under circumstances in which it would not effect the growth of population, but would be met by a sacrifice of secondary gratifications: the tax would not then shift its incidence.

Jones also discusses direct, indirect, and mixed taxes. Direct taxes are those which there is no means of escaping such as the poll tax and appear in the early stages of society. Indirect taxes are those which it is the

---

[1] *Literary Remains*, p. 277.

option of every person to avoid or incur. Mixed taxes are either indirect in form but direct in reality, or vice versa.

In the history of nations rents appear to have been the earliest subject of taxation and an increase of indirect taxation marks an increase in national wealth. Taking the tax system as a whole, he considers the three primarry portions of national wealth all taxable. "As it would not be less unjust than foolish to lay the whole burden of taxation upon rents, or profits, so it would be a false charity and a false wisdom to exempt wages altogether from taxes. Nothing is a more sure sign of a vigorous constitution and a healthy state in a country that for every member of the community to be competent to bring some contribution to the general stock. "[1] He also touches upon the diffusion theory of taxation: "All these notions about untaxable classes of men or revenues are utterly delusive. Taxes are not always paid by those on whom they are imposed; their ultimate incidence is not always the same as their apparent incidence; but still there is not one class of society, whatever be its taxation or employment, which can not be made to bear its share of the public burthens. "[2]

As has been said, Jones administrative capacity and theoretical soundness were shown in his work for the commutation of tithes. Tithes were originally a free-will offering, but gradually became compulsory, first by church law, afterwards by statutes. They were the tenth part, free of the cost of cultivation, of the yearly increase of the land. Such a system was very vexatious to both the farmers and the clergyman. [3]His interest in this

---

[1]   *Literary Remains*, p. 280.

[2]   *Literary Remains*, p. 567.

[3]   The inconvenience caused to the clergy by their being obliged to receive their dues in kind, and to collect them themselves into their tithe barns from the different farms in the parish, often produced most undesirable friction between tithe-owners and tithe-payers, between pastors and their flocks.

subject before 1831. has already been remarked in his treatment of rent. In his discussion of the Corn laws he held the opinion: "If we suppose the tithe commuted and the poor rates done away with or reduced to a very small sum, then the farmer, in estimating his peculiar burdens, would be relieved from a feeling of indefinite pressure, and from many vague fears of risk and loss, which are kept alive and irritate by the existence of those payments in their present state. Till this is done it is very much to be feared that no corn laws which are really equitable will ever appear to the farmer to give him sufficient protection, while the non-agricultural classes will be but too easily persuaded that they added exorbitantly, and unjustly to the price of provisions. "[1]

He discussed three propositions with regard to commutation of tithes:[2] first, that a commutation is desirable; second, that the future payments, in lieu of tithes, shall be applied to the same purpose and paid to the same persons as the present tithes; third, that the first step in the process shall be to transfer the liability to future payments, from the tenant to the landlords. He also defended the Government Bill by mentioning three objects of the government in the commutation of tithes. The first object was to set the capital and industry of the country completely free to extract the greatest possible amount of produce in the best manner from the soil. The second object was to remove, at the same time, any obstacles created by the actual mode of collecting their revenues. The last purpose was to promote the efficiency of the religious instruction of the people.

The landlords, the second party in the commutation of tithes, were affected directly by the measure, in a pressing manner. The prospect of re-

---

[1] *Distribution of Wealth*, p. 299.
[2] *Remarks on the Government Bill*, 1836.

moving obstacles to the freest employment of capital by the occupier of the soil and of promoting a general advance of rent were sufficient reasons for the anxiety which the landowners generally expressed for a permanent settlement of the tithe question. But the third group in the tithe question, the clergyman, had some interests of an opposite nature. They had no direct pecuniary object to gain by effecting a commutation. Considering the question as one of mere profit and loss, they would clearly gain by postponing commutation or eluding it altogether.

Jones also discussed the causes of the unpopularity of clerical income derived from this source. Tithes are represented to the tithe-payer in the form of a bread tax, enhancing the expense of cultivation. With the increasing produce of the soil, both rent and tithes increase; but they increase at very different rates: the rent slowly, the tithes faster. Where more agricultural produce is obtained by the outlay of more capital, it is found by experience that a greater proportion of the whole produce must be retained by the cultivator to replace his advances, and pay his profits on them; and the rent, although becoming gradually larger in positive amount, constitutes step by step a smaller relative proportion of the gross produce. Rent, consisting of a diminishing proportion of the raw produce, increases more slowly than tithes, which, however, greatly the produce may increase, consist always of the same proportion of the whole. Therefore, while tithes retained their then present shape there was little hope of getting rid of these various sources of irritation.

On plans for making the future tithe payments a portion of the rent, Jones mentioned two alternatives—one general and one particular. The first project purposes to establish one common proportion of future tithe payments to future rents on all soils of the kingdom. The second plan purposes to ascertain the actual proportion of tithes to rent in each particular case, and to perpetuate these various proportions. His argument against the first plan may be described as follows. If the differences in the proportions of tithes to rent were very small in particular cases, it might be possible to establish some common proportion, without any very gross violation of the rights of individual tithe-payers or receivers. But the difference between the proportions on different soils is very great. Equal quantities of produce are notoriously obtained at a very different expense from soils of different quality; from the "stiff" land for instance, at a greater expense than from light; moreover the rent of lands producing equal quantities of produce will vary with the different expense of obtaining that produce and will be small when the expense is great, and larger when the expenses have been less. The tithes, however, of equal quantities of produce must always be the same; that is, there will be the same tithes with different rents, and there can be, therefore, no universal proportion between them while the various soils of the earth yield equal crops, though to very different quantities of labor and expense. Equalize the proportion of tithes to rents on all land and very gross injustice would be inflicted upon the landowner who found his own tithes doubled, while those of his neighbor were proportionately lessened. Injustice would also be inflicted on the tithe-owners. The incomes of individual clergymen would obviously be affected most capriciously, and, it so happens, in a most undesirable direction, for the incomes, already small, of the clergy in the poorer district would be lowered, because there the actual proportion of tithes to the low rents is the greatest, while the income of the clergy in the richer districts would be proportionately augmented, since in these districts the actual proportion of tithes to rent is the smallest and the latter group must profit by the equalization which would be ruining the poorer neighbors.

As to the second plan for commuting tithes, on the basis of the various proportions tithes bear to rent on different lands, the great national object, according to Jones, of setting completely free the fresh application of capital to the soil would be fully effected. It was proposed to ascertain the reasonable value of the tithes, to compare this with the actual rent, and to declare that a like proportion of the future rent shall be always paid in lieu of tithes. Under this plan the produce obtained by such fresh capital would pay no tithes till the capitalist was secure; in other words, till such capital should return the ordinary rate of profit. The landowner would be equally secure, in that, if his rent fell, his tithe payments would proportionately diminish. In the meantime, the funds devoted to religious instruction, increasing as rent rose and cultivation improved, would increase step by step with the increasing population, not so largely, indeed, as when tithes were a fixed proportion of the gross produce, but still to an extent which might be useful in meeting the increased demand for religious instruction. It is true that, under such an arrangement, the tenants' capital would flow freely to the land, unchecked by tithes; but not so the landowners'. The landlord's outlay is always with a view to rent, and in that rent the tithe-owner would continue to share.

The success of the measure in practice must be regarded as a notable proof of the wisdom with which it was conceived, and the care and equity with which it was carried into effect.

CHAPTER VIII
JONES' CRITICS AND HIS INFLUENCE

JONES' theoretical contributions to the development of economic science consist of the recognition of a wider scope of political economy than the Classical School had manifested and a far more optimistic view of economic progress. Whenever he discussed economic institutions he took into consideration social factors as well as political conditions. His theory of rent was, in fact, a theory of income from land; although, as has been said, he did not like to confine the concept of rent to a definition. So with his theory of wages, which did not conceive of wages as a fund but as an income from labor. In his theory of profit, the accumulations of capital are treated in an exhaustive study which was later adopted by Nicholson and Edwin Cannan. His theory of population is more objective and scientific than those of any before him, being without a moral tinge, for voluntary restraint is certainly a happier term than moral restraint And his doctrine of secondary wants is a real contribution to the discussion of the distribution of wealth.

It is now about a century since Jones published his first book, *The Distribution of Wealth and the Source of Taxation*, in 1831. In making a century's estimate of his contribution to the development of political economy it is interesting to survey different opinions expressed by great economists, past and present, on Jones' system.

300

As soon as his book was published an article by McCulloch appeared in the *Edinburgh Review* expressing the latter's criticisms as follows:

"We cannot say that Mr. Jones has been very successful in his researches. His view is extensive but superficial. He never, in fact, goes below the surface. And the conclusions at which he arrives, though sometimes accurate, are, for the most part, quite foreign to the main object of his work. "①

Again McCulloch, in his *Literature of Political Economy*, condemned Jones' work with most unfavorable comments: "Perhaps it was hardly necessary to notice this work, which consists principally of a series of irrelevant and inapplicable criticisms, on the theory of rent as explained by Mr. Ricardo. " Of course, we know that McCulloch was an ardent follower of Ricardo, that his views were too extreme and unfair. Moreover, McCulloch's statements in his *Literature of Political Economy*, declares Jevons, were not alway accurate.

On the other hand, the editor of *Literary Remains*, Dr. Whewell, gave many illustrations of Jones' achievements in economic theory. He gave Jones the credit for originating the classification of rents and the inductive method in reasoning on political economy. Jones'

---

① The details of McCulloch's criticism are as follows:

1. "An account of the conditions under which land has been occupied in different ages and countries would be a work of great value and importance. But judging from the specimens of Mr. Jones' talent, we do not think that he is the very person to supply the deficiency. "

2. "Mr. Jones has treated at considerable length of the occupancy of land by Métayers, or tenants, paying a certain proportion of the produce to the landlord as a rent. But this part of his work is eminently superficial. Mr. Jones seems to imagine that cultivation by Métayers was not introduced in Italy till after the era of Columella. In point of fact, however, Métayers were well known in Italy two hundred years previously. "

3. "It was not reserved for Mr. Jones to indicate the influence of improvements on the law of decreasing fertility. But a very large portion of his work is occupied with tedious statements of principles already fully elucidated by others. "

4. "The remarks Mr. Jones has made on profits are not more original or valuable than those he has made on rent. He labors hard to show that profits have not natural tendency to fall in the progress of society. But when the law of decreasing fertility of that soil is established, the law of decreasing profits follows as a matter of course. "

5. "On the whole, we cannot say that we have derived much instruction from Jones' work. His efforts to overthrow the theory of rent have been signally abortive. "

philosophy "to look and see" was highly praised by his friend. ①

J. S. Mill adopted Jones' classification of rent, as we mentioned above, and in his *Principles of Political Economy* he referred to Jones' essay on the *Dirtribution of Wealth* as "a copious repertory of valuable facts on the landed tenures of different countries. "② Jevons also declared that

"the Essay of Richard Jones on the distribution of wealth and the forms of land tenures in different countries is a far less celebrated book, but displays all the same careful spirit of inquiry into the past or present conditions of men. "③

Perhaps the most unreserved admirer of Jones was Professor J. K. Ingram:

"The most systematic and thorough-going of the earlier critics of the Ricardian system was Richard Jones. Jones has received scant justice at the hands of his successors. J. S. Mill, while using his work, gave his merit but faint recognition. The method followed by Jones is inductive; his conclusions are founded on a wide observation of contemporary facts, aided by study of history. He is remarkable for his freedom from exaggeration and one-sided statement. "④

Professor Edgeworth considered Jones "a philosophical historian, and not a mere chronicler. He deserves to be regarded as the founder of the English historical school. " ⑤And indeed, the economists of the English historical school all tried to do justice to him. Toynbee asserted, in his *Industrial Revolution*, that "all the world had become political economists of

---

① And it is apparently highly praised today by modern statisticians. Compare Secrist's *Introduction to Statistical Method*:

"The Science of Economics is becoming statistical in its method. The advice of Richard Jones to look and see is being taken literally. " (p. 17.)

② J. S. Mill: *Principles of Political Economy*, Book I, p. 317.

③ Jevons: *Principles of Economics*, p. 193.

④ Ingram: *History of Political Economy*, p. 139.

⑤ *Dictionary of Political Economy*, Vol. Ⅱ, p. 491.

the Ricardian persuasion and the protests of Malthus and his able successor, Richard Jones, were lost in a tumult of applause. " ①

Professor Ashley also held that Jones "urged with excellent soberness
the need for historical investigation; but that his plea fell on the deaf ears,
and that the only trace of his influence in economic literature for many
years is to be found in J. S. Mill's treatment of peasant tenures!" ②

Professor Cannan places high value on the contribution of Jones' historical study:

"In 1831 a vigorous attack on the Ricardian theory was made by Richard Jones. Taking a much broader view of the matter than Ricardo, he surveyed the whole of history, instead of confining his attention to the circumstances of England during the war. It was, consequently, perfectly evident to him that the necessity of employing less productive agricultural industry was neither the only possible nor the most important actual causes of rise of
rent, since in the last three hundred years, for example, rent in England has risen enor-
mously, although the least productive agriculture employed was no less productive than it
had been at the beginning of the period…" ③

Marshall's attitude towards Jones was fair and balanced.

"Richard Jones had not fully grasped the modern distinction between generality of doctrines, or dogmas, and generality of analytical conceptions and ideas; and his own position
has his own defects. But he said what was wanted at the time, and his influence, though
little heard of in the outer world, largely dominated the minds of those Englishmen who
came to the serious study of economics after his works had been published by Dr. Whewell

---

① Toynbee, *Industrial Revolution*, p. 9.
② *Dictionary of Political Economy*, Vol. II, p. 310.
③ Cannan: *History of the Theories of Production and Distribution*, 333.

in 1859. "①

In his *Principles of Economics*, Marshall adopted Jones' views on the subject of the source of saving:

"But even in modern England rent and the earnings of professional men and hired workers are an important source of accumulation, and they have been the chief source of it in all the earlier stages of civilization. "②

Jones' emphasis upon the importance of both time and space and the relativity of economic doctrines has been admired by J. N. Keynes in his classical work. *The Scope and Method of Political Economy*, ③while Professor Taussig, in his book *Wages and Capital* mentioned Jones as a most important figure in attacking the wage-fund doctrine. ④

As regards the use and the originality of the phrase, "The Balance of Bargains," two well-known economists agreed to give Jones credit for it.

---

① Marshall: "The Old Generation of Economists and the New. " *Quarterly Journal of Economics*, 1897.

Jones' influence, however, was very slight. In a recent book, entitled *A Guide to the Printed Materials for English Social and Economic History* by Professor J. B. Williams, Jones' *Literary Remains*, is not mentioned at all.

② Marshall: *Principles of Economics*, 8th Edition. p. 229.

③ "Jones especially insisted on the limited applicability of the Ricardian theory of rent as regards both place and time. A theory based upon the assumption of individual ownership and freedom of completion could not, be pointed out, apply to Oriental stages of society in which joint ownership is the rule and rents are regulated by custom, nor even to those instances nearer home in which land is held in a customary tenure, as in the metayer system. Similarly, as regards limitation in time, he showed that the Ricardian law could not hold good in a condition of affairs such as existed in Mediaeval economy, where land was to a great extent held in common, and the relations between the owners and the tillers of soil were not controlled by free competition. " (*Scope and Method of Political Economy*, p. 298, 4th Edition, 1917) .

④ "A much more vigorous protest than came from either Senior or Malthus or Chalmers, against the general doctrine in vogue, was made by Richard Jones. Jones was an able and scholarly thinker, with views broadened by a wide knowledge of history and an appreciation of the lessons of history. His attitude on the wage-fund doctrine as the doctrine stood at that date, is significant. "

(*Wages and Capital*, p. 208) .

Cossa speaks of Jones' "invention of the happy phrase, Balance of Bargain."[1] And the same epithet was applied by Nicholson.[2]

On taxation, Jones made the least effort to contribute anything. Professor Seligman, however, gives him credit for being "one of the first to deny the Ricardian doctrine of incidence, as he was the first to dispute Ricardo's theory of distribution."[3]

Finally, Jones' institutional economics is gradually coming to be appreciated. And it is significant that Professor Mitchell, the leading quantitative economist, attributes an important position to him in the history of economics.

"Among Ricardo's contemporaries was Richard Jones, a clergyman of the Church of England, who knew enough of English history and of contemporary conditions outside of England to appreciate that Ricardo's whole System applied to an institutional situation recent in its development and limited in its scope. Accordingly Jones set himself to broaden the basis of economic theory by studying the distribution of wealth in other times and other lands...."[4]

After a survey of so many favorable opinions expressed by economists on Jones' system of political economy, it may well be asked: Did Jones have great influence upon contemporary or later writers? In truth, we must

---

[1]   *An Introduction to Political Economy*, p. 198.

[2]   Nicholson states that Jones "very happily styled ⋯ (this) ⋯ the Balance of Bargains system." (*Dictionary of Political Economy*, Vol I, p. 84).

[3]   Seligman: *The Shifting and Incidence of Taxation*, p. 195.

[4]   Mitchell: "Prospects of Economics" in *The Trend of Economics*, edited by Tugwell, 1924 (p. 17).

answer that his influence, if any at all, is insignificant. ①Except that J. S. Mill and Fawcett adopted his classification of peasant proprietors, there was no contemporary or later economist who could be called his disciple. He might have had some indirect influence upon the change in economic conceptions; but he had no direct influence on the general course of economic studies in England. This ineffectiveness was due to three causes, namely, his procrastination in writing his book, his practical activities, and the unsuitability of his economic theory to English conditions of that time. "

We must admit his slowness in writing his book. Dr. Whewell's letters show very clearly Jones' mental inactivity. A letter from Whewell dated September 9, 1828, runs as follows:

"Have you been cultivating rent, profit and wages, and getting them ready for undying type? You must have been doing this, for all things call upon you. I have been reading a pamphlet, which you very likely know, as I read the third edition, concerning the True Theory of Rent by Thompson. If you have not, read it forthwith on various accounts. Now one inference to be made from this same pamplet is how ripe the world is for your speculations, and how they will become less striking and original by all delay. Here you have the fallacy of rent being the excess of rich soil, the case indicated of rent in countries where this does not apply, the bearing of taxes in the various cases, the influence of moral causes and national habits. All these topics, no doubt, very slightly touched and with no consciousness of their extent and general principles, but still showing how the opinions of clear headed and inquiring men tend. On this account especially it is that you, who are in posses-

---

① Professor Price in his *Short History of Political Economy in England* made a less cheerful estimate of Jones:

Richard Jones, the successor of Malthus at Haileybury, controverted many of Ricardo's positions on the theory of rent in his Essay on the Distribution of Wealth and on the Source of Taxation. But Ricardo's influence on the general course of English economic opinion remains unshaken. " (*Short History of Political Economy*, p. 64).

sion of the general views which connect and systematize these apercus, and of the collections of instances which illustrate them, should linger no longer. In the same way, so far as I can understand concerning Mr. Sadler from the Quarterly Review, he has got hold, probably combined with much folly, of some of the true circumstances of the progress of population, and of the preventive checks. All these fermenting principles must converge to system and unity before long; the political economists are not all the war; ——if they will not understand common sense because their heads are full of extravagant theory, they will be trampled down and passed over; and it will be the height of indolence and bad management if you allow other heels to take the pass of yours in this most meritorious procession. "①

ones was indeed a procrastinating author. Without the nest encouragement of his friend, it is doubtful ether Jones would have brought out his book. In aner letter, dated July 31, 1829, Whewell wrote: "I bew every now and then an especial act of recollection I good hope upon your political economy, which from this time is, I expect, destined to have no stop on its progress. "② Two weeks later Whewell sent him another fascinating letter in which the most valuable and friendly inspiration was shown by an intimate friend. The letter runs as follows:

"It is rather cloudy, but through a little hole in the clouds I can see you very tolerably. You are looking with great satisfaction at a half sheet draft of your political economy and just beginning to discover the merit and difficulty of a proper division into paragraphs. You have got some shockingly ill written heaps of paper lying beside you, which you are going to make more seemly to look at as soon as you have done correcting your press. Mrs. Jones is asking in vain for the meaning of various ejaculations which escape you from time to time. Be a good boy and take pains with all the base and mechanical parts of your task, and do not, as I did, execute it so imperfectly that you are impatient till a second edition

---

① Dr. Whewell: *Writings and Letters*, Vol. II, p. 93.
② Dr. Whewell: "*Writings and Letters*," Vol. II, p. 101.

enables you to correct your blunders. "①

From these letters we gather that Jones was lazy and slow in writing the portion of his book dealing with rent. He did not publish any further portion of his *Distribution of Wealth* in a substantial form, though he more than once furnished a compendious statement of some of his views in the form of a syllabus of his lectures, and, as we have mentioned earlier, these were collected and published in his *Literary Remains*. But he has left no large and systematic development of his doctrines, and this is, of course, one of the chief reasons why Jones' influence was so insignificant.

A second reason for his obscurity is that when he was appointed Professor of Political Economy and History at Haileybury College, he was also, at the same time, taking charge of the commutation of tithes; he had removed his interests from speculative to practical political economy. But on the occasion of his being appointed Tithe Commissioner, he had received permission from the directors of the East India College to continue to hold his professorship. He went on injecting his speculations into his lectures, for that purpose often writing them over in altered forms. Due to this habit, the papers which he left contain much repetition.

Jones cherished the hope of giving something of a complete and systematic character to his system of political economy of nations, but the execution of all such projects was prevented by his engagement in practical life, and by his fondness for social intercourse, to which reference has been made in Chapter II. In addition a great obstacle to his constructing a systematic doctrine was his impatience of the labor which was requisite in order to give literary symmetry to his writings.

---

① Dr. Whewell: *"Writings and Letters,"* Vol. II, p. 102.

Above all, he was not influential because his economic discussions were based upon the study of economic institutions of other nations than England; his chief interest was not centered on English economic problems of the day. Owing to the high cost of subsistence the economists of the period had come to regard the funds for the maintenance of labor as the most important component of capital. Jones, on the contrary, put much more emphasis upon the importance of auxiliary capital than on that of circulating capital. In propounding his theory of rent, he attached himself to the support of the landlord, who was defeated by the repeal of corn laws in 1846. In his theory of wages he gave more space to the discussion of unhired laborers and paid dependents than to the English type of laborer, hired by capital. Any kind of economic theory, if divorced from its functional relation to economic problems of the day, will fail to secure public sanction. Jones could not be an exception.

All these causes—his mental slowness or impatience, his daily activities, and his peculiar system of political economy of nations, unsuitable to the English situation of that day—combined to minimize Jones' influence in the minds of the English Classical economists. [1]He did, however, distinctly see in the far distance a goal worthy of his toil; he had applied his shoulder to the task of advancing the car of knowledge, though only one span's length in its career. If in the road to truth through observation and induction, he remarked that men can advance only by slow and laborious steps, it is at least the privilege of those who tread it to see through its long vista a cheering spectacle of final triumphs. It is now one hundred years since

---

[1]   While Jones has not received due recognition among the English economists, it should be stated that as a prominent figure of the historical school of economics, he could hardly be placed on an equal footing with Schmoller & Roscher of the German Historical School.

the publication of his work, and at last a prominent school of institutional econonmics has grown up, emphasizing the inductive method of study, the statistical approach and the historical treatment which were advocated by Jones a century earlier. Perhaps it may be said with a fair degree of certainty that in the near future Jones will occupy the place in economic thought which he so well deserves.

APPENDIX A

1. Detailed study of Jones' threefold classification will rel his turn of mind as well as his economic doctrines. following list illustrates his classificatory economics.

    There were three errors of the Ricardian school. ①

    A. There is assumed a constantly decreasing power in the agricultural occupation as nations multiply and become more civilized.

    B. The laboring classes of the earth are maintained exclusively on funds saved from income.

    C. The diminishing rate of profit observable as nations become numerous and rich indicates a decreasing power of accumulating fresh resources.

2. Jones mentioned three disadvantages of cottier rents. ②

    A. The want of any external check to assist in repressing the increase of the peasant population beyond the bounds of an easy subsistence.

    B. The want of any protection to their interests from the influence of usage and prescription in determining the amounts of their payments.

    C. The absence of the direct common interest between the owners and the occupiers of the soil.

3. There are three different modes in which farmers' rent may increase. ③

    A. An increase of the produce from the accumulation of larger quantities of

① *Distribution of Wealth*, *Preface*.
② *Distribution of Wealth*, p. 139. Also *Literary Remains*, p. 209.
③ *Disstribution of Wealth*, p. 178.

      capital in its cultivation.

B. The more efficient application of capital already employed.

C. The dimunition of the share of the producing classes in that produce, and a corresponding increase of the share of the landlord.

4. Three fallacies in connection with a supposed indication of the decreasing efficiency of agricultureal labor. [1]

A. A fall in the rate of profits.

B. A rise in the relative value of raw produce, compared with other domestic commodities.

C. An increasing money value of raw produce, compared with the prices of other countries.

5. There are three facts showing the increase of rents in England has proceeded from the increase of agriculture produce [2]

A. There has been a spread of tillage, accompanied by a rise in the general rental of the country.

B. There has been a diminution of the proportion of the people employed in agriculture.

C. There has been a decrease in the landlord's proportion of the produce.

6. The labor fund may be divided into three comprehensive classes. [3]

A. Revenues which are produced by the laborers who consume them, and never belong to any other persons.

B. Revenues belonging to classes distinct from the laborers, and expended by those classes in the direct maintenance of labor.

C. Capital in its limited and proper sense of stock or accumulated wealth employed with a view to profit.

---

[1] *Distribution of Wealth*, p. 241.

[2] *Distribution of Wealth*, p. 264

[3] *A Syllabus of a Course of Lectures on the Wages of Labor to be Delivered at King's College*, 1833.

7. Laboring cultivators may be divided into three groups: [1]

   A. Hereditary Occupiers.

   B. Proprietors.

   C. Tenants.

8. Tenants may again be divided into three classes: [2]

   A. Serfs.

   B. Métayers.

   C. Cottiers.

9. There are three errors concerning the accumulation of capital or rate of profit in the Ricardian school of economics: [3]

   A. A mistaken notion that accumulation from profits must be slow where the rate of profits is low, and rapid where it is high.

   B. A mistaken belief that profits are the only source of accumulation.

   C. A mistaken belief that all the laborers of the earth subsist on the accumulations and savings from revenues, and never on the revenue itself.

10. There are three causes which determine the efficiency of labor: [4]

    A. The continuity with which it is applied.

    B. The skill by which it is directed.

    C. The power by which it is aided.

11. The laborers of the world may be divided into three great, but unequal, classes. [5]

    A. Unhired laborers, who till the ground they occupy as peasant cultivators, and live on self-produced wages.

    B. Paid dependents, who are paid out of the revenue or income of their

---

[1] *Syllabus* p. 46.
[2] *Syllabus* p. 48.
[3] *Syllabus*, p. 51.
[4] *Literary Remains*, pp. 9, 347, 189, 402.
[5] *Literary Remains*, p. 13.

employers.

C. Hired laborers, who are paid out of the capital of their employers.

12. There are three conditions governing the increase of auxiliary capital:①

A. It must return its wear and tear with a profit.

B. It must appear in a new form.

C. It must make a better application of known forces.

13. There are three major problems in the discussion of population. ②

A. The causes which affect the progress of population generally.

B. The causes which affect the progress of the labor population in particular, and among these the influence on population of fluctuations in the rate of wages.

C. The causes, which, under different circumstances, determine who shall ultimately pay the taxes laid on commodities consumed by the laboring classes.

14. There are three conditions determining the peasant laborer's wages. ③

A. The size of his holding.

B. The fertility of the land.

C. The efficiency of his labor.

15. There are three causes which determining the accumulation of capital ④

A. The source from which capital is accumulated.

B. The causes determining the inclination to acumulate.

C. The conditions favorable or unfavorable to accumulation.

16. There are three obstacles in the promotion of social fandings:⑤

A. Distinction of blood and race.

① *Literary Remains*, p. 70.
② *Literary Remains*, pp. 94, 471.
③ *Literary Remains*, pp. 124, 218.
④ *Literary Remains*, pp. 53, 316, 390.
⑤ *Literary Remains*, p. 383.

B. Paucity of non-agricultural occupations.

C. Vicious legislation and regulations as to the privilege of carrying on these occupations.

17. To create new habits of consumption among a population put in possession of increasing means, three things must concur. ①

A. The people must acquire a knowledge of, and a familiarity with, a new list of commodities suited to their tastes.

B. These commodities must be presented to them at such reasonable price as to be within the reach of the successive additions to their means.

C. There must be no insuperable physical or moral obstacles, such as distances, roads, fiscal or other regulations, which throw difficulties in the way of their attaining these new commodities.

18. Jones suggested three propositions in connection with the commutation of tithes. ②

A. That commutation is desirable.

B. That the future payments, in lieu of tithes, shall be applied to the same purposes and paid to the same persons as the present tithe.

C. That the first step in the process shall be to transfer the liability for those future payments from the tenant to the landowner.

19. Jones mentioned three parties concerned with the commutation of tithes: ③

A. The government, as representing the whole population and all the national interests.

B. The landowners.

C. The tithe owners.

20. Jones set forth three objects of the government in the commutation of

---

① *Literary Remains*, p. 480.

② *Remarks on the Government Bill for the Commutation of Tithes*, 1836.

③ Ibid.

tithes: ①

A. The setting of the capital and industry of the country completely free to extract the greatest possible amount of prodtice in the best manner from the soil.

B. The removing at the same time, of any obstacles created by the actual mode of collecting their revenues.

C. The efficiency of religious instruction.

---

① Ibid.

APPENDIX B

THE DIFFERENCES BETWEEN RICARDO AND JONES ON THE THEORY OF RENT

JONES	RICARDO
1. Rent proceeds from the employment of an additional quantity of capital and labor with an equal proportional return.	1. Rent invariably proceeds from the employment of additional quantity of labor and capital with a proportionally less return.
2. Increase of produce and rise of rent.	2. Increase of produce and decrease of rent.
3. Agricultural improvement beneficial to landlords.	3. Agricultural improvement detrimental to landlords.
4. The rise of rents is the creation of wealth.	4. The rise of rents simply the transfer of wealth already in existence.
5. National produce increasing while rent rising.	5. National produce stationary while rent rising.
6. Inferior soils present a boundary to the rise of rent.	6. Inferior soils cause rise in rent.
7. To minimize the importance of the law of diminishing returns.	7. The law of diminishing returns is regarded as the foundation of the theory of rent.
8. The rise of rent is independent of the alteration in the relative fertility of the soils.	8. The rise of rent is due to the alteration in the relative fertility of the soils.

JONES	RICARDO
9. The cultivation of poor soil is the consequence of the increased efficiency of capital which is the cause of the rise of rent.	9. The cultivation of poor soil is the consequence of the law of diminishing returns (in the old soil) which is the cause of rise in rent.
10. Rent rises as the fertility of soils increases.	10. Rent rises as the fertility of soils decrease.
11. The interests of landlords not in opposition to that of other classes. Theory of social harmony.	11. The interests of landlords always opposed to that of other classes. Theory of class struggle.
12. The increase of rent from the total quantity of produce, that is, the mass of rent.	12. The increase of rent from the margin of different soils: the wider the margin the higher the rent.
13. Emphasis upon the productive power of agriculture in the theory of rent.	13. Emphasis upon the share in distribution in the theory of rent.
14. Rent as a surplus profit from capital investment.	14. Rent as a differential return from cultivation.
15. Using addition or multiplication to estimate the total quantity of rent, the mass.	15. Using subtraction or division to calculate the rate of rent, the margin.
16. Close relation between wages and rent in the peasant rent: one determines the other. But this relation ceases in the farmer rent.	16. Close relation between rent and profit, one rises as the other falls. Their movement tends in opposite directions.
17. Emphasis on human institution. The origin of farmer rent due to the rise of capitalist class. Pecuniary interpretation.	17. Emphasis on physical constituents of the soil. Physical interpretation.

INDEX

BIBLIOGRAPHY

I. PRIMARY SOURCES

es, Richard, *An Essay on the Distribution of Wealth and the Sources of Taxation*, 1831. London. J. Murray.

An Introductory Lecture on Political Economy, Delivered at King's, College, London, 1833.

Lectures on Capital and Labour.

Lectures on Population.

"Primitive Economy in England," *Edinburgh Review*, 1847.

A Short Tract on Political Economy, Including Some Account of the Anglo-Indian Revenue System.

Text Book of Lectures on Political Economy of Nations, Delivered at the East India College, Haileybury, in 1852.

Tract on the Incidence of Taxes on Commodities Consumed by the Labouring Class.

above-mentioned seven lectures were collected in one book, enl *Literary Remains*, edited by Whewell) . 1859. London.

Syllabus of a Course of Lectures on the Wages of Labour, Proposed to be Delivered at the East India College.

A Few Remarks on the Proposed Commutation of Tithes, with Suggestions of Some Additioal Facilities, 1833.

A Letter to Sir R. Peel.

An Essay on the Law of Bailments.

Observations on the English Tithe Bill.

"Peasant's Rent" in *Ashley's Economic Classics*, 1895. New York and London, Macmillan & Co.

Remarks on the Government Bill for the Commutation of Tithes, 836. London.

Remarks on the Manner in Which Tithes Should Be Assessed to he Poor's Rate, 1838. London, Shaw & Sons.

II. SECONDARY SOURCES

A. Books:

rson, J. , *Enquiry into the Nature of Corn Laws*, 1777.

al Register, 1855, vol. 97.

Ashley. W. J. , *An Introduction to English Economic History and Theory.* 4th edition, 1923, London, Longmans, Green & Co.

——, *Economic Organization of England*, 1915. London. Longnans, Green & Co.

Bagehot, W. , *Postulates of Political Economy In Economic Studies*, 1880. London, Longmans, Green & Co.

Bailey, S. , *A Critical Dissertation on Value*, 1825. London, Hunter.

Banfield. T. C. , *The Organization of Industry*, 1844. London.

Bastable, C. F. , *Theory of International Trade*, 4th ed. , Rev. 1903, Macmillan.

Bonar, J. , *Malthus and His Work*, 1924, N. Y. , Macmillan.

Boucke, O. F. , *The Development of Economics*, 1750-1900-1921. N. Y. Macmillan & Co.

Buckle, H. T. , *History of Civilization*, Vol. ji , 1868. D. Appleton & Co.

Bygone Sussex, W. E. A. Alon, 1897. M. Bygone Series, vol. 27.

Cairnes, J. E. , *The Character of Logical Method of Political Economy*, 1875, Harper & Brothers.

——, *Leading Principles of Political Economy.* 1879. London, Macmillan & Co.

Cannan, E. , *History of the Theories of Production and Distribution*, 1924. P. S.

King & Son, London.

Cassel, G. , *The Theory of Social Economy*, 1924. Harcourst, translated by Mc-Cabe.

Cossa, L. , *An Introduction to the Study of Political Economy*, 1893. Macmillan.

Craig, J. , *Remarks on Some Fundamental Doctrines in Political Economy*, 1821. London.

Cunningham, W. , *The Growth of English Industry and Commerce.* 3 vol. , 5th edition, 1912. London.

Dictionary of National Biography, vol. 30. 1885. London, Elder. Smith & Co.

Davenport, H. J. , *Value and Distribution*, 1908. Chicago, University of Chicago Press.

Edgeworth, F. Y. , *The Objects and Method of Political Economy*, 1891.

Edgeworth, M. , *Memoirs*, 1820. London.

Edie, L. D. , *Economic Principles and Problems*, 1927. N. Y. , Thomas Y. Crowell Co.

Ely, R. T. , "land Economics," in *Economic Essays in Honor of J. B. Clark*, 1927. N. Y. , Macmillan & Co.

Fetter, F. A. , *Economic Principles*, 1915. N. Y. , Century Company.

Gide, C. and Rist C. , *History of Economic Doctrines* 1915. N. Y. , D. C. Heath & Co.

Haney L. H. , *History of Economic Thought*, 1920. N. Y. , Mactmillan.

Hare, A. J. C. , *The Life and Letters of Maria Edgeworth*, 1895. Boston.

Hollander J. H. , *David Ricardo*, 1910. Baltimore, Johns Hopkins Press.

——, *Ricardo's Notes on Malthus' Principles of Political Economy*, *Introduction*, 1928. Baltimore, Johns Hopkins Press.

Ingram, J. K, *History of Political Economy*, 1915. London.

Jervons, W. S. , *Principles of Economics*, 1905. N. Y. and London, Macmillan.

——, *Principles of Science*, 1874. London.

——, *Theory of Political Economy*, 1911. London, Macmillan.

326

Johnson, A. S. , *Rent in Modern Economic Theory*, 1903. N. Y. , Columbia University.

Keynes, J. N. , *Scope and Method of Political Economy*, 4th edition, 1917, Macmillan.

List, F. , *The National System of Political Economy*, 1904. Longmans, Green & Co, London.

Malthus, T. R. , *An Essay on the Principle of Population* 1890, London.

——, *An Inquiry into the Nature and Progress of Rent and the Principles by Which It Is Regulated*, 1815. London, J. Murray.

——, *Principles of Political Economy*, 1820. London, Murray.

Marshall, A. , *Principles of Economics*, 8th edition, Macmillan.

Mayo-Smith, R. , "*Methods of Investigation in Political Economy*," *Science Economic Discussion*, 1886.

McCulloch, John R. , *Literature of Political Economy*, 1845. London.

Mill. J. S. , *Early Essays*, 1897. London, Y. Bell & Sons.

——, *Logic*, vol. II .

——, *On the Definition of Political Economy*, *In the Essay on Some Unsettled Question*, 1877. 3rd edition.

——, *Principles of Political Economy*. 1920. London, Longnans, Green & Co.

Nicholson, J. S. , *Tenant's Gain Not Landlord's Loss*, 1883. Edinburgh D. Douglas.

Patten, S. N. , *The Premises of Political Economy*, 1885.

Patton, F. L. , *Diminishing Returns in Agriculture*, 1926. N. Y. , Columbia University.

Price, L. L. , *A Short History of English Political Economy*, 12th ed. , Methuen & Co. . 1924.

Ricardo, D. , *Principles of Political Economy and Taxation*, Gonner's Ed. 1908. London, George Bell & Sons.

Rogers, J. E. T. , *Economic Interpretation of History*, 1888. N. Y. , Y. P.

Putnam's Sons.

———, *Six Centures of Work and Wages* 1884. N. Y. , Putnam's Sons.

Roscher, W. , *Principles of Political Economy*, 1878. N. Y. , Holt (2 vols) .

Secrist, H. , *Introduction to Statistical Methods*, 1925. N. Y. , Macmillan.

Seligman, E. R. A. , *Economic Interpretation of History*, 1902. Columbia University Press.

———, *Essays in Economics*, 1929, N. Y. , Macmillan.

———, *Principles of Economics*, 10th edition, N. Y. , Longman's, Green & Co.

———, *The Shifting and Incidence of Taxation*, 1910 Columbia University Press, 3rd edition.

Sidgwick, H. , *Scope and Method of Political Economy*, 1904. Macmillan.

Taussig, F. W. , *Wages and Capital*, 1896. N. Y. , D. Appleton & Co.

Thompson, T. P. , *The True Theory of Rent in Opposition to Ricardo and Others*, 1826.

Torrens, R. , *Essay on the Production of Wealth*, 1821. London.

Toynbee, A. , *Industrial Revolution*, 5th edition, 1905.

Tugwell, R. G. , *The Trend of Economics*, 1924 N. Y.. Knopf.

Veblen, T. , *Theory of the Leisure Class*, 1917. N. Y. , Macmillan.

———, "Peasant's Rent" is Ashley's *Economic Classics*, 1895. New York Ward. T. H. , *Men of the Reigh*, 1885. London, and N. Y. , Routledge & Sons.

Weber, M. , *General Economic History*, translated by F. H. Knight, 1927. Greenberg.

West, S. E. *The Application of Capital and Labor to Land*, 1815.

Whewell, W. , *Writings and Lettters*, ed. by Todhunter. 2 vols. , 1876. London.

Young, A. , *Travels*, vol. ii. 1793. Dublin.

II. Articles

Ashley, W. J. , "The Enlargement of Economics," *Economic Journal*, vol. 18.

——, "The Historical School of Political Economy. " *Dictionary of Political Economy*, *vol.* ii.

——, "On the Study of Economic History," *Quarterly Journal of Economics*, 1893.

——, "Place of Economic History in University Studies. " *Economic History Review*, vol. i.

Bohm-Bawerk, "The Historical vs. the Deductive Method in Political Economy. " *American Academy of Political and Social Science*, Annals, 1890.

Camp, W. R. , "The Limitations of the Ricardian Theory of Rent. " *Political Science Quarterly*, vol. 33.

Cannan, E. , "The Origin of the Law of Diminishing Returns. " *Economic Journal*, 1892.

on, F. T. , "The Rent Concept, Narrowed and Broadened. " *Quarterly Journal of Economics*, 1907.

J. B. , "Distribution as Determined by a Law of Rent. " *Quarterly ournal of Economics*, 1890.

C. G. , "A History of Political Economy. " *American Academy of Political and Social Science*, Annals, 1894.

worth, E. Y. , "Richard Jones. " *Dictionary of Political Economy*. vol. ii, p. 491.

L. D. , "Some Positive Contributions of the Institutional Concept. " *Quarterly Journal of Economics*, 1927.

R. T. , "Land Income. " *Political Science Quarterly*, 1928.

"Landed Property. " *American Economic Review*, 1917.

r, F. A. , "Price Economics vs. Welfare Economics. " *American Economic Review*, 1920.

lent, P. , " The Law of Non-proportional Returns; Its Evolution and Improvements. " *Review of Political Economy*, 1928.

emen's Magasine, March 1855.

ngs, F. H. , "The Sociological Character of Political Economy. " *American Economic Association Publication*, 1888.

er, E. C. K. , "Ricardo and His Critics. " *Quarterly Journal of Economics*, 1889.

N. S. B. , "The Rise and Development of Economic History. " *American History Review*, vol. i.

ilton, W. H. , "The Institutional Approach to Economic Theory. " *American Economic Review*, 1918.

s, H. G. , "Land Rent and the Price of Commodities. " *American Economic Review*, 1927.

Dn, J. A. , "The Law of Three Rents. " *Quarterly Journal of Economics*, 1890.

lndet, J. H. , "The Present State of the Theory of Distribution. " *American Economic Association Publication*, 1906.

e R. F. , "The Historical Method vs. Historical Nerrative. " *Journal of Political Economy*, vol. 14.

rm. J. K. , *Presidential Address; Journal of the Statistical Society.* 1878.

s. W. S. , "The Future of Political Economy. " *Fortnightly Review.* 1878.

e, T. E. C. , "Economic Science and Statistics. " *Athenaeum*, 1873.

"The Known and the Unknown in the Economic World. " *Fortnightly Review*, 1879.

"On the Philosophical Method of Political Economy. " *Hermathena*, 1876.

"Political Economy and Sociology. " Fortnightly Review.

Loos, J. A. , "The Historical Approach to Economics," *American Ecoconomic Review*, 1918.

Mackenzie, J. S. , "Historical Method. " *Dictionary of Political Economy* vol. ii.

Marshall, A. , "On Rent. " *Economic Joutnal*, vol. iii.

——, "The Old Generation of Economists and the New. " *Quarterly Journal of Economics*, 1897.

McCulloch. J. , "Jones' Distribution of Wealth. " *Edinburgh Review*, 1831.

Mitchell, W. C. , "Quantative Analysis in Economic Theory. " *American Economic Review*, 1925.

Nicholsen, J. S. , "The Accumulation of Capital. " *Dictionary of Political Economy*, vol. i.

——, "The Balance of Trade. " *Dictionary of Political Economy* vol. i.

Patten, S. N. , "The Making of Economic Literature. " *Economic Bulletin*, vol. i.

Price, L. L. , "Some Aspects of the Theory of Rent. " *Economic Journal*, vol. i.

——, "The Study of Economic History. " *Economic Journal*, vol. 16.

Seligman, E. R. A. , " On Some Neglected English Economists," *Economic Journal*, 1903.

Sommer, L. , "Theoretical and Historical Methods in Economics. " *Schmoller's Jahrbuch*, August, 1928.

Taussig, F. W. , "Exhaustion of the Soil and the Theory of Rent. " *Quarterly Journal of Economics*, vol. 31.

Turner, J. R. , " Henry C. Carey's Attitude toward the Ricardian Theory of Rent. " *Quarterly Journal of Economics*, vol. 26.

Veblen, T. , "The Preconception of Economic Science. " *Quarterly Journal of Economic.* 1899.

——, Why is Economics Not an Evolutionary Science?" *Quarterly Journal of Economics* , vol. 12.

Viner, J. , "Some Problems of Logical Method in Political Economy. " *Journal of Political Economy*, 1917.

Wagner, A. , "On the Present State of Political Economy. " *Quarterly Journal of Economics*, vol. i.

Young, A. A. , "Economics as a Field of Research. " *Quarterly Journal of Economics*, 1927.

——, "English Political Economy. " *Economica*, March, 1928.

VITA

The author of this dissertation was born in Hangchow, China, on March 28, 1897. He received his early education from a private tutor under the old Chinese educational system. He taught Chinese literature in the Peking Anhwei Academy from 1918 to 1920 and was employed as a compiler in the National Bureau of Historical Research in Peking from 1920 to 1922 while he was attending the Peking National Government University. He received the B. A. degree in the above mentioned university in 1922. He taught economics in the Min-Kuo University, Peking from 1922 to 1923. He came to the United States in 1923 and received the degree of M. A. in Columbia University in 1924. From 1925 to 1929 he has been studying in the same institution and attending the seminar conducted by Professors, Seligman, Seager, Mitchell and Simkhovitch.

五十年来美国经济思潮的主流
——制度经济学派

（一）引言

在二十世纪以前，美国的经济思想大都从英国播迁而来，尚未脱离传统观念的羁绊。不过美国为新兴之国家，有其特殊之素质，举其大者而言，约有四端：

一、经济的环境　美国的经济环境与欧洲国家不同。美洲为新开发之园地，天然资源十分丰富，土地肥沃，农作简易。

二、政治的构造　在十八世纪，欧洲国家之政治制度大都为君主专制或君主立宪，惟美国革命独立之后，以民主自治为天下倡，其政治构造视英国遂亦大有不同。

三、社会的组成　美国的人民均由欧洲移殖而来，故美国的民族分子非常复杂，各有其风俗习惯，历时久之，遂融合而组成特殊之社会。

四、教育制度　美国的教育制度注重实验教育，以养成技术人才为目的，颇能迎合社会的需要。

以上几端均足以影响其经济思想之发展，由此蔚成独特之见解，遂使美国的经济学家与英国的古典经济学家颇有持论各异之处：

一、从大体言，美国经济学家之观点，富有乐观的色彩。盖因美国地旷人稀，富源充足，衣食无虞，社会称安，国家有新兴之气象，人民有进取之精神。此种乐观的色彩之流露于经济理论者有二点：其一，美国的经济学家大都不承认报酬递减律之重要性。其二，对于马尔萨斯的人口说表示怀疑。

二、美国经济学家对于英国古典派所倡导之一般工资率与一般利息率，均予以否认，其理由因新大陆幅员辽阔，各洲各区域所流行之工资率及利率颇不相等。

三、美国土地广大，同时人民富有民主自治的思想，因此产生了一种极富有流动性的土地所有权制度。土地的租赁及其债值，在自由竞争之下，与市场发生了深切的关系。此种情形颇与英国的土地制度不同，故美国经济学家对于土地与资本的区别，不似英国古典派之严格。

四、大多数美国经济学家均接受分配理论上的边际生产力说。推其原因，实缘于美国当时生产上的稀少因素乃是劳动，而非土地。故对于劳动注意于节省与经济，对于劳动的生产力必须详加分析。研究的结果，遂产生了工资的生产能力说。

五、新大陆处于比较孤立的地位，国内市场大可发展，遂形成了一个极坚强的保护主义。

六、新大陆的奠定和建设，其功绩皆出于富有理想之志士。若辈或因其在本国有宗教上信仰之殊异，或因与旧社会之环境不适合，或因政治上见解之冲突，遂不惜远离乡井，来此乐土，以求解放。故皆有冒险之精神与较高之理想，个人主义的勃兴，良非偶然。

在二十世纪初叶，美国经济思想大体上采取折衷的理论。奥国学派的边际分析与克拉克（J. B. Clark）氏的特殊生产能力说配合，颇能收融会贯通之效。英国马薛尔所倡导之新古典派学说，亦被许与历史学派之理论互相调和而共存。但由于公司企业之发达，会计制度之确立，与夫统计资料之搜集，商业经济学遂应运而生。同时就经济体系加以分析，遂形成邰文扑脱（Davenport）的企业经济学与费暄（Fisher）氏所倡导之数理会计经济学（Mathematico-Accounting Economics）。第一次欧战以后，幸福经济学与制度经济学，经霍柏生（Hobson）与樊勃伦（Veblen）之鼓吹，康孟斯（Commons）之擘画，寖成为美国现代经济思潮之重心。兹述制度经济学，盖以其就美国环境言最富代表性也。

（二）　制度经济学的理论

制度经济学的理论，是要将经济秩序的整体作一普遍的广泛描绘，对于习惯演变的历程，尤加注意。谓习惯乃由日常生活的教训而养成；这种习惯，若为社会大多数人民所采取，即称谓制度。所以制度乃是为一般人民所接受之一种惯例，而为维系社会秩序不可或缺之物。制度经济学之所研究，不仅在检讨双方买卖的交易行为，并须对于经济体系的特性所以使某种事件在某条件下产生者，予以透彻的分析。凡组成经济秩序的传统习惯和思想的方式，以及行为的规范，皆属于研究范围之内。关于现代工业社会之组织中所有各种制度间的关系，尤必剖解详明。

制度经济学家所提倡之理论，虽亦彼此颇有出入，惟下列数点为一般所公认：

1. 经济行为的研究

经济学必须根据人类行为（Human Behavior）去作研究，盖所谓制度系指团体行为之传统的方法而言。这种制度，即表示系大多数人民共循之习惯。这是一种大量的现象，最适合于经济学之研究。倘若我们想了解全体人民的经济行为，则经济制度的检讨实为必要。在各种社会科学中，吾人颇注意于过去人类行为之变迁，并致力于将来可能的发展的探讨。大凡社会生活的变动，皆缘于行为之变动。现代国家大多数人民之生活所以异于其祖先者，并非因为现代国家大多数人民之智慧聪明胜于古代之人民。吾人之感应（反躬作用）、本能，以及学习的才能，实与巢居穴处之初民并无二致。吾人之所以能处理日常生活而得到更高水准的经济幸福与物质享乐，推其原因，乃由于现代人之团体的思想习惯与团体的活动习惯与古代人之思想习惯及活动习惯迥然不同。吾人经过了很悠久的累积变动之历程，获得了更有效率的方法，去训练吾人禀赋的才能。这些普遍流行的社会习惯，历代相传，颇有变更，使现代人民之行为异于古代者，必将使将来人民的行为亦异于现代。吾人既对于社会的变动极感兴趣，吾人乃集中注意力于经济制度中人类行为之累积的变动与发展。盖因习惯不仅在吾人经济活动中占重要位置，即在社会生活之其他部门，亦有极大影响。试观吾人消费上的支出，此行为并非完全出于个人的理智，实际上受社会习惯之支配者正多。个人乃社会的产物，个人决不能以自然的欲望满足了便自觉满足；人的嗜尚往往依其群的社会心理而移动。吾人行为的大部分皆是摹仿的，他人有行之者，乃从而效之。货币经济的制度在人类的本性上已经烙印了它的模型，使吾人受到某一种的刺激即采取模型中某一方法去反应。重赏之下，必有勇夫，就是一个好的例证。不仅此也，吾人对于真美善的观念，也都要受习惯的影响。在三十年前女子如有赤脚露臂披发者，即视为大逆不道，而今则司空见惯，不以为奇。所以制度一名词表示最标准化最重要的社会习惯。故从经济行为的观点，经济理论的研究应从经济制度入手。制度经济学者对于"人类行为"的看法有几点意见：

（1）他们承认人类的行为时刻在变动之中，因此经济理论的真确性必须相对于时间和空间。

（2）他们相信经济学的重要主题乃是团体的行为，而非商品的价格。

（3）他们注重风俗、习惯与法律乃所以组成经济生活之范型。

2. 经济管制的检讨

经济管制问题之所以引起人们的注意，其理由一半由于承认制度乃是社会的一种安排，而可以随时变更之者；一半由于认识经济活动从前以为意志自由者，其实皆受了繁复的传统与思想的习惯之管治。经济学之研究，正与其他科学相同，其目的在追求知识，以为管理之工具。所谓管理，其意即欲促成吾人经济生活的进化，使其适合于民族发展的意识。吾人之经济生活至为错综复杂，而各种产业之状况尤为参差不齐，决不能采用一种方式或一种组织可以普遍适用于各种场合。自由竞争的演变已经不是一个满意的有力的保障，能使购买人得到良好的物品和公平的价格，使出售者得到劳力和资本的合理报酬。

在现代经济组织之下，吾人感觉到若干困难。现代工业社会之最显著的特征，即为其不确定性。盖因消费者欲望之变动，以及商业循环的周转，每使商品的需求无法推测。因此生产事业所负之风险，因需求之失调而日益严重。经济生活之需要管制，其程度视前世纪遂更为迫切。

制度经济学者从历史发展的观点来检讨管理问题。初民之世的氏族，不过是一种扩大的家庭，由血统的结合而成，其中管理的机构相当贴切而完善。故初民的社会经济制度颇有共产主义的色彩。在中古时期，市镇中之重要的管理机关为行会的商人及职工或手艺行会，对于成品的制造有严格的管制。同时教堂倡公正价格，使消费人与生产人俱能得到公平的待遇。迨后重商主义兴起，即采用取缔的或管制的经济体系。意谓任何有用的生产部门都应当得到人为的维护，而最有利益的生产部门当首推国际贸易和航运业。反对重商主义之干涉与取缔者为个人主义正统学派。但是为古典派领袖的斯密亚当，他对于企业自由的经济体系亦不认为至善尽美。斯密氏曾根据国防重于国富的理由，也承认几种经济的管制有其需要。

现代的工业与国计民生休戚相关，但是在生产与消费过程中，公家利益决非个人主义所提供者能给予保证。因此社会公家自有充足的理由，采取有效的管制方法，使吾人经济生活的计划得以重行安排，藉以保护或增进社会的利益。吾人对于经济生活之某部门如欲加以管制，则对于特殊的经济制度非有相当的知识不可。例如吾人欲检讨通货膨胀的问题，企为求一合理的解决，自非对于一国的金融组织有深切的了解不为功。由此可知为经济管制的问题着想，经济学家的任务必须对于现存制度的运用详加分析，因此经济理论的轮廓之描述遂成了制度的累积变动之研究。

3. 经济过程的研究

制度经济学非常着重经济的过程。这是一个动态的概念，认为经济的现象常在变动的过程中。制度经济学不仅探讨进化的过程，而且研究波浪形的变动。所谓进化的过程，即指经济社会中，在极大扰乱的因素不存在时，所有一切的变动循一定之方向而发展，并不重复，如人口之增殖，即其例也。所谓波浪形的升降变动，即指各种变化在其进行时，常改变方向，而且往往重复，如物价水准之变动，即其例也。

制度经济学之研究变动的过程，必须考虑数量的变化与品质的变化。在若干情形之下，品质的变化其重要性实甚于数量的变动。因为社会结构其形态随时代而不同，例如土地之所有权，由共有而渐变为个人独占之绝对权益，此中意义深长，对于财富分配的影响极大。在其他情形之下，物价之涨落，利率之高低，以及所得之大小，此类数量的变动，对于国计民生极其重要，其有赖于统计编制上之进步与推广者甚钜。吾人研究经济学，切不可疏忽吾人所检讨之经济现象绝不可能永远保持其固定之内容，不仅要受外界事物的搅动，就是他们自己内部的事物因此亦常在变化之中。所以进化论的经济学必须对于经济的过程予以详细的分析，因此与其说经济科学是机械的，毋宁说它是生物的。

（三）制度经济学与其他学派的联系

制度主义的概念相当含糊，人们对之尚无明确的认识，遂有将它与其他学派与主义相提并认者。与古典派经济学持不同见解之数量经济学、幸福经济学以及新心理学派，均尝被认为与制度经济学产生了联系。

1. 制度经济学之所以与数量经济学发生联系，推其原因实由于密吉尔教授（Mitchell）的著作之被人误解。其实一般数量经济学家与制度主义的经济学家，虽抱共同之愿望，均在追求经济学中更大的现实，但是二者之间仍有相当的距离。盖数量经济学之追求现实，其道是或将新古典学派之理论用更正确之方法表示之，或将旧体系中所包涵之相互关系用数量描述之。至于制度经济学家其对于各种制度的相互关系，乃欲求知其更深切的意义。制度经济学家决不与数量经济学家持一般的见解，将其所研究之范畴限于可以计算之现象，或限于能得到供给之统计资料。因此，制度经济学与数量经济虽观点上并无冲突，但决不可混为一谈。

2. 制度经济学之所以与幸福经济学发生联系，推其原因实缘于皮戈教授（Pigou）的著作之被人误解。须知皮戈氏的经济体系是完全利用新古典派所采取之工具与范畴的。即使皮戈氏对于经济幸福发生了很大的兴趣，其浓厚之程度高于检讨理想的生产量所要具备之有利的条件或均衡的维持，以未必即采用各种"经济关系间的新的概念"。退一步言，纵使大部分经济学家未尝不以制度为研究之对象，同时若干制度经济学家抱了一种愿望，求推广经济组织的社会管理，吾人亦不能即凭一种偶然的事实而谓此二者为同一范畴。

3. 制度主义之兴起，虽由于新古典经济学的乐利主义招致了不满，因而深受刺激，不过乐利主义或理智主义的心理之被摒弃，并不一定即是说必须采取完全新的方法去研究经济学。新心理学派的经济体系固依然是继承正统派的衣钵，自不与制度经济学发生必要的联系。制度主义之涵义甚广，往往被误解为凡反抗李嘉图经济学、奥国派经济学、马薛尔经济学以及克拉克经济学者，皆为制度经济学之标志，是则不可以不辨者也。

（四）制度经济学评价

制度主义之研究经济问题，在说明各种社会制度间的彼此作用，将经济现象直陈出来，而依此予以有次序的排列。樊勃伦的著作对于经济现实颇多深刻之批评，颇思对于经济制度的发展作一溯源的研究。马克斯伟勃（Max Weber）即系采溯源法而分析资本主义的经济体系者，虽然溯源法不过是制度经济学中的一种新观点。与此有同等重要性者，有克拉克氏（J. M. Clack）之"固定成本经济学"，从技术的制度来检讨在短期中其所产生经济上的影响如何。至于康孟斯教授之巨帙《制度经济学》，积三十年之研究，阐明了法庭的判例对于经济社会之进化所产生之影响如何，使法制经济学与制度经济学发生了密切的联系。

制度经济学之研究，可以供给对于经济现象及其相互之关系，一个更为正确而详尽之报告，使经济学之内容更为充实。制度经济学欲在理论上有所成就，必须自创一种体系或结构，使各种专题研究所作的贡献都能包括在内，各取得其相当之地位，期成为一整个的有机体。过去正统派经济学未尝没有完整的体系，可引以为鉴的，是机械观的经济学发生了几种流弊：

1. 专注于经济法则或经济行为规律的发现，此种规律又每每是超乎任何特殊之经济组织的，故现存的特殊结构之个性遂往往被忽视而不加以分析。

2. 集中注意于均衡势力的研究，而对于所以酿成不均衡的各种势力以及新的不同的均衡，均予忽略而不加以检讨。

3. 养成了心理上的惰性，殊不顾对于现存的体系或结构加以革新，遂使经济理论陷于停滞不前的状态中，墨守旧说，不敢改弦更张，缺乏勇气与毅力去搜集、分类以及解释关于社会行为的新资料。似以为辟新园地用力多而收获少，不若追随旧的蹊径，免致有迷失路途之虞。

制度主义的经济学家标立范畴，求在范畴内将各种不同的社会所有的特殊经济现象彼此间之相互关系，解释个明白，并按照生物学家分析"个别生命的形态"之方法来检讨各种"社会生命形态"，尤其是对于社会生命中的经济形态，为创立适宜的规范，以为分类的标准。吾人必须寻出某种社会具何基本特性，依以决定社会各部门间之相互关系，其主要象征为何。经济理论既然要适合于实际的经验，所以对于社会的病理，也应做一番解剖工作。对于过去经济理论的大前提，遂应重加考虑。其要点有可举者：

1. 社会政策的标准必须依据统计资料而予设立。

2. 边际效用的理论乃是心理的假说，并非经济的假说，这种过于重视理智的心理假说有重加检讨之必要。

3. 供求的法则只能适用于若干种市场，而且仅能表示近似的程序。吾人必须认清价格体系中的相互关系，与夫将来价格对于目前供求的影响。吾人更须明白若干市场既不是完全竞争的市场，也不是完全独占的市场，实乃竞争与独占的混合物。

4. 边际生产能力的学说充满了伦理道德与正义的情调，并不是客观的事实；固定的成本常使自由竞争受到了限制。因此实际上社会分配并不依据边际生产能力的基础而行决定。

无论静态的研究或动态的研究，必须采取制度主义的观点。任何一时代，在其进行之途径中，所有生产、分配及消费，在社会中各种制度的堤坝以内展其流转。这些制度的堤坝常常从古典经济学所提示的均衡趋势设置阻碍。另一方面，这些制度的堤坝，又为将来的变动指出了沟道。过去马薛尔、克拉克及其他经济学家自也承认制度的存在，但他们都未能将制度的影响加以充分的叙述。吾人必须明白，任何体系的经济理论，不问它着眼于社会的管理，或只作现象的解释，均不能不认清经济制度的重要性及其在理论中所应占之地位。对于人类行为，我们应当予以较大量的揉性。

制度主义是一个比较新的名词，其涵义尚不甚明确。樊勃伦称制度主义为进化的经济学，包括一种文化进展的理论。此种文化进展以经济上的利益为出发点，用经济过程来解释经济制度的累积连续性。根据樊勃伦的意见，所谓制度，即指习惯或流行的思想方式与行为方式。或谓现代制度经济学决不能死守一种方式，以为经济制度固若是也，如有过失，其过失盖潜伏于人类本性之中；另一方面，亦不能说人类的本性固若是也，如有困难，其困难当归咎于承袭下来的制度。我以为，一位制度经济学家应认明，人类的品性本身即是一个社会制度。经济制度有他自己的连续性与生命的过程，虽不必即特异于个别的人类，但当承认两者间自有显著的不同。

或谓近三十年来制度主义成了一种信仰，凭是信仰遂以为搜集了经济资料，采用了进化的过程加以分析之后，即可发现经济之原则，对于过去有系统的经济理论所描述的经济关系，持着一种否定的态度。而且这种否定的态度，不仅于观念论为然，即对于组成经济理论整体所采取之方法论，亦复如此。我以为制度主义的经济理论家并不是凭空去创造他们的经济体系，他们也不是从经济生活中赤裸裸的事实开始做他们的研究工作。他们心目中固仍存有若干概念与先入之见，以为事实选择的标准。

制度经济学派对于"人的因素"，注重"人格（Personality）"

的分析更甚于"人（Man）"的分析。从人格来观察，人实在是权利的势力之结晶。也就是说，必须从其在制度中的地位对个人加以观察，才能了解社会的真相。按照这个看法，所谓人格，各有其不同之重要性，其广狭，其浓淡，时在变化之中。个人可以利用若干制度以辅助其行动，以逞其心中之所欲，其人格将因其能利用更多之制度而逐渐提高。此际吾人必须认清者，在社会制度中有若干制度，其效能远较其他制度为高，因之若干制度显得生动活跃，另有若干制度则黯然无生气。吾人之人格即因能利用活跃的制度而表露得广大，因只能利用不活跃的制度而表露得狭小。社会制度中之富有经济的意义者，言其重要者如次：

1. 在社会制度中，最明显的，利用之可以扩大吾人之人格者，莫若私有财产制度。有财产即可享受经济上及政治上之特权。能享受这些权利的人们，他们的人格，在某种意义上，是扩展的。

2. 因吾人有占有的欲望和管理的欲望，遂产生了信用制度。信用的使用能使个人的势力范围为之扩大，因为信用能增加吾人经济活动的效率。

3. 第三个重要的经济制度，就是公司组织。有了这个公司组织，一方面可使财产权分散，一方面可供管理权集中，使人们（不论其为个人，或为团体）的人格更为扩大而加强。

4. 其他一切政治经济的制度，凡足以表示民主及自由的理想者，皆足以影响吾人生活的幅度，或增加若干人们的权利，或减少若干人们的权利，或扩大若干权利所能行使之范围，或缩小若干权利所能行使之范围。形形色色，不一端而足。

倘若所有制度均是密切附着于人们的，所有制度皆不过是一种工具，用以实现人们的意志与增加意志的力量的，那么，制度经济学必须对于人格的分析特别注意。

经济学家所负之使命，在于检讨社会结构内各阶级利益冲突之根源。所感困难者，若干经济学家或因金融上的联系，或因情感上的缠绻，每与某一个团体相联合，故其所贡献之意见，为一方所接受者，必为他方所拒绝。因为在一个存有阶级制度的社会里，决没有一个普遍幸福的标准，或一种普遍的社会政策，可以适用于国民全体。吾人所了解的论理观念，亦很难浸濡于经济理论之全部，除非社会的阶级不存在。

制度主义的经济学，并不与古典派经济学完全相枘凿。马薛尔、约翰·弥尔及李嘉图均在其短节文句中或注脚中偶尔谈经济制度的一部分。现代的制度经济学家只是将古典经济学中的注脚扩充而成一书，反将古典经济学变成注脚罢了。吾人从经济研究的技巧上观察，可以承认制度主义的确比新古典主义富有活力。制度主义利用统计资料的帮助，能将学理参以事实的证明。

吾人对于经济生活的研究，可能有两个途径，即平面的研究与垂直研究是也。所谓平面的研究，即于特定的时间内注重经济生活的横切面，亦即普通所谓静态的研究。至于垂直的研究，乃注意经济生活上历史的发展，即普通所称动态的研究。一般学者之采用垂直的研究者，皆以为经济学的研究，应与生物学发生联系。至于采用平面的研究者，皆以为经济学之研究，应与物理学发生联系。制度主义的经济学即属于前者。

制度主义的经济学家，对于本能与制度，详加分析，尤以工巧的本能（Instinct of Workmanship）特别邀注重。至于理智，乃是一种补充本能的工具而已。有时制度可以抑制本能，甚至于可以改变本能，此际制度即可以收管制人类行为之效。但制度有时可以，有时不能与流传的经验相调整，此文化的落后（Cultural Lag）往往促成阶级利益的紧张与冲突。在初期，技术的知识，公开于大众。遂后工业技术发达，生产超过了必需，于是财产权利被掠夺阶级所利用，争取剩余，供一己奢侈之生活。此际私人的利益，遂与公众利益相冲突。生产的机器，也逐渐受货币利益的支配。资本家以遥领主人翁的资格，主持生产企业，采用限制生产量或规定价格，以及金融上的操纵，掠取不正当的利润。而且过分提高资本的价值，以冀获投机的利益，影响所及，酿成经济恐慌。

所以，在社会上即存有一个基本的阶级利益之冲突，此种利益的冲突即存于两阶级之间。一阶级努力于社会的生产事业，其他一阶级藉争夺的手段，享其优裕的生活，赖资本的力量，指挥生产上之技术。谓为"有闲阶级"，谁曰不宜。此种利益的冲突，即存于商业的运用（Business Operation）与机器生产的过程（Machine Process）二者间的不协调。亦即由于两种经济制度的磨擦。这两种经济制度就是：

1. 财产制度　财产制度表示商业的关系（Business Relations）。这个制度与人类掠夺的本能相联系。

2. 技术的制度　技术的方法表示工业的关系（Industrinl Relations）。这个制度与人类技巧的本能相联系。

制度主义经济学家提出"生命"是在继续不断地动荡中，不知其所自，亦不知其所归。吾人不能在任何点上踌躇满志地认为这是平衡水准。吾人研究经济现象必须采取动态的观点，用进化论的概念，去解释变动的历程。凡行为之表现于经济制度者，应予以密切之注意，并且采用相对论之原则，说明时空之限制。

原载于《国立北京大学五十周年纪念论文集》（法学院）1948 年 12 月